Where Does the
Money Go?

SIXTEENTH ANNUAL YEARBOOK
OF THE AMERICAN EDUCATION FINANCE ASSOCIATION
1995

Where Does the Money Go?

Resource Allocation in Elementary and Secondary Schools

Editors

Lawrence O. Picus
James L. Wattenbarger

CORWIN PRESS, INC.
A Sage Publications Company
Thousand Oaks, California

For information address:

Corwin Press
A Sage Publications Company
2455 Teller Road
Thousand Oaks, California 91320
E-mail: order@corwin.sagepub.com

SAGE Publications Ltd.
6 Bonhill Street
London EC2A 4PU
United Kingdom

SAGE Publications India Pvt. Ltd.
M-32 Market
Greater Kailash I
New Delhi 110 048 India

Printed in the United States of America

Library of Congress Cataloging-in-Publication Data

Main entry under title:

Where does the money go?: Resource allocation in elementary and
  secondary schools/editors, Lawrence O. Picus, James L.
  Wattenbarger.
      p. cm.—(Annual yearbook of the American Education Finance
  Association; 16th)
    Includes bibliographical references and index.
    ISBN 0-8039-6162-6 (alk. paper)
    1. Education—United States—Finance. 2. Resource allocation.
  I. Picus, Larry, 1954-   . II. Wattenbarger, James Lorenzo, 1922-
  . III. Series.
  LB2825.W415 1995
  379.1'1'0973—dc20   95-22874

This book is printed on acid-free paper.

96 97 98 99 10 9 8 7 6 5 4 3 2 1

Corwin Press Production Editor: Diane S. Foster

Contents

Preface

Across the United States, there is growing pressure for greater accountability in how schools spend the tax funds they receive. Policy makers often point out that despite considerable growth in real per-pupil expenditures during the past three decades, student performance measures have remained flat or declined. These policy makers, along with the business community and the public in general, want to know where this tax money is going and what it is buying. Former Secretary of Education William Bennett's claim that half of all educational expenditures are lost in an "administrative blob" rang true to many.

Unfortunately, both the education community and the school finance research community have done little to convince the public that its tax dollars are being used wisely. State accounting systems for school districts focus on object-level accounting categories and are designed to make sure funds are not misappropriated. Frequently they provide little information about the flow of resources to schools and classrooms, focusing instead on district-level expenditures.

Similarly, school finance research has focused on spending at the district level, measuring the relationship between district property wealth and spending, and comparing the level of spending across districts in a state. Little research has been done to analyze spending differences at the school and/or classroom level, nor has there been much research into the distribution of the quality of the resources those funds actually purchase.

It seems unlikely that the education community will be able to garner support for additional funding unless it is able to show in more detail how the money it already receives is spent. This book summarizes the emerging research in educational resource allocations at the district, school, and classroom level. This important research will help the public schools explain how the funds they receive are used for the education of our nation's children. It is my hope that this information will help inform the debate over how much we should spend on our children's education and to what purpose those funds should be used.

Overview of Contents

The 13 chapters of this volume address the important issue of how schools and school districts allocate their resources. The first chapter, by Picus and Fazal, summarizes the current work of the Finance Center of the Consortium for Policy Research in Education and the work of others in attempting to discern how school districts allocate and use educational resources, including funds, personnel, and other educational resources.

Chapters 2 and 3 continue the important debate over whether or not money matters in education. In Chapter 2, Eric Hanushek discusses the school finance implications of his belief that there is no systematic relationship between spending and student performance, arguing that it is important for schools to use their resources efficiently if money is to matter. In Chapter 3, Laine, Greenwald, and Hedges summarize the findings of a number of new studies and provide further evidence to support their view that money does matter.

Chapters 4 through 9 describe a number of current initiatives in determining how educational resources are used at the school and classroom level. In Chapter 4, Linda Hertert describes her analysis of school-level equity in California. She shows that despite the tremendous gains the state has made in district-level school finance equity, when spending patterns are analyzed at the school level, considerable inequities still exist. In Chapter 5, Yasser Nakib describes a 3-year study of resource allocation patterns in the state of Florida. Florida has the most detailed school-level data system in the nation. Nakib shows that district- and even school-level spending are highly equalized, but when one probes more deeply into how educational resources are actually used, there are considerable differences across school districts and schools. In Chapter 6, Sheree Speakman and colleagues describe the most detailed analysis of spending patterns in New York City to date. Their analysis shows how funds are allocated throughout the nation's largest school system.

Perhaps the single most important resource purchased with education dollars is teachers. In Chapter 7, Theobald and Gritz describe how district resource allocation decisions affect the employment behavior of new teachers and policies that can help retain teachers early in their careers. David Anderson uses Chapter 8 to describe in detail one approach, the quadriform, for measuring the efficiency of school district resource allocation decisions. In Chapter 9, Thomas Timar describes the resource allocation and school finance implications of the current litigation in Ohio.

The remaining chapters describe the implications of this growing area of research on important policy issues in education and in school finance in particular. In Chapter 10, Wood and Maiden discuss how school-level resource allocation data could be used in school finance litigation, and in Chapter 11, Wohlstetter and Van Kirk show how this information can be used to make site-based management more effective. Because Florida has more experience in school-level data collection than any other state, Carolyn Herrington uses Chapter 12 to discuss the state public policy implications of such data systems. Finally, James Guthrie summarizes the importance of school-level data collection and analysis in the last chapter.

Acknowledgments

As with the previous American Education Finance Association (AEFA) Yearbooks, this volume is a product of the work of many individuals. I thank each of the contributors to this volume for the time and effort they put into their individual chapters. By showing the diversity of approaches to understanding how educational resources are used, we have all gone a long way in helping schools find the most efficient way to use the funds they receive.

Special thanks are due to Phil Kearney, past president of AEFA, for asking me to edit this edition of the *Yearbook* and for believing that I could produce a volume distinguished enough in quality to join the previous 15 published by the association.

I also thank the staff at the Center for Research in Education Finance at the University of Southern California. Without their dedication and help, this book would never have been completed. In particular, I thank Carolyn Bryant for managing all the small details necessary to get the manuscript to the publisher on time, Eric Shaw Quinn for putting the manuscript into final form, and Erick Garcia for dealing with all the last-minute details we faced.

Finally, I thank my wife Susan and my year-old son Matthew for their patience and understanding as the book was completed. I hope this work will in some small way make Matthew's public school education a stronger and more rewarding experience.

Lawrence O. Picus

About the Contributors

David M. Anderson is Assistant Professor at Salisbury State University, Maryland, in the School of Education and Professional Studies. He earned a B.A. and an M.S. in physics and worked as a research physicist before turning to teaching and educational research. He received a doctorate in education from the University of Michigan in 1992 and held the position of Associate Director of Assessment for the National Science Foundation Systemic Initiative in South Dakota and of Executive Associate for Assessment and Research at the National Board for Professional Teaching Standards. In addition to school finance, his interests include educational technology, science education, educational reform, and the social foundations of education.

Bruce S. Cooper is Professor of Education Administration, policy, and urban education at the Graduate School of Education, Fordham University, New York, NY.

Minaz B. Fazal is a doctoral student in the Department of Educational Psychology and Technology at the University of Southern California School of Education. She is also a statistics programmer for the university's Center for Research in Education Finance. She holds an M.S. in educational psychology and technology from the University of Southern California, an M.A. in clinical psychology from Bombay University, India, and a B.A. in psychology and philosophy from Jai Hind College in Bombay, India.

Brian Glass, of Coopers & Lybrand, specializes in computer analysis technology.

Rob Greenwald is a Searle Fellow at the University of Chicago. His primary research interests are in the efficacy of court decisions. His current research investigates the question of whether existing measures of equity are adequate to assess whether state supreme court decisions in school finance litigation have their intended effect. He is trained in biochemistry and ecology, and his experience in public and private education has included teaching in middle school, high school, and college.

R. Mark Gritz is Senior Research Scientist at Battelle Memorial Institute. Prior to joining Battelle, he was an Assistant Professor of Economics at the University of Washington. He earned a B.S. from Colorado State University and a Ph.D. in economics from Stanford University. His research interests include teacher labor markets, the development of performance indicators for education and training programs, the evaluation of alternative employment and training policies, and school-to-work transitions.

James W. Guthrie is Professor at Vanderbilt University and Director of the Peabody Education Policy Center. Prior to assuming these positions in the fall of 1994, he was a Full Professor at the University of California, Berkeley, and cofounder of PACE (Policy Analysis for California Education). His research interests include educational policy studies, school governance and finance, organizational analyses, and international development education. He has held positions in Washington, DC, as a Special Assistant to a cabinet secretary and as Education Specialist for the U.S. Senate Subcommittee on Equality of Educational Opportunity, has testified in numerous significant education-related trials such as *Bradley v. Miliken* and *Serrano v. Priest,* has served as a consultant to state education departments and local school districts, and has advised overseas governments such as those of South Africa, Chile, Romania, and Guyana. Among his books are *Schools and Inequality, New Models for American Education, Educational Administration Policy,* and *Education Finance.* He has served as Vice President of Division A of the American Educational Research Association (AERA), as two-term editor of *Education Evaluation and Policy Analysis,* as Chair of the Government and Professional Liaison Committee, and as a member of the AERA council.

Eric A. Hanushek is Professor of Economics and Public Policy and Director of the W. Allen Wallis Institute of Political Economy Policy at the University of Rochester. From 1983 through 1985, he was Deputy Director of the Congressional Budget Office. His research involves applied public finance and public policy analysis, with special emphasis on education issues. His publications include *Making Schools Work, Modern Political Economy, Educational Performance of the Poor, Improving Information for Social Policy Decisions, Statistical Methods for Social Scientists,* and *Education and Race,* along with numerous articles in professional journals.

Larry V. Hedges is the Stella M. Rowley Professor of Education and Social Sciences at the University of Chicago. His primary research interests are the application of statistical methods, particularly the combination of replicated empirical research studies (meta-analysis) and multivariate analysis, to a wide range of problems, including cognitive science, education, and medicine. He is currently Associate Editor of the *Journal of Educational Statistics* and an American Statistical Association Research Fellow. He has previously served as Chair of the Department of Education at the University of Chicago, Quantitative Methods Editor of the *Psychological Bulletin,* and Visiting Fellow of the Russell Sage Foundation. Among his books are *Statistical Methods for Meta-Analysis* (with Ingram Olkin) and *The Handbook of Research Synthesis* (with Harris Cooper).

Carolyn D. Herrington holds appointments as Associate Professor in the Department of Educational Administration and Research Fellow for Policy in the Learning Systems Institute at Florida State University. In 1992 she served as the American Educational Research Association Program Chair for the Fiscal Issues, Policy, and Education Finance Special Interest Group and edited the monograph *The Political Economy of Educational Finance: The 1993 State of the States.* Her research focuses on school reform, fiscal policy, and politics, and she has published numerous articles, book chapters, and technical reports. She is currently coauthoring a book on the politics of integrating children's services.

Linda Hertert is Assistant Professor of Educational Administration at the University of Cincinnati, where she teaches and writes in the fields of school finance and educational policy. A recent postdoctoral fellow for the Consortium for Policy Research in Education at the University of Wisconsin-Madison, she is the 1994 recipient of the American Education Finance Association's Dissertation Award.

Hunt Holsomback, of Coopers & Lybrand, specializes in technical and data management issues.

Richard D. Laine is Associate Superintendent for Policy, Planning, and Resource Management for the Illinois State Board of Education. Previously he was Executive Director of the Coalition for Educational Rights, the only statewide organization in Illinois dedicated to reforming the current education funding system, and Executive Secretary of the Committee for Educational Rights, an organization composed of 75 school districts that are currently challenging the constitutionality of Illinois's public education funding system. His graduate education has focused on public and private sector roles in reforming and supporting public education. He has received an M.B.A. from the Graduate School of Business and an M.A. from the Graduate School of Public Policy Studies and is currently working on his doctorate in education, all at the University of Chicago.

Jeffrey Maiden is Assistant Professor, Department of Educational Leadership and Policy Studies, College of Education, University of Oklahoma, where he teaches courses in public education finance and school business management. He has been a classroom teacher as well as an administrator in higher education. His doctorate is from the University of Florida, where he was a research associate with the UCEA Center for Education Finance. He has conducted research in education finance litigation in several state cases and has presented his research at the American Education Finance Association (AEFA). He has served as the editor of the AEFA conference proceedings.

Jay May, of Coopers & Lybrand's K-12 Education Team, is experienced in crisis management and process analysis.

Yasser A. Nakib is Assistant Professor at the University of Delaware and a research fellow with the Finance Center of the Consortium for

Policy Research in Education (CPRE). He was recently a research fellow at the Center for Research in Education Finance at the University of Southern California. He was an economist at Economic Research Services, Inc., a labor-related-issues consulting firm in Tallahassee, FL. He has taught economics and education courses at various universities, most recently at the University of California-Los Angeles. He has published and presented research in the area of the economics of school finance and policy.

Lawrence O. Picus is Associate Professor in the School of Education at the University of Southern California (USC), specializing in school finance, school business administration and budgeting, and the economics of education. He is the director of the Center for Research in Education Finance, a School of Education research center whose purpose is to study issues of school finance and productivity as they relate to school reform. He is also a senior research fellow with the Finance Center of the Consortium for Policy Research in Education and coordinator of the USC School of Education's annual Summer Superintendents' Conference. He is coauthor, with Allan Odden, of *School Finance: A Policy Perspective*. In March 1995 he was elected to the position of president-elect of the American Education Finance Association.

Robert Sampieri, of Coopers & Lybrand's K-12 Education Team, has central management experience in the Los Angeles Unified School District and was former chief operating officer of the Chicago Public Schools.

Sheree T. Speakman is partner, Coopers & Lybrand L.L.P., in charge of the K-12 Education Team. She has years of experience in corporate restructuring and mergers and acquisitions practices.

Neil D. Theobald is Associate Professor of Educational Administration at Indiana University, teaching graduate courses in education finance and the economics of education. He earned his B.A. from Trinity College and his M.Ed. and Ph.D. from the University of Washington. His research interests in educational finance and the economics of education are reflected in numerous articles published in professional journals. He received the Jean Flanigan Dissertation Award from the American Educational Finance Association (AEFA) for the outstanding doctoral dissertation in the study of educational finance in 1990, and currently serves on the AEFA Board of Directors.

Thomas B. Timar is Visiting Associate Professor of Educational Policy and Administration at the University of California-Berkeley. His work in school finance has focused on the relationship between the allocation of resources and the political processes that make those kinds of determinations. His principal research interests are policy and politics of education and how they shape organizational behavior.

Amy Van Kirk is a doctoral student in the policy and organization Ph.D. program at the University of Southern California School of Education and is a research assistant with the Center on Educational Governance. Formerly a math teacher, she is currently interested in the political and organizational issues surrounding school-based budgeting.

James L. Wattenbarger is currently a Distinguished Professor Emeritus in the Department of Education Leadership at the University of Florida. He has been an active contributor to the community college movement in Florida and the United States. He has served on the Board of Directors of the American Association of Community Colleges (AACC) and the Commission on the Future of the Community College, has been Chair of the Council of State Directors of Community/Junior Colleges, and was awarded the prestigious Leadership Award from AACC. He was the first director of the Division of Community Colleges for Florida and served as Director of the Institute of Higher Education at the University of Florida for 24 years. He has authored more than 200 articles, books, monographs, and other publications on issues influencing higher education in the United States and abroad.

Priscilla Wohlstetter is Director of the University of Southern California's Center on Educational Governance and Associate Professor in the School of Education. She is internationally recognized for her work on school-based management (SBM), particularly in the areas of politics, organizational policies, and school-based budgeting. Her recent research has included several large-scale evaluations of SBM and a national study of charter school laws. She is author of *School-*

Based Management: Organizing for High Performance (with Susan Albers Mohrman), as well as numerous journal articles.

R. Craig Wood is Professor in the Department of Educational Leadership and Codirector of the UCEA Center for Education Finance at the University of Florida. He has published over 150 articles and texts, including *Principles of School Business Management, Education Finance Law: Constitutional Challenges to State Aid Plans,* and *Fiscal Leadership for Schools: Concepts and Practices.* He serves as the Chair of the Editorial Advisory Board of the Association of School Business Officials as well as on the Board of Directors of the American Education Finance Association. He serves on the review boards of *Education Law Reporter* and the *Journal of Education Finance.* He has delivered numerous general sessions at major academic conferences, including the National Center for Educational Statistics and the National Conference of State Legislatures. He is a Director of Wood, Thompson & Associates, Inc.

ONE

Why Do We Need to Know What Money Buys?
RESEARCH ON RESOURCE ALLOCATION PATTERNS IN ELEMENTARY AND SECONDARY SCHOOLS

LAWRENCE O. PICUS

MINAZ B. FAZAL

Spending on K-12 public education in the United States is approaching $300 billion a year. These funds are used to employ 2.4 million teachers and some 400,000 additional instructional staff to educate over 42 million children (National Center for Education Statistics [NCES], 1993a). Despite this tremendous commitment to the education of our children, we know surprisingly little about how these funds are actually used, or how new or additional funds are likely to be spent by the nearly 16,000 school districts and more than 100,000 schools across the United States. Although school districts are required to maintain detailed revenue and expenditure budgets for their operations, state-level fiscal reporting requirements vary dramatically, making comparisons difficult. Moreover, there are generally few state-level requirements governing the level of detail for which districts must keep school-level fiscal information. Although a few states, most notably Florida (Picus & Nakib, 1993), have begun requiring uniform fiscal reporting at the school level, they are the exception, not the rule.

1

This means that very little information is available to policy makers interested in understanding how resource allocation patterns differ across schools, districts, states, and the nation, and with what effects. Although there are a number of national data collection efforts undertaken on a regular basis, Barro (1992) pointed out that incompatibilities across the major collection efforts result in a situation in which "there is not a fully satisfactory way to answer even so seemingly straightforward a question as 'How much of total expenditure for elementary and secondary education in the United States goes to pay teachers' salaries?' " (p. 2). Odden and Picus (1992) argued that there is a great deal of information about how dollars are distributed to school districts, but insufficient information on how to put dollars to productive use in districts, schools, and classrooms. Moreover, there is little information on the equity of resource distribution to school districts across states.

This chapter offers a summary of what we currently know about the allocation and use of educational resources in K-12 public education. It summarizes research that has been conducted over the past 4 years by the Finance Center of the Consortium for Policy Research in Education (CPRE). The findings are described in three sections. The first analyzes the levels and sources of education spending across the United States. It includes aggregate data on all 50 states. The second section discusses spending disparities across school districts and schools, beginning with a national sample from the Schools and Staffing Survey (SASS) and providing additional discussions of spending disparities at the district and school level in California and Florida. The third section considers in detail how schools utilize the resources available to them, summarizing findings to date across the United States and in Florida, California, and New York.

Levels and Sources
of Education Spending

NCES estimates that by 1997 or 1998, public elementary and secondary schools in the United States will spend more than $300 billion a year to educate children in grades K-12 (NCES, 1993b). In 1992 to 1993, NCES estimated that K-12 public school districts spent approximately $218 million in current expenditures, or $5,721 per pupil in average daily attendance.

Although there is a general perception that funding for public education has declined in recent years, the data show quite the opposite. Using data collected and published by NCES, Table 1.1 shows the change in per-pupil expenditures for the United States between 1959 to 1960 and 1993 to 1994. These figures are adjusted for both inflation and changes in student enrollments. This table shows the dramatic increase in spending that occurred during the past three decades. Despite a slowdown in growth in the 1990s, per-pupil expenditures for education have continued to outpace inflation. On average, real per-pupil spending for K-12 public schools increased by over 207% between 1960 and 1992.

Table 1.1 also shows that this dramatic growth was not consistent across states. New Jersey experienced the highest rate of growth, with real expenditures increasing by over 411% between 1959-1960 and 1992 to 1993. At the other extreme, Utah's real per-pupil expenditures increased by just over 100% during the same time period. Interestingly, two of the states that adopted highly centralized, state-controlled school finance systems in the 1970s, California and Washington, experienced growth rates considerably lower than the national average.

Over time, there has been a dramatic shift in who pays for K-12 education. Table 1.2 shows how the shares of school district revenue from federal, state, and local sources have changed between 1959-1960 and 1990 to 1991. NCES estimates that in 1990 to 1991, 47.3% of total school district revenue came from the state, 46.5% from local sources, and 6.2% from the federal government. The state share of elementary and secondary education funding surpassed the local share for the first time in 1978-1979, the first year that California's Proposition 13 was implemented. Proposition 13 dramatically shifted the source of school support away from local taxes and to the state of California, beginning in 1978-1979. State revenues as a percentage of total school district funds reached a peak of 49.7% in 1986 to 1987 and have declined slightly since that time.

Spending Disparities

Disparities Within States

In analyzing disparities in per-pupil expenditures across the 50 states in 1989 to 1990, Barro (1992) found a ratio of 2.9:1 between the

Table 1.1. Changes in Real Expenditure Per Pupil in Average Daily Attendance (ADA) in Public Elementary and Secondary Schools, by State, 1959-60 to 1991-92 (Constant 1991-92 Dollars)

State	Current Expend. per ADA 1959-60 ($)	Current Expend. per ADA 1991-92 ($)	% Change 1959-60 to 1991-92
United States	1,765	5,421	207.14
Alabama	1,134	3,616	218.87
Alaska	2,570	8,450	228.79
Arizona	1,898	4,381	130.82
Arkansas	1,059	4,031	280.64
California	1,994	4,746	138.01
Colorado	1,863	5,172	177.62
Connecticut	2,051	8,017	290.88
Delaware	2,144	6,093	184.19
Dist. Columbia	2,028	9,545	370.66
Florida	1,494	5,243	250.94
Georgia	1,192	4,375	267.03
Hawaii	1,527	5,420	254.94
Idaho	1,363	3,556	160.90
Illinois	2,062	5,670	174.98
Indiana	1,734	5,074	192.62
Iowa	1,730	5,096	194.57
Kansas	1,636	5,007	206.05
Kentucky	1,096	4,719	330.57
Louisiana	1,749	4,354	148.94
Maine	1,330	5,652	324.96
Maryland	1,847	6,679	261.61
Massachusetts	1,923	6,408	233.23
Michigan	1,952	6,268	221.11
Minnesota	2,000	5,409	170.45

highest- and lowest-spending states. When these figures are adjusted for price differentials across states, the ratio decreases to 2.3:1. Odden and Kim (1992) found considerable differences in both per-pupil expenditures and the level of effort made by taxpayers across the states. They proposed that the federal government consider a greater role in equalizing spending differences across states.

Table 1.1. Continued

State	Current Expend. per ADA 1959-60 ($)	Current Expend. per ADA 1991-92 ($)	% Change 1959-60 to 1991-92
Mississippi	969	3,245	234.88
Missouri	1,618	4,830	198.52
Montana	1,932	5,423	180.69
Nebraska	1,585	5,263	232.05
Nevada	2,025	4,926	143.26
New Hampshire	1,633	5,790	254.56
New Jersey	1,823	9,317	411.08
New Mexico	1,706	3,765	120.69
New York	2,642	8,527	222.75
North Carolina	1,116	4,555	308.15
North Dakota	1,725	4,441	157.45
Ohio	1,717	5,694	231.62
Oklahoma	1,465	4,078	178.36
Oregon	2,109	5,913	180.37
Pennsylvania	1,926	6,613	243.35
Rhode Island	1,944	6,546	236.73
South Carolina	1,035	4,436	328.60
South Dakota	1,631	4,173	155.86
Tennessee	1,120	3,692	229.64
Texas	1,563	4,632	196.35
Utah	1,517	3,040	100.40
Vermont	1,618	6,944	329.17
Virginia	1,290	4,880	278.29
Washington	1,978	5,271	166.48
West Virginia	1,216	5,109	320.15
Wisconsin	1,943	6,139	215.95
Wyoming	2,118	5,812	174.41

SOURCE: National Center for Education Statistics, 1994, Table 166.

Although these differences are important, school finance has typically considered spending disparities across districts within individual states. Hertert, Busch, and Odden (1994) analyzed spending in school districts in each of the 50 states for 1989-1990 and found

Table 1.2. Source of Revenues for Public Elementary and Secondary
Schools, 1959-60 to 1990-91

	% of Total Revenue From		
Year	Federal Sources	State Sources	Local Sources
1959-60	4.4	39.1	56.5
1969-70	8.0	39.9	52.1
1979-80	9.8	46.8	43.4
1989-90	6.1	47.3	46.6
1990-91	6.2	47.3	46.5

SOURCE: National Center for Education Statistics, 1993a, Table 156.

substantial differences in the disparities that exist within different
states. Their findings are summarized in Table 1.3. Using standard
school finance equity measures, the authors found considerable variation in equity across districts within the states. For example, the
coefficient of variation, which is the standard deviation divided by the
mean, ranged from a high of 43.81% in Alaska to a low of 6.79% in
West Virginia. In fact, they found that only 4 states met the equity
standard of a coefficient of variation of 10% or less postulated by
Odden and Picus (1992). The federal range ratio, which is the per-
pupil spending of the district at the 95th percentile minus the spending level of the district at the 5th percentile divided by the value of the
district at the 5th percentile, was over 100% in 6 states and above 75%
in 9 additional states. Hertert et al. (1994) found that the federal range
ratio was less than 50% in 16 states.

In Florida, Nakib and Picus (1994) and Nakib (Chapter 5 of this
volume) found relatively small differences in per-pupil spending across
districts. For example, spending per weighted pupil in the lowest-
spending quintile of schools in Florida averaged $3,361, whereas in
the highest-spending quintile it averaged $5,513 per pupil in 1991-
1992. The coefficient of variation for district-level expenditures per
weighted pupil that year was estimated to be 5.43%. Spending disparities across schools in Florida are greater than the district-level
spending variation, but the coefficient of variation for school-level
spending per weighted pupil was 13.64%, considerably better than
the coefficient of variation across districts in most states calculated by
Hertert et al.(1994).

In California, Hertert (1993) found that although there is consider-able equity across school districts in the state, with a coefficient of variation of 10.69% for all districts, the distribution of expenditures across schools within districts is less equitable. She found that within districts, the coefficient of variation among schools averaged 18.47% and the federal range ratio 66.49%. When the data for individual schools were analyzed across districts, the coefficient of variation increased to 22.60% and the federal range ratio to 114.0%. Moreover, she found that although pupil-teacher ratios did not vary dramatically across schools (coefficient of variation of 10.33% within districts and 13.64% across districts), there were considerable differences in course offerings, particularly in higher-level math and science.

Disparities Across States

Picus (1993a) analyzed per-pupil spending disparities in a national sample of over 4,000 school districts using data from the school and staffing survey (SASS) and the U.S. Bureau of the Census of Govern-ments. He found that there is substantially less equity in educational expenditures per pupil among school districts across the entire United States than is apparent from an analysis of state-level fiscal databases. Specifically, Picus found that district per-pupil expenditures for educa-tion ranged from under $1,000 per pupil to over $50,000 in 1987-1988, the most recent year for which SASS data were available (Picus, 1993a). The coefficient of variation for per-pupil expenditures was 52.4%. When adjusted for differences in the cost of education across states, the coefficient of variation declined to 47.6%. Even this cost-adjusted figure is considerably larger than the coefficient of variation found in any individual state, the largest of which was 43.8% in Alaska. This implies that a considerable school funding equity problem continues to exist across our nation.

Picus's district-level analysis also found that spending tends to be higher in larger metropolitan areas and that suburban districts sur-rounding large and very large cities tend to spend more than the central cities they surround. The opposite is true in medium-sized cities, but for small and medium cities, overall spending levels are below those for large and very large cities and their suburbs. Finally, rural areas have the second lowest per-pupil spending level, exceed-ing only the average spending of school districts in small cities.

Table 1.3. Equity Statistics by State for Per-Pupil Expenditures, 1989-90

State	Mean Per-Pupil Expenditures ($)	Federal Range Ratio (%)	Coefficient of Variation (%)
Alabama	3,490	41.43	10.40
Alaska	7,914	174.12	43.81
Arizona	3,358	98.19	20.87
Arkansas	2,995	54.62	13.52
California	4,457	61.14	17.21
Colorado	4,307	51.07	13.63
Connecticut	6,726	55.83	13.38
Delaware	5,229	34.75	9.91
Dist. Columbia	6,845	n/a	n/a
Florida	4,758	33.39	10.26
Georgia	3,930	82.42	18.80
Hawaii	4,288	n/a	n/a
Idaho	3,085	55.77	17.67
Illinois	4,180	139.31	29.86
Indiana	4,105	52.62	14.03
Iowa	4,063	25.57	8.29
Kansas	4,139	57.90	14.69
Kentucky	3,022	58.52	15.96
Louisiana	3,617	41.65	11.17
Maine	4,585	59.96	15.27
Maryland	6,202	53.36	15.95
Massachusetts	5,248	109.72	23.97
Michigan	4,419	89.91	21.48
Minnesota	4,677	49.93	14.15
Mississippi	2,944	41.96	11.99
Missouri	3,391	138.03	27.75

Analysis of district spending across the nation also showed that spending is highest in the smallest districts. There is a pattern of declining expenditures in general until enrollments reach approximately 25,000, when per-pupil expenditures begin to increase again.

Hertert et al. (1994) found similar results for disparities across the country. Using data for the 1989-1990 school year from virtually all school districts in the country, they found that for low-spending

Table 1.3. Continued

State	Mean Per-Pupil Expenditures ($)	Federal Range Ratio (%)	Coefficient of Variation (%)
Montana	4,282	142.40	32.16
Nebraska	4,451	88.77	22.38
Nevada	3,828	19.45	10.68
New Hampshire	4,795	61.09	16.31
New Jersey	6,560	76.25	18.49
New Mexico	3,965	56.84	17.20
New York	7,396	91.04	22.09
North Carolina	4,064	36.05	10.16
North Dakota	3,815	97.95	24.46
Ohio	4,343	109.75	24.29
Oklahoma	2,976	45.07	15.52
Oregon	4,862	74.34	18.59
Pennsylvania	5,503	98.29	20.92
Rhode Island	5,655	39.15	8.66
South Carolina	3,910	37.63	10.84
South Dakota	3,522	72.85	19.96
Tennessee	2,985	63.35	16.35
Texas	3,645	50.56	15.99
Utah	2,606	43.53	13.35
Vermont	5,081	84.87	19.17
Virginia	4,698	66.46	21.39
Washington	4,336	43.36	12.55
West Virginia	3,549	22.63	6.79
Wisconsin	5,417	47.17	14.73
Wyoming	5,206	63.17	19.67

SOURCE: Hertert, Busch, & Odden, 1994.

districts, it would cost $8.1 billion to bring their spending up to the median spending in their individual states, and some $13.2 billion to bring the spending in all districts below the national median up to the national median spending level in 1989-1990. Although these appear to be very large numbers, they represent only 4% and 6.6%, respectively, of total current operating education expenditures in that year.

Uses of Dollars in Schools

Spending by Function

How educational resources are spent is an important question. This section analyzes elementary and secondary school spending by function from a variety of perspectives. What is evident from this discussion is the consistency of the findings regarding how educational resources are used. All of the studies reported here find that approximately 60% of total resources are devoted to direct instruction. As the discussion below shows, this finding is consistent regardless of how the analysis is approached.

Spending on Instruction

Table 1.4 displays the shares of total expenditures allocated to different functions in 1991-1992 for all schools in the country. It shows that spending for instruction represented just over 60% of current expenditures. This is similar to Picus's (1993a) finding that approximately 60% of total district expenditures is devoted to instruction. Picus's analysis of SASS and census data found considerably less variation in the share of expenditures devoted to instruction than in the total spending per pupil. The coefficient of variation was only 10.6%, indicating that very little variation exists in the share of total resources that is devoted to instruction. Not only is this an important finding, but its consistency is surprising. It means that as their revenues increase, districts continue to spend each additional dollar in roughly the same proportion as the dollars they received previously. The strength of this finding is remarkable.

The national databases analyzed by Picus do not provide sufficient detail to conduct an analysis of noninstructional spending. To resolve this problem, CPRE researchers also analyzed spending by function in Florida, California, and New York. In Florida, where school-level data were available, the total per-pupil expenditures for an average Florida school were $4,022 in 1991-1992. Of that amount, 58.43% or $2,350 was devoted to direct instruction (Nakib & Picus, 1994). In California, Picus, Hertert, and Tetreault (in press) found that almost 60% of district expenditures was devoted to instruction in 1990-1991, and in New York, Monk and Roellke (1994) estimated that

Table 1.4. Total K-12 Expenditures by Function: 1990-91

Category	Expenditures (Thousands of Dollars)	% of Total Expenditures	% of Current Expenditures
Current expenditures	201,549,624	88.04	
Instruction	122,214,281	53.38	60.64
Student services	70,419,509	30.76	34.94
Students	8,933,843	3.90	4.43
Instructional support	8,467,453	3.70	4.20
General admin.	5,781,474	2.53	2.87
School admin.	11,680,254	5.10	5.80
Operation & maint.	21,323,871	9.31	10.58
Student transportation	8,666,697	3.79	4.30
Other	5,565,916	2.43	2.76
Food services	8,276,621	3.62	
Enterprise operations	639,213	0.28	
Other current	3,298,439	1.44	
Capital outlay	19,770,913	8.64	
Interest on school debt	4,314,321	1.88	
Total	228,933,297		

SOURCE: National Center for Education Statistics, 1993a, Table 160.

instruction represented just over 60% of spending in New York City and approximately 52% of total spending in districts across the rest of the state.

The finding that school districts spend approximately 60% of their resources on instruction is remarkably consistent across all studies that have attempted to ascertain how educational resources are allocated by school districts. A study by Cooper (1993) of eight school districts across the country looked closely at district and school spending patterns by function. Within eight sample districts, Cooper found that between 79.6% and 94.1% of total per-pupil expenditures was spent at school sites and that overall between 57.9% and 62.8% of total expenditures was devoted to instruction. Cooper's methodology analyzes school district spending from the "bottom up" by aggregating school-level expenditures. His methods have also found that instruction consistently accounts for 60% of a district's spending. Similarly, Sherman, O'Leary, and Lancaster (1992) found that in 1988-1989, school districts spent an average of 61.3% of their resources for instruction, and the California Department of Education (1987) estimated that in 1985-1986, 63.0% of that state's K-12 educational expenditures was allocated to direct classroom expenditures.

Odden, Palaich, and Augenblick (1979) found that spending for instruction represented about 60% of state/local operating expenditures per pupil in New York in 1977-1978 and that high-spending districts devoted a slightly higher percentage of their resources to instruction than low-spending districts (63% for the highest decile compared to 58% in the lowest-spending decile). Hartman (1988) found similar spending patterns in Pennsylvania, with two exceptions. Instructional spending as a percentage of total expenditures was approximately 60%, but the higher-spending districts tended to spend a slightly lower percentage of their funds on instruction compared with the low-spending districts (58.1% in the high-spending districts, compared with 61.3% in the low-spending districts). Also, Pennsylvania districts seemed to spend more on reducing class size and less on increasing teacher salaries as the level of funding increased.

These findings do not mean that all children are treated equally, however. As the data presented above indicate, there are dramatic disparities in the level of per-pupil expenditures across school districts. This means that a district spending $10,000 per pupil still has twice as much money to spend on instruction as a district spending $5,000 per pupil. Not surprisingly, we found that as a district's expenditures increase, the average class size declines, and average teacher salary increases somewhat. Moreover, one would expect additional services for children to be more readily available in high-spending districts than in low-spending districts. Barro (1992) estimated that districts that have an additional dollar of revenue to spend will devote approximately half of it to instruction, using 40 cents to reduce class size and 10 cents to increase teacher salaries.

Spending on Other Functions

If school districts spend 60% of their resources on instruction, then where does the remaining 40% go? Is there an administrative "blob," as some have argued? CPRE's research in Florida, California, and New York shows that administration, both central and school-site, represents only part of the story. The balance of the dollars spent on our schools is used for a number of other essential items, including operations and maintenance, transportation, and student services. Below, some of the major components of functional expenditures are described.

Administration

Table 1.4 shows that nationally, approximately 5.8% of total expenditures is devoted to school-site administration and 2.9% to central administration. These figures are similar to the findings in New York and Florida, where despite some differences in how they are divided up, the total for administration is approximately 8%. In New York, a slightly higher share of administrative costs is found at the central office (Monk & Roellke, 1994), whereas in Florida, a slightly higher share is devoted to school-site administration (Nakib & Picus, 1994).

The figures are different and substantially higher for California. This may be due not to higher administrative costs in that state, but to the fact that data analyzed for that state did not include the state's considerable categorical expenditures, which amount to approximately 25% of total expenditures. If the bulk of administrative costs is funded through a district's general fund, then these findings make the administrative expenditures in California appear artificially high (Picus et al., in press).

A criticism frequently levied against large urban school systems is the high cost of their administrative structures. Yet Monk and Roellke (1994) found that administrative spending in New York City is lower than the average for the rest of the state. Data from Florida's largest district, Dade County (the fourth largest district in the nation), shows a similar but somewhat weaker trend. Central administration represents 1.1% of Dade County's expenditures, and site administration another 6.3%. This is somewhat lower than the statewide average for spending in these two categories (Nakib & Picus, 1994). Earlier research on California by Picus (1991) found that administrative spending in the Los Angeles Unified School district was among the lowest in the state when considered as a percentage of total revenues.

Instructional Support

The evidence from Florida, New York, and California indicates that spending for instructional support varies widely across the states. In

Florida, instructional support, which in that state's accounting structure includes pupil personnel, instructional media, curriculum development, and staff training, amounts to almost 10% of total expenditures (Nakib & Picus, 1994). On the other hand, in California, instructional support represents only 1.56% of expenditures (Picus et al., in press). Supplies, training, and pupil services are accounted for in different locations in that state, and many of the services included in Florida's list are probably provided through the extensive categorical program in California. New York school districts spend approximately 4% of their funds on instructional support (Monk & Roellke, 1994). The only exception to this is New York City, which spends only 1.4% on instructional support.

Operations and Maintenance

Operations and maintenance expenditures averaged between 7.5% and 12.84% of district expenditures in all three states. Again, it is possible that California's numbers are high because of the missing categorical funds.

Pupil Transportation

Nationally, transportation expenditures averaged just over 4% of total spending across the United States, with New York school districts devoting somewhat more to transportation (Monk & Roellke, 1994) and California districts devoting somewhat less (Picus et al., in press).

Pupil-Teacher Ratios and Reported Class Size

A cursory review of the most recent edition of the *Digest of Education Statistics* (NCES, 1993a) shows that the average pupil-teacher ratio for K-12 public schools in the United States was 17.6:1 in 1993. Moreover, the data provided in the *Digest* suggest that this ratio has declined consistently since 1955, when it stood at 26.9 pupils per teacher (NCES, 1993a, p. 74). In fact, except for an increase of 0.1 pupils per teacher between 1961 and 1962, and slight increases from 17.2:1 in 1990 to 17.3:1 in 1991 and 17.6:1 in 1993, the average pupil-teacher ratio across the United States has declined in every year since 1955.

Picus (1993a) found that district-level pupil-teacher ratios declined as expenditures per pupil and expenditures per pupil for instruction increased. However, as the percentage of expenditures devoted to instruction increased, a similar pattern did not emerge. Because expenditure data were not available at the school level in the national databases, Picus (1993b) compared school-level pupil-teacher ratios with district per-pupil expenditures. He found that at the elementary, intermediate, and secondary school levels, there is a trend toward lower pupil-teacher ratios as expenditures increase.

The typical policy maker views the pupil-teacher ratio as a proxy for class size. Yet despite what would thus appear to be small class sizes, teachers across the nation claim their classes are much too large. They argue that if they are to succeed in making dramatic improvements in student achievement, class sizes must be reduced. They often describe classes with 30 or more students and talk of the impossibility of meeting the needs of individual students under such conditions. The explanation for this difference between what teachers say and what the national averages seem to indicate is that the national averages often include special education classes, which generally have many fewer students, and in many districts itinerant teachers who provide special pull-out services for children through a variety of programs, including Chapter 1, gifted and talented education, and art and music instruction. Also, these national averages often include certificated personnel who have nonteaching assignments, such as counselors or curriculum development specialists.

Perhaps the most important finding from Picus's (1994) analysis of the SASS teacher questionnaire data is the confirmation of teachers' arguments that they have much larger classes than most national and state-specific pupil-teacher ratio data indicate. Picus found that at the district and school level, the pupil-teacher ratio for elementary grades (K-6) is between 17.68 and 18.77. However, the mean teacher-reported class size for self-contained classrooms is 24.21, some 29% to 36% larger than estimates based on district and school data.

Similarly, the average secondary school pupil-teacher ratio as reported on the district-level SASS questionnaires was 14.41. At the school level, the mean pupil-teacher ratio was 16.38 for intermediate schools and 16.55 for secondary schools. On the other hand, the self-reported average class size for departmentalized classes amounted to 22.65. The difference between self-reported class size and the pupil-teacher ratios computed through district and school averages, though disconcerting, was not unexpected, given that teachers have been making similar claims for a number of years (see Hertert, Chapter 4 of this volume, for more detailed information on this particular line of research).

In Florida, Nakib and Picus (1994) found an average of 21.37 pupils per regular teacher at the district level and 13.9 pupils per teacher if specialists were included in the count of teachers for 1991-1992. In California, the average district pupil-teacher ratio in 1990-1991 was estimated at 23.26 by Hertert (1993).

Average Teacher Salaries

Teacher salaries represent the largest single component of school district budgets. Picus (1993a) reported that there was considerable variation across districts in salary levels. He found that there was a close correlation between the salary level on each of the steps on a districts teacher salary schedule and average salary in the district. He also found that district location had a major impact on salaries, as did the overall level of per-pupil expenditures.

Expenditure by Program

Nakib and Picus (1994) also reported expenditures by program across Florida school districts. Table 1.5 summarizes their findings. The table shows that approximately 55% of total expenditures in Florida school districts is devoted to K-8 education and that another 19% goes toward 9-12 education. It is somewhat surprising that high schools receive a substantially smaller portion of total spending than do the K-3 or 4-8 program areas. Expenditures on programs for exceptional children represent almost 15% of spending, whereas programs for at-risk students and vocational education consume just over 11% of district spending.

Conclusion

This summary of the research conducted to date by the Finance Center of CPRE shows that over the past 35 years, real per-pupil

Table 1.5. Share of Total Expenditures by Program:
Florida School Districts, 1991-92

Program	% of Total Expenditures
Grades K-3	27.42
Grades 4-8	27.54
Grades 9-12	19.05
At-risk	5.01
Exceptional	14.72
Vocational	6.33

SOURCE: Nakib & Picus, 1994.

expenditures for education across the United States have increased by over 207%. Although the rate of increase has varied across the 50 states, real spending has increased in each of the states during the past three and a half decades. Over that period of time, the federal share of education funding has increased from just over 4% in 1959-1960 to nearly 10% in 1979 to 1980 and then declined again to today's level of approximately 6.2%. During the same period of time, state revenues have become the largest source of K-12 education revenues, accounting for over 47% of total revenue in recent years. In 1978-1979, state revenues became, for the first time, the single largest source of funding for school districts.

It appears that most of the money expended by school districts for education is spent at the school level. Data from studies by Cooper (1993) indicate that between 80% and 90% of a district's funds are spent at the school level. This figure is remarkably consistent across districts, regardless of location, spending level, or demographic composition of the student population.

The noninstructional dollars represent not an administrative "blob," as some have claimed, but spending for important functions such as maintenance and operations, student transportation, site administration, and instructional support in the form of staff to help teachers and students. Moreover, there is growing evidence that central office administration as a percentage of total district expenditures is lower in large urban districts. Although large urban districts' administrative expenditures are quite high, they are spread over even larger student and employee bases.

Districts that have more money tend to spend about half of it on additional instruction, with approximately 40% devoted to reducing class size and 10% to increase teacher salaries (Barro, 1992). The balance of these additional funds is used to provide more of existing services outside the classroom.

As we attempt to understand the impact of educational resources on student outcomes, gaining a stronger knowledge of how existing resources are used by school districts is important. The studies conducted under the "What Money Buys" banner have provided a great deal of new data on how resources are allocated. The next step is to learn how those resources affect student outcome, and to find ways to direct future educational resources toward methods that improve student performance.

References

Barro, S. M. (1992). *What does the education dollar buy? Relationships of staffing, staff characteristics, and staff salaries to state per-pupil spending.* Washington, DC: SMB Economic Research.

California Department of Education. (1987). *The cost of a California school.* Sacramento: Author.

Cooper, B. (1993, March). *School-site cost allocations: Testing a micro-financial model in 23 districts in ten states.* Paper presented at the annual meeting of the American Education Finance Association, Albuquerque, NM.

Hartman, W. T. (1988). District spending: What do the dollars buy? *Journal of Education Finance, 13,* 436-459.

Hertert, L. (1993). *Resource allocation patterns in public education: An analysis of school level equity in California.* Unpublished dissertation, University of Southern California.

Hertert, L., Busch, C., & Odden, A. (1994, March). *School financing inequities among the states: The problem and the potential for federal solutions.* Paper presented at the annual meeting of the American Education Finance Association, Nashville, TN.

Monk, D. H., & Roellke, C. (1994, March). *The origin, disposition and utilization of resources within New York State public school systems: A progress report.* Paper presented at the annual meeting of the American Education Finance Association, Nashville, TN.

Nakib, Y. A., & Picus, L. O. (1994, March). *Allocation and use of K-12 education funds: A summary of "what dollars buy" in Florida.* Paper presented at the annual meeting of the American Education Finance Association, Nashville, TN.

National Center for Education Statistics. (1993a). *Digest of education statistics: 1993.* Washington, DC: U.S. Department of Education.

National Center for Education Statistics. (1993b). *Projections of education statistics to 2004.* Washington, DC: U.S. Department of Education.

Odden, A. R., & Kim, L. (1992). Reducing disparities across the states: A new federal role in school finance. In A. R. Odden (Ed.), *Rethinking school finance: An agenda for the 1990s* (pp. 260-297). San Francisco: Jossey-Bass.

Odden, A. R., Palaich, R., & Augenblick, J. (1979). *Analysis of the New York State school finance system, 1977-78.* Denver, CO: Education Commission of the States.

Odden, A. R., & Picus, L. O. (1992). *School finance: A policy perspective.* New York: McGraw-Hill.

Picus, L. O. (1991). Cadillacs or Chevrolets? The effects of state control on school finance in California. *Journal of Education Finance, 17,* 33-59.

Picus, L. O. (1993a). *The allocation and use of educational resources: District level evidence from the schools and staffing survey* (Working Paper No. 34). Los Angeles: Consortium for Policy Research in Education, Finance Center.

Picus, L. O. (1993b). *The allocation and use of educational resources: School level evidence from the schools and staffing survey* (Working Paper No. 37). Los Angeles: Consortium for Policy Research in Education, Finance Center.

Picus, L. O. (1994). Estimating the determinants of pupil/teacher ratios: Evidence from the schools and staffing survey. *Educational Considerations, 21*(2), 44-52.

Picus, L. O., Hertert, L., & Tetreault, D. (in press). *An analysis of resource allocation patterns in California schools and school districts.* Los Angeles: Center for Research in Education Finance.

Picus, L. O., & Nakib, Y. A. (1993). *The allocation and use of educational resources at the district level in Florida* (Working Paper No. 38). Los Angeles: Consortium for Policy Research in Education, Finance Center.

Sherman, J. D., O'Leary, M. B., & Lancaster, M. (1992, March). *Trends in state expenditures for elementary and secondary education.* Paper presented at the annual meeting of the American Education Finance Association, Williamsburg, VA.

TWO

The Quest for Equalized Mediocrity
SCHOOL FINANCE REFORM
WITHOUT CONSIDERATION
OF SCHOOL PERFORMANCE

ERIC A. HANUSHEK

Although school finance had a history prior to *Serrano v. Priest* (1971), that history has been displaced almost completely by the more recent developments across the states. Today, school finance is synonymous with court action to alter funding patterns or, at times, state legislation designed to deal with past or prospective court actions about funding patterns. Although school finance discussions might bring in issues of student performance, the focus remains unabashedly on the distribution of educational revenue. Along with the implicit concentration on variations in school revenue patterns across districts has come the sense that this discussion must precede any other policy activities of the state because finance is a "necessary" if not "sufficient" condition for the improvement of schools. Unfortunately, no matter how convincing the case for inequities in school outcomes, no evidence supports the notion that financing reform of the type typically promoted will cure these inequities. Moreover, there is reason to believe almost the opposite—that reform as commonly conceived could actually be harmful. The reason for this is simple: None of the discussion or policy initiatives deals directly with student performance.

A Brief History

The California case of *Serrano* was born in the late 1960s and was a very natural extension of the War on Poverty. The arguments were straightforward and compelling. Poor and disadvantaged students were not competing well in schools—as measured by school attainment, achievement tests, and popular testimonials. Moreover, as state school finance systems had evolved, the local property tax was used extensively to finance a system of local public schools, and this tax instrument implied that rich jurisdictions—property-wealthy ones— could more easily raise funds than poor ones. It was then straightforward and natural to put these two observations together and to deal with the problems of inequitable outcomes through the system of financing schools. This approach also had real advantages from a policy perspective. Defining the school-financing formula and the distribution of school funds is the type of school policy intervention that state legislatures are accustomed to doing. It is also the type of issue that the courts can take on if they are determined that the legislature has not fulfilled its constitutional obligations.

As is well known, subsequent actions of the U.S. Supreme Court in *San Antonio Independent School District v. Rodriguez* (1973) eliminated issues related to the U.S. Constitution, and all of the debate turned to issues in individual states. When the finance issue is placed in the separate states, each with a different constitutional provision and history, it is more difficult to make overall judgments about the lessons of the legal history. Indeed, different states have reached different judgments about the constitutionality of their financing arrangements. But this fact should not be surprising because both constitutional requirements and financing arrangements differ widely across states. Enough common policy issues nevertheless remain so that analysis of general financing issues is useful.

School finance cases have spread across the states over the quarter century of their recent form. Indeed, some states have had more than one case, not counting the lengthy appeals and reappearances of individual cases. The form of the arguments in the cases has evolved somewhat. Most cases retain a core set of arguments revolving around variations in the ability of local jurisdictions to raise tax revenues. Most recently, however, a new element—"adequacy"—has been introduced. Though no standard definition of adequacy has yet to emerge, the central argument is simply that even if funding were

equalized across jurisdictions, the funding available would be insufficient to accomplish the purposes of schools. Adequacy may be
applied to argue that the overall level of a state's spending is too low
to accomplish the state's constitutional mandate with respect to schools.
Or it may be applied to argue that equal spending is not the objective
because some districts require additional funds to deal with an especially hard-to-educate student population.

Each of the traditional arguments for striking down local funding
of schools comes complete with appealing slogans. For the core arguments about local revenue-raising ability, the overriding argument is
that "the quality of a student's education should not be a function of
the wealth of the student's neighbors." For adequacy, it is simply that
"we should not handicap students for life by failing to provide resources sufficient for a first-class education for all." These slogans are
simultaneously appealing, misleading, and, at times, damaging to the
cause of ensuring a high-quality, equitable schooling system.

The court arguments and the related popular discussion of school
finance reform rely on three key but unstated assumptions. First, local
revenue-raising capacity is the key determinant of variations in school
spending across districts. It is easy to present simulations of property
tax bases across jurisdictions that suggest that raising an equal amount
of funding in all jurisdictions implies quite divergent tax rates. But, of
course, tax rates are not the only thing to come into play in determining actual spending decisions, as the preferences of citizens, the
efficiency of the schools in using funds, the needs of the student
population, and a variety of other factors influence patterns of school
spending. Moreover, as discussed later, individuals are not simply
placed in districts with their differences in revenue bases, but exercise
some considerable choice in where they decide to reside. Second,
general discussions of finance assume that revenue capacity of a
district is directly related to the incomes of students in the jurisdiction.
The impression often conveyed is that the property tax base is largely
dictated by residential property and that a large tax base is an indicator of large homes and high incomes. Yet this assumption is far from
being true. The distribution of commercial and industrial property is
very important in determining local property wealth, but this nonresi-
dential wealth is not very directly related to either residential wealth
or household incomes in jurisdictions. Thus, property wealth, the
usual measure of tax capacity employed in these considerations, does
not equate in any simple manner to the distribution of household

income and wealth across jurisdictions. Moreover, the relationship between property tax base and family incomes or poverty varies within and across states, making simple generalizations impossible. The implications of the incorrectness of both these assumptions are considered later, but the main focus of this chapter is the final implicit assumption.

The most critical assumption of all school finance discussions is that spending is a good measure of school quality. This assumption permits direct and easy evaluation of the distribution of school quality within a state. It also makes remedies obvious because "low quality" can be corrected by increasing the resources going to the district. This notion is appealing and commonsensical, just not supported by the evidence. Moreover, pursuing policies that flow from the presumed relationship between spending and school performance can actually do long-run harm to a state's schools.

School Expenditure
and Student Performance

Analysis summarized in *Making Schools Work* (Hanushek et al. 1994) demonstrates clearly that education is valuable to individuals and society as a whole. The economy's valuing of skilled individuals leads directly to high relative earnings in the labor market and low relative unemployment rates of the more educated. Over the past two decades, the earnings advantages associated with more schooling have soared (see Kosters, 1991; McMahon, 1991; Murphy & Welch, 1989). These facts on their own justify general investment in schooling, but they are only part of the story. More educated members of society are generally healthier, more likely to become informed citizens who participate in government, less likely to be involved in crime, and less likely to be dependent on public support (see Haveman & Wolfe, 1984; Wolfe & Zuvekas, 1995). Moreover, the education level of the workforce affects the rate of productivity growth in the economy, and thus the future economic well-being of society. These latter factors, while further justifying schooling investments, provide reasons for governmental support and finance of education (as opposed to purely private finance).

If schooling has been such a good investment, why is there so much dissatisfaction with our schools? Much of the analysis of the effects of education on earnings and the economy relates exclusively to the amount of schooling obtained by the population, typically measured just as years of schooling attained. But the previous growth in school attainment of the population has virtually stopped, and with it the debate has become much more directed at quality differences. The issues now center on whether students are learning sufficient amounts during each year of schooling and whether learning is sufficient given the resources devoted to schools.

The strongest evidence about the effects of school quality relates to individual earnings. Better skills of individuals, which can be directly related to the quality of schooling, are rewarded in the labor market. There is also evidence that such skills are becoming more important over time as an increasingly technical workplace looks for people to fill jobs.[1] Finally, school quality directly affects the amount of school an individual completes, with students from better schools seeking postsecondary education and thus enjoying the added rewards of increased quantity (Hanushek, Rivkin, & Taylor, 1995). These benefits again justify investments in school quality.

The overall story about what has been happening in schools is clear: The rapid increases in expenditure on schools in the past three decades have simply not been matched by measurable increases in student performance. Moreover, detailed studies of schools have shown a variety of inefficiencies that, if corrected, could provide funds for a variety of improvement programs.

There has been a dramatic rise in real expenditure per pupil over the entire century. Figure 2.1 shows that, after allowing for inflation, expenditures per pupil have increased at almost 3.5% per year for 100 years (see Hanushek & Rivkin, 1994; Hanushek, Rivkin, & Jamison, 1992). This remarkable growth is not explained away by such things as increases in special education or changes in the number of immigrant students in the school population, though those have had a noticeable impact on school expenditures.

The spending increases that have occurred have come from three basic sources. In terms of direct instructional staff expenditure, both declines in pupil-teacher ratios and increases in the real salaries of teachers have been very important. These are the primary elements behind the lower portion of the graph in Figure 2.1, which plots instructional staff and other expenditures per student. Throughout the century, teachers have been used more intensively, as a result both of direct programs to reduce class size and of the introduction of new

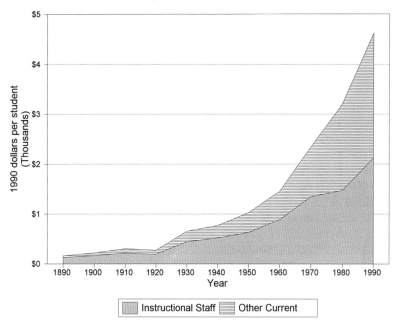

Figure 2.1. Instructional Staff and Other Expenditures per Student in the United States, 1890-1990

supplementary programs that expand on teacher usage. Real teacher salaries have also grown, although in a somewhat complicated way. The increases in teacher salaries have not been uniform, for periods in which salaries do not keep up with inflation are offset by periods of more rapid increase. Moreover, even with general improvement, salary growth has not kept up with growth in salaries in other occupations. Thus, although teacher wages have put cost pressure on schools, school salaries have been competitive with a smaller proportion of outside jobs over time.

The top portion of Figure 2.1 identifies in a general way the third source of cost increases. Expenditures outside those for instructional staff have increased even more rapidly than those for instructional staff. Between 1960 and 1990, instructional staff expenditure fell from 61% to 46% of total current expenditure. Unfortunately, what underlies this trend is unclear because there are very poor data on these expenditures. Though it is often convenient to attribute them simply to "increased bureaucracy," the available data neither confirm nor deny this interpretation, because these expenditures include a variety of items that are legitimately classroom expenditures (such as teacher health and retirement funds or purchases of books and supplies) in addition to administrative and other spending. The aggregate effects are clear, however: If these expenditures had grown between 1960 and 1990 at just the rate of instructional staff spending—which itself includes significant increases in resource intensity—total spending per pupil would have been 25% lower in 1990.

Matched against the growth in spending, student performance has at best stayed constant and may have fallen. The pattern of performance change is easiest to see with the scores for various subjects on the National Assessment of Educational Progress, or NAEP. (See Figure 2.2; U.S. Department of Education, 1994.) While aggregate performance measures are somewhat imprecise, all point to no gains in student performance over time.

There have also been a series of embarrassing comparisons with students in other countries. The comparisons of U.S. and Japanese students in the early 1980s showed, for example, that only 5% of American students surpassed the average Japanese student in mathematics proficiency (see McKnight et al., 1987; National Research Council, 1989). In 1991 comparisons, Korean 9-year-olds appeared closer to U.S. 13-year-olds than to U.S. 9-year-olds, hardly the kind of performance that would suggest that U.S. students will soon be top in the world in mathematics performance (National Center for Education Statistics, 1994).

The problems of performance are particularly acute when considered by race or socioeconomic status (Congressional Budget Office, 1986). Even though there has been some narrowing of the differences in performance, the remaining disparities are huge and incompatible with society's goal of equity. During the 1980s, there was a broad-based convergence of black-white score differences on the SAT and NAEP, but most recent data suggest that convergence may have ceased.

The aggregate results, in which expenditure increases have not been accompanied by improvements in student performance, are confirmed in more detailed studies of schools and classrooms (see the summaries in Hanushek, 1986, 1989). These more detailed studies document a variety of common policies that increase costs but offer no assurances of commensurate improvements in student performance. The wide range of careful econometric studies reviewed indicate that key resources—ones that are the subject of much policy attention—

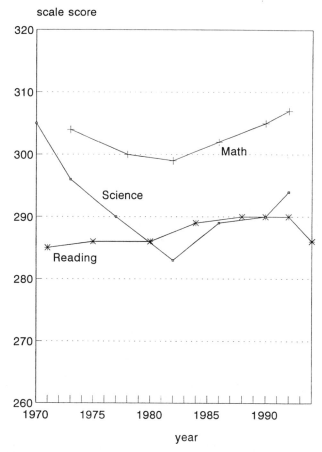

Figure 2.2. National Assessment of Educational Progress (NAEP) Performance of 17-year-olds, 1970-1994

are not consistently or systematically related to improved student performance.

Perhaps the most dramatic finding of analyses of schools is that smaller class sizes usually have no general impact on student performance, even though they have obvious implications for school costs. Moreover, the basic econometric evidence is supported by experimental evidence, making it one of the clearest results from an extensively researched topic.[2] Though some specific instruction may

Table 2.1. Percentage Distribution of Estimated Effect of Key Resources on Student Performance (377 Studies)

Resources	Number of Estimates	Statistically Significant		Statistically Insignificant		Insignificant, Unknown Sign
		+	-	+	-	
Teacher-pupil ratio	277	15%	13%	27%	25%	20%
Teacher education	171	9%	5%	33%	27%	26%
Teacher experience	207	29%	5%	30%	24%	12%

be enhanced by smaller classes, student performance in most classes is unaffected by variations in class size in standard operations of, say, class sizes between 15 and 40 students.[3] This lack of relationship is evident in Table 2.1, which includes a tabulation of the 277 available estimates of the effects of teacher-pupil ratios.[4] Few of the estimates give any confidence that there is a real relationship (i.e., few are statistically significant). Moreover, positive estimates are almost equally matched by negative estimates. Nevertheless, even in the face of high costs that yield no apparent performance benefits, the overall policy of states and local districts has been to reduce class size in order to try to increase quality (see below).

A second, almost equally dramatic, example is that obtaining an advanced degree does little to ensure that teachers do a better job in the classroom. It is essentially as likely for a teacher with a bachelor's degree to elicit high performance from students as it is for a teacher with a master's degree. Only 16 of 171 separate estimates of the effects of teacher education find positive and statistically significant effects, and 9 find negative and statistically significant effects (see Table 2.1). Again, because a teacher's salary invariably increases with the completion of a master's degree, this is another example of increased expenditure yielding no gains in performance.

The final major resource category with a direct impact on school spending (through salary determination) is teacher experience. The evidence on the effectiveness of experienced teachers is more mixed than for the previous categories, but it does not provide convincing support of a strong relationship with performance.

These resource effects are important for two reasons. First, variations in instructional expenditure across classrooms are largely de-

Table 2.2. Public School Resources, 1961-1991

Resource	1960-61	1965-66	1970-71	1975-76	1980-81	1985-86	1990-91
Pupil-teacher ratio	25.6	24.1	22.3	20.2	18.8	17.7	17.3
% teachers with master's degree	23.1	23.2	27.1	37.1	49.3	50.7	52.6
Median years teacher experience	11	8	8	8	12	15	15
Current expenditure/ADA (1992-93 $s)	$1,903	$2,402	$3,269	$3,864	$4,116	$4,919	$5,582

SOURCE: National Center for Education Statistics, 1994.

termined by the pupil-teacher ratio and the salary of the teacher (which in turn is largely determined by the teacher's degree and experience). If these factors have no systematic influence on student performance—which the evidence shows they do not—expansion of resources in the ways of the past is unlikely to improve performance. Second, either explicitly or implicitly, schools have pursued a program of adding these specific resources. Table 2.2 traces these resources over the past several decades. The schools currently have record-low pupil-teacher ratios, record-high completion of master's degrees, and more experienced teachers than at any time at least since 1960. These factors put in resource terms the result of many specific programs that have contributed to the rapid growth in per-pupil spending. But they have not led to improvements in student performance. Schools do not regularly ensure that increased student performance flows from increased expenditure.

Recent discussions of the existing literature reinforce these conclusions, although some readers may lose the central message in the technical discussions that have surrounded the debate. The discussions of existing work in Hedges, Laine, and Greenwald (1994) and Laine et al. (Chapter 3 of this volume) provide evidence that some school systems appear to use money effectively in the sense of getting positive effects from increased real resources or expenditure, but that many others provide no basis for believing that money will be spent effectively. Even though written to suggest differences in results, these analyses are entirely consistent with the findings and conclusions here. The key element of their analysis, which unfortunately receives no discussion until their conclusions, is that they ask whether there is evidence *anywhere* that expenditure *ever* matters. In essence, they devote all of their attention to the fact that 15% of the studies in Table 2.1 find positive and significant effects of larger teacher-pupil ratios—as contrasted with the 5% that would be expected by statistical tests if no school ever used small classes effectively. Unfortunately, they completely ignore that 85% of the estimated effects of teacher-pupil ratios, 91% of the estimated effects of greater teacher education, and 71% of the estimated effects of teacher experience give no confidence of a positive effect and that some proportion even give confidence of a perverse negative effect. These latter comparisons are the key to policy considerations centered on overall changes in resources allocated to schools.[5]

The researchers' array of tables confirms that money appears sometimes to be used effectively. Though some of the assumptions behind this statistical analysis are clearly unwarranted by the data, their central finding that some districts use money effectively and many do not is the entire point of this discussion. Said differently, there is no reason to presume that adding extra resources to a district employing the existing decision-making structure will improve student achievement. In some instances it may. In others it may not. In still others, achievement may actually fall. The overwhelming majority of results suggest, however, that we should have no confidence that adding resources will consistently and systematically improve student performance. In the face of such general uncertainty about the effects on student performance of added expenditure, consideration of the potential magnitude of effects implied is clearly misleading and useless.[6]

None of this accumulated evidence suggests that any minimum level of resources is needed for promoting student achievement. Nor is there any suggestion in the underlying data that there are significant nonlinearities—say, through diminishing marginal returns to resources—in the relationship between expenditure and student achievement.[7] These conclusions follow directly from the underlying studies, regardless of the specific method used to summarize the results. And they underscore why simple resource policies—by themselves or related to policies of school financing—are likely to be ineffective.

A final aspect of this analysis deserves attention. Even though there has been a concerted effort to identify specific aspects of schools and teachers that systematically improve student performance, no such factors have been reliably identified. Individual studies tend to find one or more specific factors that are correlated with performance, but factors thus identified seldom hold up to further scrutiny in other studies. Furthermore, no systematic evidence is available to indicate why some districts tend to make better choices—ones leading to heightened student performance—than other districts make.

Although there is no consensus about what specific factors affect student performance, there is overwhelming evidence that some teachers and schools are significantly better than others. For example, within inner-city schools, progress of students with a good teacher can exceed that of students with a poor teacher by more than a year of achievement during a single school year (Hanushek, 1992). The dramatic differences in performance are simply not determined by the training of teachers, the number of students in the classroom, or the overall level of spending. Resource differences do not describe the differences in performance across teachers and schools. Therefore, the measures of resource differences cannot be used to indicate potential problems (such as underfunding or resource shortages). Nor can they be used to describe policies that will yield better student results. A primary task of school reform is increasing the likelihood that a student ends up in a high-learning environment.

The lack of overall relationship between resources and performance surprises many people, but perhaps it should not. The most startling feature of schools—a feature distinguishing them from more successful parts of our economy—is that rewards are only vaguely associated with performance, if at all. A teacher who produces exceptionally large gains in her students' performance generally sees little difference in compensation, career advancement, job status, or general recognition when compared with a teacher who produces exceptionally small gains. A superintendent who provides similar student achievement to that in the past while spending less is unlikely to get rewarded above what would be the case for spending the same or more. If there are few incentives to obtain improved performance, it should not be surprising to find that resources are not systematically used in a fashion that improves performance.

As more completely described in *Making Schools Work* (Hanushek et al. 1994), these results reflect the structure and operating procedures of schools observed in the existing settings. A different organizational structure with different incentives could produce very different results. For example, almost every economist would support the position that increasing teacher salaries would expand and improve the pool of potential teachers. However, whether this improves the quality of teaching depends on whether schools can systematically choose and retain the best teachers from the pool (see Ballou & Podgursky, 1995). The results on salary differentials presented previously might be very different if schools faced a greater incentive to produce student achievement and if mechanisms for teacher selection were altered. In other words, there seems to be little question that money *could* count. It just does not systematically do so with the current organization of schools.

Moreover, the consistency criterion used to judge the results and the potential for policy improvements does not suggest that money never counts. The results are entirely compatible with some schools using funds effectively and others not. But unless some way is found to change the districts that would squander additional funds into districts that would use them effectively, added resources are not likely to lead to any improvement in average performance. Good uses of funds are balanced by bad uses within the current structure.

The current inefficiencies of schools, with too much money spent for the student performance obtained, indicate that schools can generally make improvements in their performance at no additional cost. They need simply to use existing resources in more effective ways. These inefficiencies also indicate that continuing the general policies of the past, even if dressed up in new clothing, is unlikely to lead to student performance gains, even though cost pressures will continue to mount. Though it may be appropriate to increase spending on schools in the future, the first priority is restructuring how existing resources are being used.

Implications for School Finance

The evidence on school performance indicates that variations in school expenditure are exceedingly poor measures of the variations in education provided to students. Most directly, when learning of students is the concern, the conventional evidence about interdistrict disparities in spending does not identify where educational deficiencies are to be found, and such evidence is generally irrelevant for either an equal-protection or an educational disparity court case. Such evidence about expenditure simply does not indicate differential provision of education. Therefore, showing how expenditures vary either absolutely or with characteristics of districts and students does not have much use.

We must be quite precise about the interpretation of expenditure. As previously noted, most economists, including myself, would readily accept that differences in spending would be directly related to the education provided that schools were operating efficiently. The previously presented evidence indicates clearly, however, that assuming efficiency in spending is entirely inappropriate.

Although there are many alternative ways to define and measure educational equity, only the most narrow of these would call for paying attention to expenditure variations in the face of the evidence that such expenditure variations are unrelated to the education provided. The standard employed would have to be a rigid one linked to dollars, with total disregard for the quality of schooling received by students. In other words, equity and efficiency are inextricably linked. It is not possible to ignore efficiency issues under the guise of just being concerned about equity (see Hanushek, 1991, 1993).

Discussions of "adequacy" founder on the same problems. Current knowledge does not permit specifying any definitive minimum level of resources that is needed. Nor does it permit identifying how much more expenditure disadvantaged students may require above that for more advantaged students.

There is another side to this discussion: What is likely to happen if we disregard the evidence on the interpretation of expenditure differences and simply make policy on the basis of expenditure differences? This consideration is prompted by a few sometimes-heard arguments such as "The educational problem of the poor is serious, and equalizing expenditure cannot hurt," or "We should at least give everyone the same chance to make mistakes." The policies flowing from such notions do, unfortunately, have a downside to them.

First, a likely reaction to any move to lessen variation in expenditure is to increase the total level of expenditure on schools. This is just the outcome found by Downes and Shah (1995). The reason is simple: A state legislature, faced with a need to alter expenditure patterns, finds it much easier to redistribute a larger pie than a fixed pie. This is, in the school finance debate, frequently referred to as "leveling up," or bringing the low-spending districts up to where the top districts are. The arguments behind the policy are generally ones either of the need to do better or of pure political necessity. On the other hand, because of the potential for disruption and the obvious divisiveness of "leveling down," there is seldom much interest in such ideas. The previous evidence indicates, however, that such added funds will on average be dissipated on things that do not improve student achievement (at least unless other, larger changes are also made). Teachers, administrators, and, perhaps, taxpayers in some districts gaining funds will probably be happier, but the average state taxpayer and parent will not find that the resulting changes do much more than increase tax bills.

Second, there is no assurance that the new funds will go to the schools of poor children. As indicated previously, one of the pervasive views of finance "reform" is that poor children will be helped (or at least will have a better chance by virtue of larger funding). But reform schemes designed to follow district wealth patterns can lead to unexpected outcomes because there is frequently not a strong relationship between district wealth and the concentration of student poverty.

Some states find that wealthier districts in terms of property wealth per student also have concentrations of poorer families and children. New York State provides a good illustration. Consider the six largest cities in New York State: New York City, Buffalo, Rochester, Yonkers, Syracuse, and Albany. Albany and Yonkers have tax bases in which real property per student is greater than the state average; New York City, Rochester, and Syracuse have tax bases per student only slightly below the state average; and Buffalo is left with a tax base 30% below the state average. Yet all of these districts except Yonkers have poverty rates for children above the state average. For example, whereas the average poverty rate in New York State for children 18 or younger in 1980 was 19.0%, it was over 36% in New York City and over 30% in Buffalo.[8] The largest districts in the state intervened (unsuccessfully) on the side of the plaintiffs in the *Levittown v. Nyquist* (1982) case and introduced a new argument, municipal overburden, in order to protect their funding.

In other states, property wealth and poverty may be negatively correlated—that is, high property wealth tends to be found in districts with a small poverty population—but even in these states the overall pattern clearly does not hold jurisdiction by jurisdiction. Therefore, although not a necessity, it is likely that many districts serving poor children are hurt in spending terms by plans to neutralize expenditure on the basis of district wealth. Moreover, because of a combination of federal and state grants, districts with concentrations of poor students frequently have above-average spending, regardless of their property wealth or overall economic health. Programs to limit variations in expenditure could operate to cut back existing compensatory spending for disadvantaged students.

Third, spending differences may not even accurately reflect the real resources each district is able to deliver (i.e., the actual educational inputs). This is the simple result of possible cost differentials facing individual districts. That is, if districts face different prices for things they might buy, from teachers to buildings and equipment, dollar variations themselves do not indicate variations in available real resources. As a simple example, if the schools in one city are less pleasant and desirable than those in other cities, it will be necessary to pay a higher salary to get a teacher of equal quality.[9] An extension of this involves districts faced with concentrations of students who are more difficult to educate because of a variety of preexisting educational deficiencies. These, like cost differences for inputs, lead to expenditure variations in districts behaving in an otherwise identical manner. (Indeed, many state funding formulas recognize such issues and attempt to adjust for input cost differences or for differences in student preparation, handicap status, and the like, even though the magnitude of any real cost differences is poorly understood and measured.)

Fourth, districts themselves are not entities to which we should gear educational policies. Individuals choose among districts when they enter an area and move among districts after they live in an area. In fact, there is extensive evidence that individuals make choices among districts in part to satisfy their demands for various public services. Some people who generally place considerable weight on schooling search for districts that seem to emphasize quality schooling. Others who emphasize other goods or even low public expenditure seek districts that provide an agreeable level and pattern of the services they are looking for. Certainly, this system has some drawbacks. Moving can be expensive, and some might find it difficult to move to the districts they would like—say, because of housing prices, commuting costs, or discrimination. Nevertheless, the fundamental fact for this discussion is that individuals generally have considerable latitude in choosing schools. They are not inextricably tied to a particular district and are not doomed to whatever expenditure levels currently exist in a specific district. Finally, individual districts change their expenditure in line with the desires of the population and with population shifts, so that districts may increase or decrease their expenditure over time. For example, it is possible to trace the movement of district expenditure in the state of Indiana between 1977 and 1987. Only 43 of the 76 top spending districts in 1977 remained in the top quartile in 1987; only 42 of the 76 bottom-quartile districts remained there from 1977 through 1987. Thus policy discussions that speak generally of the population as captives of districts (with undesirable spending patterns) tend to miss an extremely important feature of the political economy of local jurisdictions. (The special problems of "mobility-constrained" groups, such as the poor, are discussed below.)

Fifth, the preferences and movements of citizens across district boundaries have direct ramifications for the observed distribution of property wealth. Specifically, districts that appear to offer a particularly favorable tax and school quality package will appear relatively attractive to many people. This will lead to a bidding up of housing prices in such desirable jurisdictions because they are in demand, other things being equal. In fact, it is well documented that "otherwise identical" houses will sell for different amounts *because of* citizens' evaluations of the taxes and the schooling being offered (see Oates, 1969; Rosen & Fullerton, 1977; Tiebout, 1956; Walker, 1995; Wendling, 1981). Another way of saying this is that some people pay for their schooling up front through the capitalization of school advantages into the price of homes. Some places that initially look attractive from the vantage point of just the tax rate are really less attractive because the low rate is multiplied by a high valuation (relative to the other attributes of the home). This has, among other things, a direct effect on the property tax base of the community—something that is often entered into the discussion of the "inequities" of the school finance system. Moreover, reform changes in the funding formula of the state imply distributing somewhat arbitrary capital gains and capital losses across the jurisdictions in the state. Some places will be made more fiscally attractive and some less by major changes in the financing laws, leading to changes in the capitalization of the fiscal differences.

Sixth, in most states spending levels reflect a wide variety of things, including the preferences of the citizens. Though it is common to argue that local property wealth is the primary determinant of expenditure differences, that simply is not the case. For example, even though New Jersey and Indiana have relied on local property taxes to fund schools, rough estimates indicate that less than one fifth of the variation in expenditure would be eliminated by totally equating local property wealth per student.[10] A combination of local preferences, differences in student needs, curricular choices, cost differentials, and a variety of other factors completely dominates property wealth in the determination of the pattern of expenditure.

Seventh, differences in tax rates across communities bear no direct relationship to the degree of educational equity. Most important, school finance reform has been based on perceived differences in the quality of education available, and the quality of education is not related in any simple way to tax rates. The tax rate provides an indication of the price that residents face to raise funds for schools, and high tax rates might indicate that some districts find it more difficult than others to raise funds through the property tax. But tax rates differ according to a variety of factors, including community preferences, community income and wealth, and the amount of non-residential wealth in the tax base. The pattern of tax rates may be an issue from the standpoint of various notions of "taxpayer equity," but it seldom has much to do with considerations of equity in education. Further, although the education clauses of state constitutions may place requirements on states to provide certain levels of education, they never indicate that school tax rates must be equalized across a state.

The overall thrust of this listing of likely ramifications is to underscore the point that simple alterations in expenditure patterns can have consequential and undesirable effects. From what we know about the educational process and about behavior of local jurisdictions, we arrive at the inescapable conclusion hinted at previously. The general assumptions behind early school finance reform are at best misleading.

Conclusions

A simple argument undergirds much of the current school finance discussion. Because the lack of consistent relationship between spending and student performance cannot be easily dismissed or ignored, those who would argue for rearranging (and increasing) school revenues fall back on the blithe comment, "Of course, we do not advocate spending money in ways that are unproductive." In giving this response, they underscore just what the real problem is. Nothing in the current structure rewards performance. Nothing automatically moves us toward better use of resources. And nothing ensures that future funds will be spent better than past funds.

Indeed, when put in the context of school finance discussions, matters are even worse. Current financing of schools does nothing to provide performance incentives and, in some cases, may even provide perverse incentives. The clearest example of perverse incentives appears when states provide categorical aid that is reduced if student performance is higher. A school doing a good job loses funds, whereas a school doing a bad job gets more funding.

The dichotomy between the good intentions of school finance reform and the reality of schools is pervasive. For example, it is instructive to contrast the school finance version of Jonathan Kozol with the school policy version of Jonathan Kozol. His recent book, *Savage Inequalities*, which identified truly outrageous situations in some of our nation's schools, pointed to fixing everything simply by bringing the unsafe and unsanitary schools up to the spending level of the most opulent public schools that could be found (Kozol, 1991). On the other hand, the main theme of the equally compelling *Death at an Early Age* (Kozol, 1967) is that the current organization of schools with few incentives to improve student performance squanders the good resources that are available. Nothing in the Kozol (1991) volume indicates how the problems of the Kozol (1967) volume will be overcome.

One way that people attempt to deal with the conflict between reality and desires is to identify a specific program that appears to offer some improvement in student performance, to claim that some districts are precluded from introducing this program because of its cost, and to assert that providing extra funding would correct the situation. This line of argument typically fails on two counts. First, given extra funding, most districts would not in fact introduce the identified "productive" program. This conclusion follows immediately from past behavior, for many of the target districts could have readily introduced the program had they not favored some alternative approach for dealing with exactly the same problem. Second, experience demonstrates that many programs that appear to work in one place are not easily transferred to another. Important aspects of the program frequently are not sufficiently understood to permit easy diffusion. The result is that the transplanted program does not produce the anticipated results.

Nothing indicates that more of the same—more spending and more equalized spending—will lead to improvements in the very real problems of our schools without a series of more fundamental changes in perspective and organization. We have developed a system that is geared toward mediocrity. We neither reward success nor make much effort to uncover what is successful (Hanushek, 1994a). When we pursue the pure funding equalization strategy, we observe little in the way of equalization of student outcomes (Downes, 1992). What we typically find is that more money is spent without commensurate improvement in student performance. Changing that reality is the fundamental challenge facing schools today, and this is a challenge that the courts are particularly ill equipped to face.

Notes

1. Although the evidence on the effects of cognitive achievement is sketchier than that for cognitive skills, recent work suggests an increasingly strong impact on individual earnings. See Hanushek (1994b).

2. An early review of experimental evidence is found in Glass and Smith (1979). More recently, the state of Tennessee conducted an extensive statewide random assignment experiment of reduced class size in Grades K-3. Except perhaps for kindergarten, no gains in student performance were associated with being in the smaller classes (Word et al., 1990).

3. There may be special programs—say, ones falling outside of the range of normal operations—in which smaller classes are effective. For example, the Success for All program and the reading tutorial program of the University of Texas at Dallas show that early one-on-one instruction may be beneficial. But these are different from general reductions in overall class size or pupil-teacher ratio (see Hanushek et al., 1994; Hanushek et al., 1995).

4. This table expands on previous tabulations of evidence on resource effects. An attempt was made to include all qualified studies published by December 1994. In all, 90 separate publications with 377 studies of resource effects were included. Hanushek et al. (1995) analyzed these studies in terms of quality as proxied by aggregation of the data. The empirical results of that study are also included in the tabulations.

5. Several analytical choices are important and questionable. First, as noted above, they arbitrarily exclude a large number of studies that indicate no effect of school resources, in part because these do not fit into their chosen methodology. Thus, they select studies according to the answer they hope to produce. Second, for reasons that they point out in Hedges et al. (1994), the studies sampled are not statistically independent, as is required by their chosen analytical approach. Third, their sequential tests of one-directional hypotheses are forced by the embarrassing fact that some studies show significant effects of the wrong sign but are, at the very least, nonstandard. Fourth,

they ignore the well-known bias toward publication of statistically significant results (see Hedges, 1990). For a more complete discussion, see Hanushek (1994).

6. Laine et al. (Chapter 3 of this volume) attempt to estimate the expected change in achievement that would follow an increase in expenditure. It is difficult to understand exactly how they do these calculations, but the results are questionable at face value. They now estimate that a $1,000 increase in expenditure per pupil (1992-1993 dollars) will yield an increase in achievement of 0.3 standard deviations. On the basis of actual expenditure increases, this would imply that average achievement between 1970 and 1993 should have increased by three quarters of a standard deviation. The observed increases on the NAEP over this period ranged from minus one third of a standard deviation (science) to plus one fifth (reading). Moreover, as Grissmer, Kirby, Berends, and Williamson (1994) pointed out, the gross changes overstate the potential effects of schools because of improvements in parents' education and reductions in family size. The estimates in Laine et al. (Chapter 3) thus bear no relationship to real school experiences. Laine et al. (Chapter 3) disingenuously describe this estimated effect as "a somewhat smaller effect than was estimated from our reanalysis of Hanushek's universe of studies (Hedges et al., 1994)." Their previous estimate was a two-standard-deviation increase in student test scores from a $1,000 increase in expenditure per pupil (1991-1992 dollars). Such an effect is some *seven* times greater than the one they now report. Although they make some changes in their sample, they employ only one more estimate in the new collection, implying that the distribution of estimates in the new additions to the sample must be dramatically different to obtain such a reduction in estimated effects. More plausibly, they now realize that their previous calculations were obviously overstated and have introduced some new, but unstated, calculation methodology to bring down the estimates. The underlying point, however, is that these studies cannot give any reasonable estimate of the effect of increasing expenditure within the current structure.

7. One interpretation of estimates indicating a relationship between school resources and individual earnings (Card & Krueger, 1992) is that such a relationship held in the 1920s and 1930s when sampled individuals received their education (see Burtless, 1994). Recent analyses have, however, raised questions about the reliability of the original findings (Betts, 1994; Hanushek et al., 1995; Heckman, Layne-Farrar, & Todd, 1994; Speakman & Welch, 1995).

8. See New York State Office of the Comptroller (1983) and U.S. Bureau of the Census (1983, Tables A and C).

9. This situation, called *compensating differentials* by economists, can exist whenever jobs or job locations include different attributes such as riskiness, opportunities for learning, or favorable living conditions in the case of cities. See, for a general description, Ehrenberg and Smith (1991) or Hamermesh and Rees (1988). In the context of teachers, see Toder (1972), Antos and Rosen (1975), and Kenny (1980). Differences in the attractiveness of areas can also lead to differences in housing and land prices, thus affecting other inputs to education. See, for example, Roback (1982).

10. These calculations rely on estimates of the relationship between expenditures per student and wealth per student in districts in these states. The R^2 of simple regression in each state was less than .20, indicating that one fifth would be an estimate of the upper bound on the potential for equating spending by eliminating property tax base differences.

References

Antos, J. R., & Rosen, S. (1975, May). Discrimination in the market for teachers. *Journal of Econometrics, 2*, 123-150.

Ballou, D., & Podgursky, M. (1995). Recruiting smarter teachers. *Journal of Human Resources, 30*, 326-338.

Betts, J. R. (1994, November). *Is there a link between school inputs and earnings? Fresh scrutiny of an old literature.* Unpublished manuscript. University of California, San Diego.

Burtless, G. (1994, June). *Does money matter? The effects of school resources on student achievement and adult earnings.* Paper presented at the Brookings Institution conference, "Do School Resources Matter?"

Card, D., & Krueger, A. B. (1992). Does school quality matter? Returns to education and the characteristics of public schools in the United States. *Journal of Political Economy, 100*, 1-40.

Congressional Budget Office. (1986). *Trends in educational achievement.* Washington, DC: Author.

Downes, T. A. (1992). Evaluating the impact of school finance reform on the provision of public education: The California case. *National Tax Journal, 45*, 405-419.

Downes, T. A., & Shah, M. P. (1995, January). *The effect of school finance reforms on the level and growth of per pupil expenditures.* Paper presented at the annual meeting of the American Economic Association, Washington, DC.

Ehrenberg, R. G., & Smith, R. S. (1991). *Modern labor economics: Theory and public policy* (4th ed.). New York: HarperCollins.

Glass, G. V., & Smith, M. L. (1979). Meta-analysis of research on class size and achievement. *Educational Evaluation and Policy Analysis, 1*(1), 2-16.

Grissmer, D. W., Kirby, S. N., Berends, M., & Williamson, S. (1994). *Student achievement and the changing American family.* Santa Monica, CA: RAND Corporation.

Hamermesh, D. S., & Rees, A. (1988). *The economics of work and pay* (4th ed.). New York: Harper & Row.

Hanushek, E. A. (1986). The economics of schooling: Production and efficiency in public schools. *Journal of Economic Literature, 24*, 1141-1177.

Hanushek, E. A. (1989). The impact of differential expenditures on school performance. *Educational Researcher, 18*(4), 45-51.

Hanushek, E. A. (1991). When school finance "reform" may not be good policy. *Harvard Journal on Legislation, 28*, 423-456.

Hanushek, E. A. (1992). The trade-off between child quantity and quality. *Journal of Political Economy, 100*(1), 84-117.

Hanushek, E. A. (1993). Can equity be separated from efficiency in school finance debates? In E. P. Hoffman (Ed.), *Essays on the economics of education* (pp. 35-73). Kalamazoo, MI: W. E. Upjohn Institute for Employment Research.

Hanushek, E. A. (1994a). Money might matter somewhere: A response to Hedges, Laine, and Greenwald. *Educational Researcher, 23*(4), 5-8.

Hanushek, E. A. (1994b, June). *School resources and student performance.* Paper presented at the Brookings Institution conference, "Do School Resources Matter?"

Hanushek, E. A., et al. (1994). *Making schools work: Improving performance and controlling costs.* Washington, DC: Brookings Institution.

Hanushek, E. A., & Rivkin, S. G. (1994, August). *Understanding the 20th century explosion in U.S. school costs* (Working Paper No. 388). Rochester, NY: University of Rochester, Rochester Center for Economic Research.

Hanushek, E. A., Rivkin, S. G., & Jamison, D. T. (1992, December). Improving educational outcomes while controlling costs. *Carnegie-Rochester Conference Series on Public Policy, 37*, 205-238.

Hanushek, E. A., Rivkin, S. G., & Taylor, L. L. (1995, February). *Aggregation and the estimated effects of school resources* (Working Paper No. 397). Rochester, NY: University of Rochester, Rochester Center for Economic Research.

Haveman, R. H., & Wolfe, B. L. (1984). Schooling and economic well-being: The role of non-market effects. *Journal of Human Resources, 19*, 377-407.

Heckman, J. J., Layne-Farrar, A. S., & Todd, P. E. (1994, September). *Does measured school quality really matter?* [Mimeo]. University of Chicago.

Hedges, L. V. (1990). Directions for future methodology. In K. W. Wachter & M. L. Straf (Eds.), *The future of meta-analysis* (pp. 11-26). New York: Russell Sage.

Hedges, L. V., Laine, R. D., & Greenwald, R. (1994). Does money matter? A meta-analysis of studies of the effects of differential school inputs on student outcomes. *Educational Researcher, 23*(3), 5-14.

Kenny, L. W. (1980). Compensating differentials in teachers' salaries. *Journal of Urban Economics, 7*, 198-207.

Kosters, M. H. (1991). Wages and demographics. In M. H. Kosters (Ed.), *Workers and their wages* (pp. 1-32). Washington, DC: AEI.

Kozol, J. (1967). *Death at an early age: The destruction of the hearts and minds of Negro children in the Boston public schools.* New York: Houghton Mifflin.

Kozol, J. (1991). *Savage inequalities: Children in America's schools.* New York: Crown.

Levittown v. Nyquist, 57 N.Y.2d 27, 439 N.E.2d 359, 453 N.Y.S.2d 643 (1982).

McKnight, C. C., Crosswhite, F. J., Dossey, J. A., Kifer, E., Swafford, J. O., Travers, K. J., & Cooney, T. J. (1987). *The underachieving curriculum: Assessing U.S. school mathematics from an international perspective.* Champaign, IL: Stipes.

McMahon, W. W. (1991). Relative returns to human and physical capital in the U.S. and efficient investment strategies. *Economics of Education Review, 10*, 283-296.

Murphy, K. M., & Welch, F. (1989). Wage premiums for college graduates: Recent growth and possible explanations. *Educational Researcher, 18*(4), 17-26.

National Center for Education Statistics. (1994). *The condition of education, 1994.* Washington, DC: U.S. Department of Education.

National Research Council. (1989). *Everybody counts: A report to the nation on the future of mathematics education.* Washington, DC: National Academy Press.

New York State Office of the Comptroller. (1983). *Financial data for school districts, 1982.* Albany, NY: Author.

Oates, W. (1969). The effects of property taxes and local public spending on property values: An empirical study of tax capitalization and the Tiebout hypothesis. *Journal of Political Economy, 77*, 957-971.

Roback, J. (1982). Wages, rents, and quality of life. *Journal of Political Economy, 90*, 1257-1278.

Rosen, H. S., & Fullerton, D. J. (1977). A note on local tax rates: Public benefit levels and property values. *Journal of Political Economy, 85*, 433-440.

San Antonio Independent School District v. Rodriguez, 411 U.S. 1 (1973).

Serrano v. Priest, 5 Cal.3d 584, 487 P.2d 1241 (Super. Ct. for Los Angeles County, CA, 1971).

Speakman, R., & Welch, F. (1995). *Does school quality matter? A reassessment.* Unpublished manuscript. Texas A&M University.

Tiebout, C. M. (1956). A pure theory of local expenditures. *Journal of Political Economy, 64,* 416-424.

Toder, E. J. (1972). The supply of public school teachers to an urban metropolitan area: A possible source of discrimination in education. *Review of Economics and Statistics, 54,* 439-443.

U.S. Bureau of the Census. (1983). *County and city data book, 1983.* Washington, DC: Government Printing Office.

Walker, G. C. (1995, January). *Capitalization: An explanation for the failure of education finance-demand estimates for wealthy school districts.* Paper presented at the annual meeting of the American Economic Association, Washington, DC.

Wendling, W. (1981, March/April). Capitalization: Considerations in school finance. *Educational Evaluation and Policy Analysis, 3*(2), 57-66.

Wolfe, B. L., & Zuvekas, S. (1995, May). *Non-market outcomes of schooling* (Discussion paper 1065-95). Madison: University of Wisconsin, Institute for Research on Poverty.

Word, E., Johnston, J., Bain, H. P., Fulton, B. D., Zaharies, J. B., Lintz, M. N., Achilles, C. M., Folger, J., & Breda, C. (1990). *Student/teacher achievement ratio (STAR), Tennessee's K-3 class size study: Final summary report, 1985-1990.* Nashville: Tennessee State Department of Education.

THREE

Money Does Matter

A RESEARCH SYNTHESIS OF
A NEW UNIVERSE OF EDUCATION
PRODUCTION FUNCTION STUDIES

RICHARD D. LAINE

ROB GREENWALD

LARRY V. HEDGES

Much of the current debate surrounding education reform revolves around the issues of identifying the most educationally effective and efficient allocation of resources, attempting to remove barriers to learning, and creating concordant incentives for both students and educators. Underlying these issues is the belief that there is a relation between the structure, processes, and resources in education and the level of student achievement. The historic lack of clarity in these relations has fueled the debate surrounding what constitutes the most effective educational reform and the level of resources that is necessary to support and ensure successful change.

The relation between school expenditures (and the resources money may buy) and student achievement has proven difficult to determine. Systematic efforts to do so began 35 years ago with Project Talent (Flanagan et al., 1964) and reached widespread public awareness with *Equality of Educational Opportunity* (Coleman et al., 1966). Most of the work in the ensuing three decades has employed similar methodology, using regression analysis to estimate the relation between school resources and student achievement while controlling for student or family background characteristics. These studies, using the metaphor of the factory, view schools as producing some amount of achievement from a certain level and mix of school resources and student characteristics, and employ the term *education production function* to describe the relation between school resources and student achievement.

The diverse literature presenting the results of education production functions has yielded mixed conclusions about the relation between school resources and student achievement. Coleman's original (1966) study found that school resources had a remarkably small impact on achievement. Subsequent production function research produced results that sometimes supported and sometimes challenged Coleman's conclusions. Over the past 15 years, Hanushek (1981, 1986, 1989) published the results of a synthesis of a portion of the educational production function literature. His synthesis methods (known as vote counting) consisted of categorizing, by significance and direction, the relations between school resource inputs and student outcomes (including, but not limited to, achievement). He concluded that the evidence did not support any strong or consistent relation between school resources and student achievement.

Vote counting is known to be a rather insensitive procedure for summarizing results (Hedges & Olkin, 1980). It is now rarely used in areas of empirical research where sophisticated syntheses of research are expected. Yet although the methods Hanushek used have been shown to be flawed and outdated, his summaries continue to receive considerable exposure in the public policy and legal arenas.

Hanushek's work received several challenges (Baker, 1991; Spencer & Wiley, 1981), but none substantial enough to begin to level the playing field until a 1994 reanalysis (Hedges, Laine, & Greenwald, 1994). That article outlined significant methodological flaws in Hanushek's work that, when overcome, demonstrated that relations between school resource inputs and student outcomes, including achievement, were substantially more consistent and positive than Hanushek had been able to elucidate. The typical relation between school resource inputs and student outcomes was found to be positive and large enough to have implications for educational policy. Indeed, the median magnitude of some of the coefficients actually appeared to be too large to be plausible.

In addition to the methodological flaws, the 1994 reanalysis (Hedges et al., 1994) of Hanushek's work identified several data weaknesses included in his synthesis. Also, because the subsequent publications of Hanushek's synthesis added very few new studies to his original universe of production function studies developed in 1980, he failed to identify and incorporate into his synthesis a significant portion of the current research in this area of study.

This chapter identifies our method in developing a current and comprehensive universe of production function studies in order to overcome the data weaknesses in Hanushek's universe and reports the methods and results of our synthesis of this comprehensive collection of education production function studies. By identifying a broad and rigorously developed universe of production function studies and by applying the meta-analytic methods described in our April 1994 *Educational Researcher* article (Hedges et al., 1994), we believe we have provided the most exhaustive synthesis of education production functions to date, and thus the best evidence on the question of whether money matters in education. It does.

We must stress that the statement "money does matter" is not equivalent to saying "money always matters." We believe that our research eliminates the academic pillar relied upon by many who have maintained that money does not matter. Instead of erecting a new foundation to continue the "does money matter" debate, we hope that our findings may help move the focus of school reform beyond the hurdle of contemplating whether money matters, to the more important question of how money and the resources it may purchase may best provide a quality education for all children.

Developing a Universe of
Production Function Studies

In order to obtain the largest possible collection of education production function studies, we completed an exhaustive search of the literature. The new universe was constructed from articles and books identified from (a) studies in the universe Hanushek assembled; (b) electronic databases in education, psychology, and economics; (c) literature reviews; and (d) citations from articles under review.

Studies in the universe Hanushek constructed (Hanushek, 1989) were assessed for quality. Nine of the 38 studies were discarded due to weaknesses identified in the decision rules for inclusion described below. Although the remaining 29 studies were retained, many equations and coefficients that Hanushek utilized did not meet the decision rules we employed. Thus, although nearly three quarters of the studies in Hanushek's universe were retained, the number of coefficients from his universe was reduced by two thirds.

Three electronic databases were extensively researched: (a) ERIC (which indexes journal and technical literature from *Resources in Education* and *Current Index to Journals in Education*), (b) PsychLIT (which corresponds to the American Psychological Association's *Psychological Abstracts*), and (c) EconLit (which is compiled from the American Economic Association's *Journal of Economic Literature* and the *Index of Economic Articles*). These databases were utilized to identify abstracts of potential interest. The abstracts were read to determine whether the article or book was likely to present relevant information. Those documents (a) containing useful data, (b) presenting theories on the utility and construction of education production functions, or (c) presenting literature reviews were retained for more careful scrutiny.

The bibliographies of a number of literature reviews were used to identify other relevant publications (Averch, Carroll, Donaldson, Kiesling, & Pintero, 1972; Bridge, Judd, & Moock, 1979; Glasman & Biniaminov, 1981; Guthrie, Kleindorfer, Levin, & Stout, 1971; MacPhail-Wilcox & King, 1986; Monk, 1989, 1992). In addition, as articles were read for potential inclusion, useful publications cited were selected for retrieval.

The initial primary searches in ERIC, PsychLIT, and EconLit led to the review of more than 2,000 abstracts. From this pool, over 100 papers were retrieved. In combination with papers identified through other means, over 175 articles and books, in addition to Hanushek's original universe of 38 journal articles and books, were reviewed in order to assemble the universe of studies used in the analysis presented in this chapter.

Narrowing the Universe of Studies: Decision Rules for Inclusion

From the articles and books reviewed for inclusion, only 31, in addition to 29 articles and books from Hanushek's most complete universe (Hanushek, 1989), both met our decision rules and contained the data necessary to perform the meta-analytic procedures we utilized. The restriction of the universe created through the literature review was completed through the application of the following decision rules:

1. The data must be presented in a refereed journal or a book. (Two studies retained from Hanushek's universe were published by research institutes at universities [Heim & Perl, 1974; Maynard & Crawford, 1976]. These were retained in the new universe.)

2. The data must originate from schools in the United States. This rule was established due to our desire to apply the results to the United States and the difficulty in attempting to take into consideration the cultural and structural differences of educational systems in foreign countries.

3. The outcome measure must be some form of academic achievement. Although it is true that there are a multitude of objectives for public schools, we have attempted to focus on a specific outcome of students, the results of standardized achievement tests.

4. The level of aggregation must be the level of school districts or smaller units. Moving beyond the level of school districts greatly limits the validity of the relation between inputs and outcomes. (Note that one study in the universe, Sander & Krautmann [1991], utilized counties as the level of aggregation. Their data, however, were developed using district-level inputs aggregated to the county level only for the purpose of controlling for socioeconomic status [SES] variations due to the absence of district-level SES data.)

5. The model must control for socioeconomic characteristics or be either longitudinal (including a pretest and a posttest) or "quasi-longitudinal" (including IQ or a measure of earlier achievement as an input). In order to avoid having student ability and background confound the findings, each production function was required to account for either or both of these factors.

6. The data must be stochastically independent. The issue of production functions using dependent data appeared in a number of situations. The most frequent occurrence was when a single article presented several regression equations with identical models using the same students, but varied the output (e.g., the verbal and quantitative scores on the Scholastic Aptitude Test [SAT] or the reading and math portions of the Iowa Tests of Basic Skills [ITBS]. Because the results of a single student's score on various tests are likely to be related, including multiple scores from the same student would result in stochastically dependent results. When this occurred, we calculated the median value for the regression coefficient and t ratio (absolute value) before including the data in our analysis. Although this greatly reduced the number of coefficients, it increased the validity of our findings by eliminating the bias introduced

by the inclusion of related outputs from the same population of students. A second issue with respect to dependence of results arose when researchers reported their studies, or close variations, in multiple publications. If the identical data and model were employed, one or more of the articles were discarded (Eberts & Stone, 1984, 1987, 1988; Grimes & Register, 1990, 1991; Hanushek, 1971, 1972; Levin, 1970, 1976; Register & Grimes, 1991).

Details of each of the education production function studies (articles and books) included in the universe are presented in the Appendix. The following information is provided for each study: (a) author, (b) year of data, (c) size, (d) grade(s) of the students, (e) background control, (f) input variables, and (g) specifics of the output variable.

Methods

A separate analysis was completed for each of the seven input variables examined (note that class size is separated into teacher-pupil ratio and pupil-teacher ratio, but is considered one variable). For each input variable, we identified the relevant coefficients for that variable in the education production functions and the exact p value associated with them. When two or more production functions were estimated from data from the same individuals, stochastic independence was maintained by taking the median of the corresponding regression coefficients, p values, or absolute values of the t statistics.

Both combined significance tests and combined estimation methods were used in our reanalysis (for further information, see Cooper & Hedges, 1994; Hedges et al., 1994). Combined significance tests provide a means of combining statistical significance values (p values) from studies that test the same conceptual hypothesis but that may differ in the details of their designs or measurement methods (Hedges & Olkin, 1985). The inverse chi-square (Fisher) method was used to determine if the data were consistent with either the positive or the negative null hypotheses, or both, in every study, or if there were effects in a specified direction in at least some of the studies. Two directional null hypotheses were tested for each of the resource input variables:

1. The positive case, in which the null hypothesis states that no positive relation exists between the resource input and student achievement
2. The negative case, in which the null hypothesis states that no negative relation exists between the resource input and student achievement

It is possible to reject the null hypothesis in both the positive and negative cases. Such an outcome would mean that there was evidence of both some positive and some negative relations. In order to reach the conclusion that "no strong or systematic relationship" (Hanushek, 1989, p. 47) exists between the major educational resource inputs and student outcomes, the data would have to be consistent with the null hypothesis in both the positive and the negative cases.

Effect magnitude analyses attempt to estimate the strength of the relation between inputs and outputs. Because neither input nor output variables were typically measured on the same scale in all studies, the partial regression coefficients for the resource input variables could not be combined directly. Consequently, the index of effect magnitude used for most inputs was the fully standardized regression coefficient. This coefficient measures the number of standard deviations of change in output that would be associated with a one-standard-deviation change in input. The median value of the coefficients for each variable was used as the summary statistic of the effect magnitude for that variable.

Per-pupil expenditure (PPE) and teacher salary were initially measured in dollars; hence, the inputs in these categories were directly comparable, or could be made so after a correction for inflation (National Center for Education Statistics, 1993). For these resource inputs, the "half-standardized" partial regression coefficient was used as the measure of effect magnitude (defined as $\beta_H = b/S_O$ where b is the unstandardized regression coefficient and S_O is the standard deviation of the output variable). The half-standardized regression coefficient measures the number of standard deviations of change in output associated with a one-dollar change in input. The median value of the half-standardized regression coefficients for each variable was used as the summary statistic of the effect magnitude for the variables PPE and teacher salary.

For both combined significance tests and effect magnitude analyses, the data were examined in a number of ways. In the full analysis, all independent p values or effect magnitudes were analyzed. In order to assess the robustness of the results, the central 90% of the values were analyzed to determine the impact of outlier values. In addition, because a number of the studies were based on data collected decades ago (Project Talent, 1959-60; Equality of Educational Opportunity, 1964-65), we analyzed both the full data set and the "robustness" sample in two ways: (a) including all studies, and (b) including only the subset of studies based on data collected after 1970 (for one variable, teacher salary, most of the studies were based on data collected after 1980; thus the subset of studies for this variable is of more recent vintage).

Results

Although each of the studies included in the universe provided the data required for at least one of the two methodologies (combined significance testing or effect magnitude estimation), not all studies provided the data required for both. In an attempt to assess the possibility that the results might be skewed due to the selective reporting of data from specific studies, we analyzed the distribution of the production function coefficients for each of the resource variables for each test by its statistical significance (significant or nonsignificant) and its sign (positive or negative). This analysis established that the distribution of data (*p* values, *t* ratios, and standard deviations) for each of the input variables was similar with respect to significance and sign for the combined significance testing and the effect magnitude estimation. Thus the availability of data for each of the methods of analysis was not thought to be skewed in any fashion that would alter the results.

The results of the combined significance tests are reported in Tables 3.1 and 3.2. Table 3.1 provides the data, including degrees of freedom and chi-square critical values in the center column. Table 3.2 provides a summary of results presented in Table 3.1, listing whether there was evidence of a positive or a negative effect on student achievement in each of the input variable categories. The results in Table 3.1 of the tests in the positive direction, shown on the left side of the table, reveal that the null hypothesis for the positive test (that no positive relation exists between resource inputs and student achievement) is rejected for every resource input. Thus the combined significance analyses provide evidence that there is a positive relation between each of the input variables and student achievement. This result appears to be quite robust. It holds for the full analysis sample and the robustness trimmed sample, and for the entire collection of studies and the more recent (post-1970) studies. Note that throughout the analyses, the signs of relations have been reversed for the variables pupil-teacher ratio (to make the relation tested to be consistent with teacher-pupil ratio) and school size so that positive coefficients reflect greater achievement in *smaller* classes and *smaller* schools, respectively.

Table 3.1 Results of Combined Significance Tests

Input Variable (Outcomes)	Equations (Studies)	Positive Case $(H_0: \beta \le 0)$ Full Analysis Sample	Robustness Sample[b]	$(df, \chi^2)^a$ Full Analysis Sample	Robustness Sample[b]	Negative Case $(H_0: \beta \ge 0)$ Full Analysis Sample	Robustness Sample[b]
Per-pupil expenditure							
All studies	27 (17)	236.43	190.34	(54, 72.15)	(50, 67.51)	35.91	27.66
Studies after 1970	16 (11)	144.05	121.33	(32, 46.19)	(28, 41.38)	12.47	7.62
Teacher ability							
All studies	18 (9)	428.93	382.87	(36, 51.00)	(32, 46.19)	14.19	2.04
Studies after 1970	9 (4)	239.34	NA	(18, 28.87)	NA	13.9	NA
Teacher education							
All studies	38 (24)	149.18	115.89	(76, 97.35)	(68, 88.25)	**143.05**	85.95
Studies after 1970	31 (17)	112.64	83.7	(62, 81.38)	(54, 72.15)	**126.90**	69.80
Teacher experience							
All studies	60 (29)	397.87	297.65	(120, 146.57)	(108, 126.57)	122.52	66.60
Studies after 1970	47 (19)	299.80	229.00	(94, 117.63)	(86, 108.65)	75.67	58.19
Teacher salary							
All studies	16 (8)	95.12	95.10	(32, 46.19)	(28, 41.34)	27.49	17.71
Studies after 1980	13 (5)	77.89	55.03	(26, 38.89)	(22, 33.92)	28.83	17.04
Pupil-teacher ratio[c]							
All studies	54 (28)	281.02	199.70	(108, 133.26)	(96, 119.87)	100.16	55.13
Studies after 1970	43 (20)	233.18	167.09	(86, 108.65)	(78, 99.62)	88.92	52.96
Teacher-pupil ratio							
All studies	10 (4)	46.16	29.05	(20, 31.41)	(16, 26.30)	**47.44**	**30.56**
Studies after 1970	9 (3)	35.36	NA	(18, 28.87)	NA	**47.43**	NA
School size[d]							
All studies	28 (18)	273.59	227.54	(56, 74.47)	(52, 69.83)	**113.69**	67.63
Studies after 1970	26 (16)	269.32	223.27	(52, 69.83)	(48, 65.17)	**111.99**	**65.94**
Exclude TEL[e]	24 (14)	272.57	226.52	(48, 65.17)	(44, 60.48)	33.25	17.03
Exclude TEL after 1970	22 (12)	268.31	222.26	(44, 60.48)	(40, 55.76)	31.56	15.34

NOTE: NA = Due to the limited number of equations, a robustness sample was not created for this variable. Figures in bold type indicate failure to reject the null hypothesis in the positive case and rejection of the null hypothesis in the negative case.
a. The chi-square values (χ) provided are at the $\alpha = 0.05$ level. The degrees of freedom and chi-square values are identical for the positive and negative cases.
b. The robustness subsamples indicated are the middle 90%, trimming 5% from each side of the distribution.
c. The signs have been reversed in those studies that utilize the pupil-teacher ratio or class size variable to be consistent with teacher-pupil ratio so that $\beta > 0$ means that smaller classes have greater outcomes.
d. The signs have been reversed so that $\beta > 0$ means that smaller schools have greater outcomes.
e. The "Exclude TEL" subsample was created by deleting equations with output = Test of Economic Literacy.

Table 3.2 Summary of Results of Combined Significance Tests

Input Variable (Outcomes)	Evidence of Positive Effects? Sample		Evidence of Negative Effects? Sample	
	Full Analysis	Robustness[a]	Full Analysis	Robustness[a]
Per-pupil expenditure				
All studies	yes	yes	no	no
Studies after 1970	yes	yes	no	no
Teacher ability				
All studies	yes	yes	no	no
Studies after 1970	yes	NA	no	NA
Teacher education				
All studies	yes	yes	yes	no
Studies after 1970	yes	yes	yes	no
Teacher experience				
All studies	yes	yes	no	no
Studies after 1970	yes	yes	no	no
Teacher salary[b]				
All studies	yes	yes	no	no
Studies after 1980	yes	yes	no	no
Pupil-teacher ratio[c]				
All studies	yes	yes	no	no
Studies after 1970	yes	yes	no	no
Teacher-pupil ratio				
All studies	yes	yes	yes	yes
Studies after 1970	yes	NA	yes	NA
School size[d]				
All studies	yes	yes	yes	no
Studies after 1970	yes	yes	yes	yes
Exclude TEL[e]	yes	yes	no	no
Exclude TEL after 1970	yes	yes	no	no

NOTE: Evidence of positive effects means that the null hypothesis was rejected at the $\alpha = 0.05$ level. Evidence of negative effects indicates that the null hypothesis was rejected at the $\alpha = 0.05$ level. NA = Due to the limited number of equations, a robustness sample was not created for this variable.
a. The robustness samples indicated are the middle 90%, trimming 5% from each side of the distribution.
b. The results are identical if teacher salary is divided into starting salary and average salary and separate analyses are performed. The data are combined due to the small number of coefficients. Note that a "post-1980" subsample is used for this variable.
c. The signs have been reversed in those studies that utilize a pupil-teacher ratio or class size variable to be consistent with teacher-pupil ratio so that $\beta > 0$ means that smaller classes have greater outcomes.
d. The signs have been reversed so that $\beta > 0$ means that smaller schools have greater outcomes.
e. The "Exclude TEL" subsample was created by deleting equations with output = Test of Economic Literacy.

The results of the tests in the negative direction, shown on the right side of Table 3.1, reveal that the null hypothesis for the negative test (that no negative relation exists between resource inputs and student achievement) cannot be rejected for the variables PPE, teacher ability, teacher experience, teacher salary, and pupil-teacher ratio in the combined significance analyses. Thus there is no evidence of negative relations between each of these input variables and student achievement. This finding holds for the full analysis sample and the robustness trimmed sample, and for the entire collection of studies and the more recent (post-1970) studies.

The null hypothesis for the negative test is rejected for teacher education, teacher-pupil ratio, and school size. Thus the combined significance analyses provide evidence of negative relations between each of these three input variables and student achievement. The rejection of the negative null hypothesis for teacher education appears to be the result of outliers (the negative null hypothesis for the robustness trimmed sample for this variable is not rejected).

Although there is evidence of negative coefficients for the teacher-pupil ratio variable in both the full analysis sample and the robustness trimmed sample, the sample size is quite small for this variable. Nearly 85% of the studies providing data on class size reported the data in the form of pupil-teacher ratio rather than teacher-pupil ratio. In addition, when the data for the teacher-pupil ratio and pupil-teacher ratio variables are combined (after the signs for pupil-teacher ratio are reversed), the data show evidence of a positive relation, but no evidence of a negative relation, between class size and student achievement. With the reversal of the sign, this would provide evidence that smaller classes are related to higher student achievement.

For the variable school size, the rejection of the negative null hypothesis for the full analysis appears to be the result of outliers (the negative null hypothesis for the robustness trimmed sample is not rejected). However, for the set of studies that contain data after 1970, there is evidence of negative effects in both the full analysis sample and the robustness trimmed sample. These findings are explained by the hypothesis that studies utilizing the Test of Economic Literacy (TEL) as the output measure should show a negative relation between small schools and student outcomes. This hypothesis states that larger school size may allow the recruitment of a teacher specifically trained in economics. The exclusion of studies using TEL as an outcome results in the failure to reject (the acceptance of) the null hypothesis for the negative case in school size. Thus, when the studies using the TEL as an outcome measure are excluded, the combined significance analyses provide evidence that there is no negative relation between school size and student achievement.

Table 3.2 provides the same information as Table 3.1, but in a simplified form. It summarizes the evidence, indicating whether either positive or negative effects between a specific input variable and student achievement are present. Recall that rejection of the null hypothesis in the positive case provides evidence of a positive relation between input and outcome. Similarly, rejection of the null hypothesis in the negative case provides evidence of a negative relation between input and outcome.

The results of the effect magnitude analyses are presented in Table 3.3. These are, in general, consistent with the results of the combined significance tests. The median effect (standardized or half-standardized regression coefficient) is positive for all of the resource variables except the teacher-pupil ratio variable for the post-1970 sample of studies. Note that as in the combined significance analyses, the signs of relations have been reversed for the variables of pupil-teacher ratio (to be consistent with teacher-pupil ratio) and school size so that positive coefficients reflect greater achievement in *smaller* classes and *smaller* schools, respectively.

In most cases, the magnitude of the coefficients is substantial. For example, the median half-standardized coefficient for PPE is .0003, which suggests that an increase in per-pupil expenditure of $1,000 (less than 20% of the national average) would be associated with an increase in achievement of nearly one third of one standard deviation.[1] This is a somewhat smaller effect than was estimated from our reanalysis of Hanushek's universe of studies (Hedges et al., 1994), but it is still large enough to be educationally important. The median half-standardized coefficient for the variable teacher salary is 0.0256, suggesting that an increase of $15,000 in teacher salary is associated with an increase of slightly more than one third of one standard deviation in student achievement.[2] Because $1,000 in PPE is roughly equal to $15,000 in teacher salary (assuming that class size is 30 and that teacher salaries account for 50% of PPE), the magnitude of effects for the global resource measure (PPE) and the largest single component of school costs (teacher salaries) are comparable.

Because the other input variables are expressed as fully standardized coefficients, it is more difficult to evaluate the magnitude of the

Table 3.3 Median Regression Coefficients

Input Variable (Outcomes)	Equations (Studies)	Full Analysis
Per-pupil expenditure[a]		
All studies	27 (14)	.0003
Studies after 1970	11 (8)	.0001
Teacher ability		
All studies	20 (6)	.0724
Studies after 1970	6 (1)	.2230
Teacher education		
All studies	24 (12)	.0003
Studies after 1970	15 (8)	.0430
Teacher experience		
All studies	27 (15)	.0482
Studies after 1970	11 (8)	.0984
Teacher salary[b, c]		
All studies	13 (5)	.0263
Studies after 1980	11 (3)	.0007
Teacher-pupil ratio		
All studies	9 (4)	.0100
Studies after 1970	7 (2)	−.0152
Pupil-teacher ratio[d]		
All studies	30 (18)	.0495
Studies after 1970	22 (13)	.0540
School size[e]		
All studies	31 (15)	.0299
Studies post 1970	21 (12)	.0299
Exclude TEL[f]	28 (12)	.0376
Exclude TEL after 1970	18 (9)	.0499

NOTE: These results are summaries of fully standardized regression coefficients unless otherwise indicated.
a. Half-standardized regression coefficients. Units are dollars, adjusted to 1992-93.
b. Half-standardized regression coefficients. Units are thousands of dollars, adjusted to 1992-93.
c. Note that a "post-1980" subsample is used for this variable.
d. The signs have been reversed in those studies that utilize a pupil-teacher ratio or class size variable to be consistent with teacher-pupil ratio so that $\beta > 0$ means that smaller classes have greater outcomes.
e. The signs have been reversed so that $\beta > 0$ means that smaller schools have greater outcomes.
f. The "Excluded TEL" subsample was created by deleting equations with output = Test of Economic Literacy.

effects of teacher ability, teacher education, teacher experience, pupil-teacher ratio, and school size, but these coefficients appear to be substantial in magnitude, and all are positive.

With some slight variations, the pattern of results for the newer (post-1970) studies is the same as that for the entire collection of studies. The coefficients for teacher ability, teacher education, teacher experience, pupil-teacher ratio, and school size appear to be somewhat more positive for recent studies (although the teacher ability finding is based on a single publication, Ferguson, 1991), but the coefficients for PPE appear to be smaller among the more recent studies. These findings are important because newer studies are certainly more relevant to conditions in contemporary schools and tend to utilize stronger methodology.

If we examine the results of the combined significance tests and the effect magnitude analyses together, the findings suggest a substantially positive relation between educational resource inputs and academic achievement. These results are similar to those obtained in our earlier reanalysis of Hanushek's universe (Hedges et al., 1994). The present results seem to suggest even stronger and more consistent relations between educational resources and student outcomes, however, with the single exception of teacher-pupil ratio in studies after 1970 (note again that the category pupil-teacher ratio has more than three times as many coefficients as the category teacher-pupil ratio, and shows a positive relation). We regard the results on the class size effect as sensible, particularly in light of the extensive experimental literature on class size, which suggests that smaller class size produces greater achievement (Glass & Smith, 1979; Hedges & Stock, 1983; note that these two studies and two additional class size studies [Finn & Achilles, 1990; McGiverin, Gilman, & Tillitski, 1989], which support the argument that smaller class size provides greater student achievement, were reviewed and discarded because they did not report data in a form that could be used in these analyses).

Conclusions

The general conclusion of the meta-analysis presented in this chapter is that school resources *are* systematically related to student achievement and that these relations are large enough to be educationally important. Global resource variables such as PPE show positive, strong, and consistent relations with achievement. Smaller classes and smaller schools are also positively related to student achievement. In addition, resource variables that attempt to describe the quality of the teachers (teacher ability, teacher education, and teacher experience) show very strong relations with student achievement. Indeed, the most consistently positive relation with achievement is that of teacher ability.

Although the findings of our research should provide a clear direction for policy makers—that money is positively related to student achievement—the data, methods, and results do not provide detailed information on the most educationally efficient means to allocate existing and new dollars at the school site. The data available to address detailed questions about optimal resource allocation are far from ideal. Few school districts and fewer state departments of education have developed data collection and reporting systems that track resources (both financial and programmatic) to the classroom, the level of greatest interest to those who study student learning. One consequence of the use of a set of rather undifferentiated resource variables is that much of the education reform policy debate has tended to center on the question "Does money matter?" rather than the more prescriptive question of "How does money matter?" It is only by addressing the latter question that local educators are likely to meet the specific needs of their students by the most educationally efficient means possible.

Although our findings and methods support broad policy directions, without the collection and pairing of qualitative information with more disaggregated quantitative data, this type of research will continue to have limited prescriptive capacity. Statewide policy makers, while using education production functions to help influence the development of policy, should resist the urge to use this tool to micromanage educational policy at the local level. In the best of circumstances, they should focus on (a) specifying clear goals and high standards for public education, (b) supporting and facilitating local educational decision making designed to meet the individual needs of a school's specific student population, (c) developing a funding system that ensures that all schools have the capacity and resources (both human and financial) to provide their students with the educational opportunities necessary for success, and (d) creating an accountability system built around ongoing evaluation and improvement.

Finally, we reiterate that we are not arguing that the quantity of resources is everything in education. Equally important are how educators utilize resources and the incentives we create for both children and teachers. Thus we hope that this review and synthesis of education production function studies has provided clearer direction for broad educational policy as well as raising a warning for those policy makers who wish to micromanage education reform.

Notes

1. For PPE, the median half-standardized regression coefficient represents the standard deviation change in student achievement associated with a $1 increase in PPE: Multiplying $1,000 by .0003 results in a 0.3 standard deviation increase in student achievement resulting from a $1,000 increase in PPE.

2. Teacher salary was measured in $1,000s: Multiplying 15 by 0.0256 equals 0.38.

References

Averch, H. A., Carroll, S. J., Donaldson, T. S., Kiesling, H. J., & Pintero, J. (1972). *How effective is schooling? A critical review and synthesis of research findings* (Rep. No. R-956-PCSF-RC). Santa Monica, CA: RAND Corporation.

Baker, K. (1991). Yes, throw money at schools. *Phi Delta Kappan, 72,* 628-631.

Bridge, R. G., Judd, C. M., & Moock, P. R. (1979). *The determinants of educational outcomes: The impact of families, peers, teachers, and schools.* Cambridge, MA: Ballinger.

Coleman, J. S., Campbell, E. Q., Hobson, C. J., McPartland, J., Mood, A. M., Weinfeld, F. D., & York, R. L. (1966). *Equality of educational opportunity.* Washington, DC: Government Printing Office.

Cooper, H. M., & Hedges, L. V. (Eds.). (1994). *The handbook of research synthesis.* New York: Russell Sage.

Eberts, R. W., & Stone, J. A. (1984). *Unions and public schools: The effect of collective bargaining on American education.* Lexington, MA: D. C. Heath.

Eberts, R. W., & Stone, J. A. (1987). Teacher unions and the productivity of public schools. *Industrial and Labor Relations Review, 40,* 354-363.

Eberts, R. W., & Stone, J. A. (1988). Student achievement in public schools: Do principals make a difference? *Economics of Education Review, 7,* 291-299.

Ferguson, R. F. (1991). Paying for public education: New evidence on how and why money matters. *Harvard Journal on Legislation, 28,* 465-498.

Finn, J. D., & Achilles, C. M. (1990). Answers and questions about class size: A statewide experiment. *American Educational Research Journal, 27,* 557-577.

Flanagan, J. C., Davis, F. B., Dailey, J. T., Shaycoft, M. F., Orr, D. B., Goldberg, I., & Neyman, C. A., Jr. (1964). *Project Talent: The identification, development, and utilization of human talents* (Final Report for Cooperative Research Project No. 635, U.S. Department of Education). Pittsburgh, PA: University of Pittsburgh.

Glasman, N. S., & Biniaminov, I. (1981). Input-output analyses in schools. *Review of Educational Research, 51,* 509-539.

Glass, G. V., & Smith, M. E. (1979). Meta-analysis of research on class size and achievement. *Educational Evaluation and Policy Analysis, 1,* 2-16.

Grimes, P. W., & Register, C. A. (1990). Teachers' unions and student achievement in high school economics. *Journal of Economic Education, 21,* 297-306.

Grimes, P. W., & Register, C. A. (1991). Teacher unions and black students' scores on college entrance exams. *Industrial Relations, 30,* 492-500.

Guthrie, J. W., Kleindorfer, G. B., Levin, H. M., & Stout, R. T. (1971). *Schools and inequality.* Cambridge: MIT Press.

Hanushek, E. A. (1971). Teacher characteristics and gains in student achievement: Estimation using micro-data. *American Economic Review, 61,* 280-288.

Hanushek, E. A. (1972). *Education and race: An analysis of the educational production process.* Cambridge, MA: Heath-Lexington.

Hanushek, E. A. (1981). Throwing money at schools. *Journal of Policy Analysis and Management, 1,* 19-41.

Hanushek, E. A. (1986). The economics of schooling: Production and efficiency in public schools. *Journal of Economic Literature, 24,* 1141-1177.

Hanushek, E. A. (1989). The impact of differential expenditures on school performance. *Educational Researcher, 18,* 45-65.

Hedges, L. V., Laine, R. D., & Greenwald, R. (1994). Does money matter? A meta-analysis of studies of the effects of differential school inputs on student outcomes. *Educational Researcher, 23,* 5-14.

Hedges, L. V., & Olkin, I. (1980). Vote counting methods in research synthesis. *Psychological Bulletin, 88,* 359-369.

Hedges, L. V., & Olkin, I. (1985). *Statistical methods for meta-analysis.* New York: Academic Press.

Hedges, L. V., & Stock, W. (1983). The effects of class size: An examination of rival hypotheses. *American Educational Research Journal, 20,* 63-85.

Heim, J., & Perl, L. (1974). *The educational production function: Implications for educational manpower policy* (Monograph No. 4). Ithaca, NY: Cornell University, Institute of Public Employment.

Levin, H. M. (1970). A new model of school effectiveness. In U.S. Department of Education (Ed.), *Do teachers make a difference?* (pp. 55-77). Washington, DC: US Office of Education.

Levin, H. M. (1976). *Economic efficiency and educational production: Education as an industry.* Cambridge, MA: National Bureau of Economic Research.

MacPhail-Wilcox, B., & King, R. A. (1986). Production functions revisited in the context of educational reform. *Journal of Education Finance, 12,* 191-222.

Maynard, R., & Crawford, D. (1976). School performance. In D. L. Bawden & W. S. Harrar (Eds.), *Rural income maintenance experiment: Final report* (Vol. 6, Part 2). Madison: University of Wisconsin, Institute for Research on Poverty.

McGiverin, J., Gilman, D., & Tillitski, C. (1989). A meta-analysis of the relation between class size and achievement. *Elementary School Journal, 90,* 47-56.

Monk, D. H. (1989). The education production function: Its evolving role in policy analysis. *Educational Evaluation and Policy Analysis, 11,* 31-45.

Monk, D. H. (1992). Education productivity research: An update and assessment of its role in education finance reform. *Educational Evaluation and Policy Analysis, 14,* 307-332.

National Center for Education Statistics. (1993). *Digest of Education Statistics: 1993.* Washington, DC: U.S. Department of Education.

Register, C. A., & Grimes, P. W. (1991). Collective bargaining, teachers, and student achievement. *Journal of Labor Research, 12,* 99-110.

Sander, W., & Krautmann, A. C. (1991). Local taxes, schooling, and jobs in Illinois. *Economics of Education Review, 10,* 111-121.

Spencer, B. D., & Wiley, D. E. (1981). The sense and the nonsense of school effectiveness. *Journal of Policy Analysis and Management, 1,* 43-52.

Studies Providing Data
Used in the Analyses

Baum, D. N. (1986). A simultaneous equations model of the demand for and production of local public services: The case of education. *Public Finance Quarterly, 14,* 157-178.

Bieker, R. F., & Anschel, K. R. (1973). Estimating educational production functions for rural high schools: Some findings. *American Journal of Agricultural Economics, 55,* 515-519.

Boardman, A., Davis, O., & Sanday, P. (1977). A simultaneous equations model of the educational process. *Journal of Public Economics, 7,* 23-49.

Borland, M. V., & Howsen, R. M. (1992). Student academic achievement and the degree of market concentration in education. *Economics of Education Review, 11,* 31-39.

Bosshardt, W., & Watts, M. (1990). Instructor effects and their determinants in precollege economic education. *Journal of Economic Education, 21,* 265-276.

Bowles, S. (1970). Towards an educational production function. In W. L. Hansen (Ed.), *Education, income, and human capital* (pp. 11-61). New York: National Bureau of Economic Research.

Brown, B. W., & Saks, D. H. (1975). The production and distribution of cognitive skills within schools. *Journal of Political Economy, 83,* 571-593.

Burkhead, J., Fox, T. G., & Holland, J. W. (1967). *Input and output in large-city high schools.* Syracuse, NY: Syracuse University Press.

Caldas, S. J. (1993). Reexamination of input and process factor effects on public school achievement. *Journal of Economic Research, 86,* 206-214.

Cohn, E. (1968). Economies of scale in Iowa high school operations. *Journal of Human Resources, 3,* 422-434.

Cohn, E., Millman, S. D., & Chew, I.-K. (1975). *Input-output analysis in public education.* Cambridge, MA: Ballinger.

Deller, S. C., & Rudnicki, E. (1993). Production efficiency in elementary education: The case of Maine public schools. *Economics of Education Review, 12,* 45-57.

Dolan, R. C., & Schmidt, R. M. (1987). Assessing the impact of expenditure on achievement: Some methodological and policy considerations. *Economics of Education Review, 6,* 285-299.

Dugan, D. J. (1976). Scholastic achievement: Its determinants and effects in the education industry. In J. T. Froomkin, D. T. Jamison, & R. Radner (Eds.), *Education as an industry* (pp. 53-83). Cambridge, MA: National Bureau of Economic Research.

Eberts, R. W., & Stone, J. A. (1987). Teacher unions and the productivity of public schools. *Industrial and Labor Relations Review, 40,* 354-363.

Eberts, R. W., & Stone, J. A. (1988). Student achievement in public schools: Do principals make a difference? *Economics of Education Review, 7,* 291-299.

Ehrenberg, R. G., & Brewer, D. J. (1994). Do school and teacher characteristics matter? Evidence from high school and beyond. *Economics of Education Review, 13,* 1-17.

Ferguson, R. F. (1991). Paying for public education: New evidence on how and why money matters. *Harvard Journal on Legislation, 28,* 465-498.

Fowler, W. J., & Walberg, H. J. (1991). School size, characteristics, and outcomes. *Educational Evaluation and Policy Analysis, 13,* 189-202.

Grimes, P. W. (1994). Public versus private secondary schools and the production of economic education. *Journal of Economic Education, 25,* 17-30.

Grimes, P. W., & Register, C. A. (1990). Teachers' unions and student achievement in high school economics. *Journal of Economic Education, 21,* 297-306.

Gyimah-Brempong, K., & Gyapong, A. O. (1991). Characteristics of education production functions: An application of canonical regression analysis. *Economics of Education Review, 10,* 7-17.

Hallinan, M. T., & Sorensen, A. B. (1985). Class size, ability group size, and student achievement. *American Journal of Education, 94,* 71-89.

Hanushek, E. A. (1971). Teacher characteristics and gains in student achievement: Estimation using micro-data. *American Economic Review, 61,* 280-288.

Hanushek, E. A. (1972). *Education and race: An analysis of the educational production process.* Lexington, MA: D. C. Heath.

Hanushek, E. A. (1992). The trade-off between child quantity and quality. *Journal of Political Economy, 100,* 84-117.

Harnisch, D. L. (1987). Characteristics associated with effective public high schools. *Journal of Educational Research, 80,* 233-241.

Heim, J., & Perl, L. (1974). *The educational production function: Implications for educational manpower policy* (Monograph No. 4). Ithaca, NY: Cornell University, Institute of Public Employment.

Jencks, C. S. (1972). The quality of data collected by the Equality of Educational Opportunity Survey. In F. Mosteller & D. P. Moynihan (Eds.), *On equality of educational opportunity* (pp. 437-512). New York: Random House.

Katzman, M. (1971). *The political economy of urban schools.* Cambridge, MA: Harvard University Press.

Kenny, L. W. (1982). Economies of scale in schooling. *Economics of Education Review, 2,* 1-24.

Kiesling, H. J. (1967). Measuring a local school government: A study of school districts in New York State. *Review of Economics and Statistics, 49,* 356-367.

Kiesling, H. J. (1984). Assignment practices and the relationship of instructional time to the reading performance of elementary school children. *Economics of Education Review, 3,* 341-350.

Levin, H. M. (1976). Concepts of economic efficiency and educational production. In T. Joseph, J. T. Froomkin, D. Jamison, & R. Radner (Eds.), *Education as an industry* (pp. 149-191). Cambridge, MA: National Bureau of Economic Research.

Lewis, J., & Ouellette, H. (1979). Teacher training, teacher experience and pupil achievement. *Journal of Instructional Psychology, 6,* 3-5.

Link, C. R., & Mulligan, J. G. (1986). The merits of a longer school day. *Economics of Education Review, 5,* 373-381.

Link, C. R., & Mulligan, J. G. (1991). Classmates' effects on black student achievement in public school classrooms. *Economics of Education Review, 10,* 297-310.

Link, C. R., & Ratledge, E. C. (1979). Student perceptions, I.Q. and achievement. *Journal of Human Resources, 14,* 98-111.

Lopus, J. S. (1990). Do additional expenditures increase achievement in the high school economics class? *Journal of Economic Education, 21,* 277-286.

Maynard, R., & Crawford, D. (1976). School performance. In D. L. Bawden & W. S. Harrar (Eds.), *Rural income maintenance experiment: Final report* (Vol. 6, Part 2). Madison: University of Wisconsin, Institute for Research on Poverty.

Michelson, S. (1970). The association of teacher resources with children's characteristics. In U.S. Department of Education (Ed.), *Do teachers make a difference?* (pp. 120-168). Washington, DC: Government Printing Office.

Michelson, S. (1972). For the plaintiffs—Equal school resource allocation. *Journal of Human Resources, 7*, 283-306.

Monk, D. H. (1994). Subject area preparation of secondary mathematics and science teachers and student achievement. *Economics of Education Review, 13*, 125-145.

Murnane, R. J. (1975). *The impact of school resources on the learning of inner city children.* Cambridge, MA: Ballinger.

Murnane, R. J., & Phillips, B. R. (1981). What do effective teachers of inner-city children have in common? *Social Science Research, 10*, 83-100.

Perl, L. J. (1973). Family background, secondary school expenditure, and student ability. *Journal of Human Resources, 8*, 156-180.

Register, C. A., & Grimes, P. W. (1991). Collective bargaining, teachers, and student achievement. *Journal of Labor Research, 12*, 99-110.

Ribich, T. I., & Murphy, J. L. (1975). The economic returns to increased educational spending. *Journal of Human Resources, 10*, 56-77.

Ritzen, J. M., & Winkler, D. R. (1977). The revealed preferences of a local government: Black/white disparities in scholastic achievement. *Journal of Urban Economics, 4*, 310-323.

Sander, W. (1993). Expenditures and student achievement in Illinois: New evidence. *Journal of Public Economics, 52*, 403-416.

Sander, W., & Krautmann, A. C. (1991). Local taxes, schooling, and jobs in Illinois. *Economics of Education Review, 10*, 111-121.

Schneider, B. L. (1985). Further evidence of school effects. *Journal of Educational Research, 78*, 351-356.

Sebold, F. D., & Dato, W. (1981). School funding and student achievement: An empirical analysis. *Public Finance Quarterly, 9*, 91-105.

Smith, M. (1972). Equality of educational opportunity: The basic findings reconsidered. In F. Mosteller & D. P. Moynihan (Eds.), *On equality of educational opportunity* (pp. 230-342). New York: Random House.

Stern, R. (1989). Educational cost factors and student achievement in Grades 3 and 6: Some new evidence. *Economics of Education Review, 8*, 149-158.

Strauss, R. P., & Sawyer, E. A. (1986). Some new evidence on teacher and student competencies. *Economics of Education Review, 5*, 41-48.

Summers, A., & Wolfe, B. (1977). Do schools make a difference? *American Economic Review, 67*, 639-652.

Walberg, H. J., & Fowler, W. J. (1987). Expenditure and size efficiencies of public school districts. *Educational Researcher, 16*, 5-13.

Walstad, W. B., & Soper, J. C. (1988). A report card on the economic literacy of U.S. high school students. *American Economic Review, 78*, 251-256.

Winkler, D. (1975). Educational achievement and school peer group composition. *Journal of Human Resources, 10*, 189-204.

Appendix

Table 3A Description of Education Production Function Studies

Study	Y.O.D.	Sample Size	Grade	Background Control	Inputs	Outputs
Baum (1986)	1970-71	41 SD.	Sec.	SES	PPE	Reading
Bieker & Anschel (1973)	1967-69	226 St. in 5 Sc.	Sec.	SES, Long.	PPE	Composite
Boardman, Davis, & Sanday (1977)	1964-65 (EEO)	16,456 St.	Sec.	SES	T.Abl. T. Exp. TP/PT Admin. B.Age	Composite
Borland & Howsen (1992)	1989-90	170 SD.	Elem.	Long.	T.Sal. TP/PT	Composite
Bosshardt & Watts (1990)	1987	>3000 St.	Sec.	Long.	T.Exp. S.Size	T.E.L.
Bowles (1970)	1964-65 (EEO)	1000 St.	Sec.	SES	T.Abl.	Verbal
Brown & Saks (1975)	1970-71	104,790 St. in 519 SD.	Elem.	SES	T.Ed. T.Exp. TP/PT	Created Comp. (Reading/ Math/ English)
Burkhead, Fox, & Holland (1967)	1961-62 1960-61 1960-61	39 Sc. 22 Sc. 177 Sc.	Sec. Sec. Sec.	SES	T.Ed. T.Exp. TP/PT S.Size Admin. B.Age	Reading Verbal Reading
Caldas (1993)	1989-90	737 Sc. 468 Sc. 96 Sc.	Elem. Sec. Dual	SES	TP/PT S.Size	Composite
Cohn (1968)	1962-63	377 Sc.	Sec.	Long.	T.Sal. TP/PT S.Size	Composite
Cohn, Millman, & Chew (1975)	1971-72	53 Sc.	Sec.	SES	T.Ed. T.Exp. T.Sal. TP/PT S.Size Admin.	Created Comp. (Verbal/ Math)

Table 3A Continued

Study	Y.O.D.	Sample Size	Grade	Background Control	Inputs	Outputs
Deller & Rudnicki (1993)	1985-89	139 Sc.	Elem.	SES	PPE S.Size	Composite
Dolan & Schmidt (1987)	1980-84	128 Sc.	Dual	SES, Long.	T.Sal. TP/ PPPPT Admin.	Created Comp. (Reading/ Math)
Dugan (1976)	1969-70	47 Sc.	Sec.	SES	PPE T.Ed. T.Exp. TP/PT	Created Comp. (Reading/ Math)
Eberts & Stone (1987)	1978	9468(U) St. 5411(NU) St.	Elem.	SES, Long.	T.Ed. T.Exp. TP/PT Admin.	Math
Eberts & Stone (1988)	1978	14,959 St.	Elem.	SES, Long.	T.Ed. T.Exp. S.Size Admin.	Math
Ehrenberg & Brewer (1994)	1981-82	3128(W) St. 1055(AA) St. 549(L) St.	Sec.	SES, Long.	PPE T.Ed. T.Exp. TP/PT	Created Comp. (Math/ Reading/ Vocab.)
Ferguson (1991)	1985-86	857-980 SD (2.4m St.)	Dual	SES	T.Abl. T.Ed. TP/PT S.Size	Reading
Fowler & Walberg (1991)	1984-85	293 Sc.	Sec.	SES	TP/PT S.Size	Math
Grimes (1994)	1986, 1987	1224 St.	Sec.	SES, Long.	PPE TP/PT S.Size	T.E.L.
Grimes & Register (1990)	1986-87	1626 St.	Sec.	SES, Long.	PPE T.Exp. S.Size	T.E.L.
Gyimah- Brempong & Gyapong (1991)	1986-87	152 Sc.	Sec.	SES, Long.	PPE TP/PT	Created Comp. (Math/ English)

continued

Table 3A Continued

Study	Y.O.D.	Sample Size	Grade	Background Control	Inputs	Outputs
Hallinan & Sorensen (1985)	Unk.	791 St.	Elem.	SES, Long.	TP/PT	Composite
Hanushek (1971)	1968-69	838 St.	Elem.	SES, Long.	T.Abl. T.Exp.	Composite
Hanushek (1972)	1964-65 (EEO)	471(W) Sc. 242(AA) Sc.	Elem.	SES	T.Abl. T.Exp.	Created Comp. (Math/ Verbal)
Hanushek (1992)	1971-75	441(AA) St.	Elem.	SES, Long.	T.Abl. T.Ed. T.Exp. TP/PT	Reading
Harnisch (1987)	1982 (HS&B)	18,684 St.	Sec.	SES, Long.	T.Ed. S.Size	Composite
Heim & Perl (1974)	1967-68	63 SD.	Elem.	SES, Long.	T.Ed. T.Exp. TP/PT	Reading and Created Comp. (Reading/ Math)
Jencks (1972)	1964-65 (EEO)	1030 Sc.	Elem.	SES	TP/PT	Verbal
Katzman (1971)	1964-65	56 Sc.	Elem.	SES, Long.	T.Ed. T.Exp. B.Age	Math or Reading
Kenny (1982)	1959-60 (P.T.)	4270 St.	Sec.	SES	T.Ed. T.Exp. TP/PT	Created Comp. (Math/ Reading/ Soc. Sci./ Tech./ Verbal)
Kiesling (1967)	1957-60	79-121 SD.	Dual	SES, Long.	PPE	Composite
Kiesling (1984)	1974	3374 St. in 171 Sc. in 4 SD.	Elem.	SES, Long.	T.Ed. T.Exp. TP/PT	Reading

Table 3A Continued

Study	Y.O.D.	Sample Size	Background Grade	Control	Inputs	Outputs
Levin (1976)	1974-65 (EEO)	597(W) St. in 29 Sc.	Elem.	SES	T.Abl. T.Exp.	Verbal
Lewis & Ouellette (1979)	Unk.	383 St.	Elem.	Long.	T.Ed. E.Exp.	Social Studies
Link & Mulligan (1986)	1976-77	103(L) St. 1986(W) St.	Elem.	SES, Long.	T.Exp.	Created Comp. (Reading/ Math)
Link & Mulligan (1991)	1976-77	1022(L) St. 10871(W) St.	Elem.	Long.	TP/PT	Created Comp. (Reading/ Math)
Link & Ratledge (1979)	1969-70	500 St. in 1 SD.	Elem.	SES, Long.	T.Ed. T.Exp. TP/PT	Reading
Lopus (1990)	1986-87	528 St. (PPE only) 655 St. (all other var.)	Sec.	SES	PPE T.Ed. T.Exp. TP/PT	T.E.L.
Maynard & Crawford (1976)	1971-72	18 Sc. (N.C.) 16 Sc. (Iowa)	Dual	SES, Long.	PPE T.Ed. T.Exp. TP/PT S.Size	Composite
Michelson (1970)	1964-65 (EEO)	458 (AA) St.	Elem.	SES	T.Ed. B.Age	Verbal or Math
Michelson (1972)	1970-71	110 Sc.	Elem.	SES	T.Ed. T.Exp. S.Size	Reading
Monk (1994)	1989-90	1492 St, in 51 Sc.	Sec.	Long.	T.Ed. T.Exp.	Created Comp. (Reading/ Math)
Murnane (1975)	1970-71 1971-72	410 (AA) St. 440 (AA) St.	Elem.	SES, Long.	T.Ed. T.Exp. TP/PT	Reading or Created Comp. (Reading/ Math)

continued

Table 3A Continued

Study	Y.O.D.	Sample Size	Grade	Background Control	Inputs	Outputs
Murnane & Phillips (1981)	1973-75	814 (AA) St.	Elem.	SES, Long.	T.Ed. T.Exp.	Vocabulary
Perl (1973)	1959-60 (P.T.)	3265 St.	Sec.	SES	PPE T.Ed. T.Exp. T.Sal. TP/PT S.Size B.Age	Created Comp (Ability/ Abstract Reasoning)
Register & Grimes (1991)	1986-87	1570 (U) St. 790 (NU) St. in 61 SD.	Sec.	SES, Long.	PPE TP/PT S.Size	Composite
Ribich & Murphy (1975)	1959-60 (P.T.)	8249- 8466 St.	Sec.	SES	PPE	Composite
Ritzen & Winkler (1977)	Unk.	1964-65	Elem.	SES, Long.	PPE	Reading
Sander (1993)	1989-90	154 Sc. in 113 SD.	Sec.	SES	T.Sal. TP/PT S.Size	Composite
Sander & Krautmann (1991)	1986-87	102 Counties	Sec.	SES	PPE T.Ed. T.Exp. T.Sal. TP/PT S.Size	Composite
Schneider (1985)	Unk.	493 St. in 4 Sc. in 1 SD	Elem.	Long.	T.Ed.	Created Comp. (Reading/ Math)
Sebold & Dato (1981)	1975-76	100 SD.	Dual	SES, Long.	PPE	Reading or Created Comp. (Reading/ Math/ Written Expression)

Table 3A Continued

Study	Y.O.D.	Sample Size	Background Grade	Control	Inputs	Outputs
Smith (1972)	1964-65 (EEO)	Unk.	Dual	SES	PPE T.Abl. T.Ed. T.Exp. S.Size	Verbal
Stern (1989)	1983-84 1984-85	2452-3652 Sc.	Elem.	SES	T.Sal. RP/PT S.Size	Created Comp. (Math/ Reading/ Writing)
Strauss & Sawyer (1986)	1977-78	105 SD.	Sec.	SES	T.Abl. TP/PT	Created Comp. (Math/ Reading)
Summers & Wolfe (1977)	1970-71	627 St. in 103 Sc.	Elem.	SES, Long.	T.Abl. T.Exp. TP/PT S.Size	Composite
Walberg & Fowler (1987)	1983-84	261 SD.	Sec.	SES	PPE	Created Comp. (Reading/ Writing/ Math)
Walstad & Soper (1988)	1984-86	2483 St.	Sec.	SES, Long.	S.Size	T.E.L.
Winkler (1975)	1964-65	388 (AA) St. 385 (W) St. in 1 SD.	Elem	SES, Long.	TP/PT Admin.	Reading

Coding Notes:

Y.O.D. = Year of Data: EEO = Equality of Educational Opportunity data
P.T. = Project Talent data
HS&B = High School & Beyond
Unk. = Unknown.

Sample Size: W = Whites
AA = African Americans
L = Latinos
U = Unions
NU = Nonunions
SD = School District

continued

                                     Sc = School
                                     St = Student

Grade: Elem. = grades kindergarten through eight
                                     Sec. = grades nine through twelve
                                     Dual = grades kindergarten through twelve

Output: Created Comp. = In order to eliminate stochastic dependence, for production functions that utilized the same model, same population of students, but different outcomes, we calculated the median of the results.
T.E.L. = Test of Economic Literacy

FOUR

Does Equal Funding for Districts Mean Equal Funding for Classroom Students?

EVIDENCE FROM CALIFORNIA

LINDA HERTERT

School finance research typically focuses on the distribution of dollars across districts within a given state. The primary purpose of much of this research is to quantify the perceived inequities that result from the methods states use to generate and allocate educational funds (see for example, Mitroff & Erekson, 1988; Verstegen & Salmon, 1989). Reliance on the district as the unit of analysis is understandable given that revenues are raised by and for districts and that they are distributed on the basis of district characteristics. The use of district-level data, however, may not be appropriate if the goal is to measure, and thereby promote, a more equitable allocation of funds among pupils. That is, it may be incorrect to assume that the distributional and/or spending patterns across districts mirror those existing among the schools children attend, either within a district or across a state (see,

AUTHOR'S NOTE: The research reported here was supported by the Consortium for Policy Research in Education (CPRE) Finance Center, Grant No. OERI-R117-G10039. The opinions expressed in this chapter are my own and do not necessarily reflect the views of the U.S. Department of Education, the Office of Educational Research and Improvement, or the institutional partners of CPRE.

71

for example, Ginsburg, Moskowitz, & Rosenthal, 1981; Owen, 1974; *Rodriguez v. Los Angeles Unified School District,* 1992).

The purpose of the research presented here is to test this assumption by comparing district-level equity in California, as measured by the dollars spent for regular instruction in 1990 to 1991, with the equity measured at the school level both within and across the state's districts. California provides a unique environment in which to conduct this investigation. The combination of judicial rulings, legislative action, and a taxpayers' revolt initiative has created a state funding system presumed to be generally free of interdistrict disparities. An evaluation of variations across schools in this state can thus be made with some confidence that the findings are not solely the result of funding differences between districts.

The research discussed in this chapter is drawn from a broader study intended to evaluate and compare district- and school-level equity as measured by money and a number of educational resources that money buys, specifically teachers and courses. Although the purpose here is to report those findings specifically related to the money spent in California school districts, some comments on the allocation of these additional resources are included in the "Discussion" section below. This chapter, then, is concerned with two research questions:

1. How do variations in per-pupil expenditures at the school level, both within and across districts, compare with interdistrict measures?
2. Do school characteristics, such as type and size, or pupil characteristics, such as ethnicity, explain the variation in per-pupil expenditures between schools?

This chapter first outlines the methodology of the study. Next, it briefly discusses California's system of financing public education, including an analysis of the equity of the system as measured by district-level expenditures. The research questions are then addressed individually. The concluding section discusses the findings and their implications.

Methodology

The Study Population and Sample

In 1990-1991, there were 1,012 school districts in California: 289 unified school districts (K-12), 105 high school districts (mostly 9-12, though some include 6-12), and 608 elementary school districts (K-8). The statewide average daily attendance (ADA) for pupils enrolled in regular education programs was 4,569,046. Over 68% of these pupils attended schools in unified districts.

In this study the population is defined as unified districts, and the "regular" schools within them, with at least 2,500 ADA. This population includes 190 districts with a total ADA of 3,012,498, or 66% of the state's pupils. Twenty-five districts are sampled from this population. The sample includes 1,042 schools with a total ADA of 926,740, representing 31% of the pupils in the population. The sample is well distributed by district size and geographical location: Districts range in size from four schools with a total ADA of 3,302 to 551 schools with a total ADA of 568,222; 15 districts are in northern California, 10 in the southern part of the state; and 16 of the state's 58 counties are represented.

Data Sources

Expenditures

Expenditures are defined as those used for regular instruction as reported on the state's J-380 form, and are calculated as the sum of direct costs for (a) regular education programs, (b) school instruction administration, (c) school administration, (d) instructional media, and (e) pupil services. No attempt is made to allocate central administrative costs, as the purpose here is to determine the equity of resources available and used directly by schools. Also, federal and state categorical funding is not included in the analyses because (a) the focus here is on state monies distributed on behalf of all children, and (b) California's method of tracking categorical funds makes it difficult to create an accurate data set for the many federal and more than 80 state programs.

The sample districts in this study maintain school-site information on their own initiative. Although there is variation in the method districts use to organize these data, all districts distinguish expenditures by fund and program consistent with the state reporting requirements. It is therefore possible to construct from these individual district reports a set of comparable expenditure data for each school.

Enrollments

The average daily attendance (ADA) used by the state to allocate unrestricted general fund monies is the source for pupil counts. Pupils enrolled exclusively in special programs are omitted.

Ethnicity

The California Basic Educational Data System (CBEDS), a division of the state's department of education, collects from districts a variety of data on pupils, staffing, and course offerings. The School Information Form (SIF) is a CBEDS survey taken each October, and it provides school-site information on pupil and staff characteristics, including ethnicity. The SIF data set for the 1990 to 1991 school year is the source of the pupil ethnicity data used in this study.

Measures of Dispersion

The following summary statistics are used to measure the variation in per-pupil expenditures: the range, the restricted range, the federal range ratio, the coefficient of variation, the Gini coefficient, and the McLoone index (Berne & Stiefel, 1984). Few standards of statistically defined equity are established. Evaluations of equity measures must rely on authoritative recommendations. Odden and Picus (1992) suggested that 0.1 and lower for the Gini coefficient, 0.9 and higher for the McLoone index, and 10% or less for the coefficient of variation are "desirable." These suggested standards are adopted here.

The association of school-level characteristics with per-pupil expenditures is assessed by stepwise multiple regression, with a two-tailed test of significance set at 0.05.

California's System of Financing Public Education

The Funding System

California's Assembly Bill 8, passed in 1979 in response to the *Serrano v. Priest* (1971) rulings and in the aftermath of Proposition 13, remains the statutory basis for the funding structure used in the state today (for a more detailed description of the creation of the current funding system, see Elmore & McLaughlin, 1981). With a few modifications since its inception, the financing system remains a combination of a flat grant (basic aid) and a foundation program (revenue limit). A district's revenue limit is funded through property tax revenues and state aid, which makes up the difference between local taxes and the permissible revenue limit. Districts receiving more than their basic revenue limit in property taxes plus the guaranteed flat grant are allowed to keep the excess funds.[1]

Revenue limits are based on historical expenditure patterns, and increases in funding are inversely related to the amount of money allocated through the foundation program. This "squeeze" factor has produced a gradual equalization of the monies received by districts. Increases in funding are made in accordance with a statutory cost-of-living adjustment that is based on the yearly change in personal income across the state. Revenue limits differ for each of the six court-defined school district types (referred to as *Serrano* bands): small (up to 100 ADA) and large elementary districts, small (up to 300 ADA) and large high school districts, and small (up to 1,500 ADA) and large unified districts. Allowable spending variations within each *Serrano* band are based on a court-defined amount adjusted for inflation ($299 in 1992-1993). It is believed that spending variations are within the legal parameters for at least 90% of the state's pupils. A special adjustment to the revenue limit is made for "necessary" small school districts. Additional "special-need" funding for specific student populations is provided through numerous categorical funding programs, including gifted and talented, compensatory education, and special education.

The vast majority of the money a district receives is calculated on a per-pupil basis. For example, revenue limits are based on spending patterns per child, and many categorical programs are funded at a certain cost per identified pupil. This system is not replicated in the districts. Districts allocate resources to schools on the basis of a variety of algebraic formulas that generally provide one unit of a given resource per a given number of students. For example, a district may provide one certificated staff member for every 22 children. Although some of these ratios are defined by state law, such as certain teacher-pupil ratios, those that are not are apportioned differently across districts in accordance with administrative preference.

California's current public school funding system is believed to be fairly equitable. Recently, though, the equity of the distribution of public school funds *within a district* was challenged in Los Angeles County Superior Court. In *Rodriguez v. Los Angeles Unified School District*, filed in 1986, plaintiffs alleged that the district disproportionately allocated general funds to its schools in violation of several state constitutional provisions. It was asserted that the results were lower general-program expenditures, overcrowded schools, less access to library materials, and more inexperienced and noncredentialed faculty members in schools attended primarily by minority pupils. In a 1992 consent decree, the district, admitting no wrong, agreed to allocate resources in keeping with the plaintiffs' request.

Equity of the System

California's system of financing public education was fairly equitable in 1990 to 1991, as measured here by district-level per-pupil expenditures. Table 4.1 lists the results of the equity calculations used as a basis for comparison in this study's subsequent school-level analyses. The first column shows that for all districts across the state, the weighted mean per-pupil expenditure for regular instruction was $2,643, with a range of $1,298 to $11,370 per pupil.[2] The restricted range, which excludes observations above the 95th percentile and below the 5th percentile, was $825 per pupil. The coefficient of variation at 10.69, the Gini coefficient at 0.055, and the McLoone index at 0.937 are all near or above the acceptable equity standards employed in this study.

The remaining columns in Table 4.1 list the equity measures for unified districts—the group of districts from which the study population is drawn. Unified districts spent approximately the same amount per pupil on average as did all districts in the state in 1990-1991. The spending, however, was more equitably distributed across unified districts. The improvement in the coefficient of variation is particularly striking, down from a state average of 10.69% to 8.04%. This is to be expected, as revenues and expenditures are highly correlated, and as revenues (as calculated by revenue limits) vary by law in California by district type and size. It is not surprising, then, that the equity statistics are improved in all cases when calculations are lim-

Table 4.1. Per-Pupil Expenditures for Regular Instruction Between
California School Districts, 1990-1991

| Measure | All Districts | Unified Districts | | |
		All	Large[a]	Study Population[b]
Mean ($)[c]	2,643	2,657	2,652	2,651
Median ($)	2,609	2,639	2,639	2,639
Standard deviation ($)	283	214	199	196
Minimum ($)	1,298	1,739	1,739	2,172
Maximum ($)	11,370	5,983	4,016	4,016
Range ($)	10,072	4,244	2,277	1,845
Restricted range ($)	825	693	693	691
Federal range ratio (%)	36.06	29.09	29.09	29.00
Coefficient of variation (%)[c]	10.69	8.04	7.52	7.40
Gini coefficient	0.055	0.040	0.039	0.038
McCloone index	0.937	0.951	0.951	0.951
Number of districts	1,012	289	221	190
ADA	4,569,046	3,121,08	3,074,215	3,012,498

NOTE: Variation due to rounding.
a. Greater than or equal to 1,500 ADA.
b. Greater than 2,500 ADA.
c. Mean and coefficient of variation weighted by ADA per district.

ited to expenditures for large unified districts (defined for the purposes of funding as those with at least 1,500 ADA). As shown in the last column of Table 4.1, equity improves on all measures when the analysis is further limited to those large unified districts with at least 2,500 ADA—the population from which this study's sample is drawn.

This analysis confirms the widely held but seldom tested perception that California's method of allocating funds to its school districts results in a fairly equitable distribution, at least as measured by per-pupil expenditures from unrestricted general funds. With this information, it is possible to compare the high degree of equity measured across California's unified districts with that measured across schools in these districts. The intent is to determine if equity achieved across districts is mirrored at the school level.

Findings

The following analyses show that in 1990 to 1991 substantial variations in school spending per pupil existed both within districts and
across districts in California, and that these school-level differences
were generally greater than those measured at the district level.
District organization influenced school-level variation, as spending
differences across school sites were much smaller within districts than
across them. School type was more strongly associated with expenditure differences than were school size or pupil ethnicity, but school
type explained only a portion of the variance across schools. When
school type and district boundaries were considered, school-level
variations for elementary schools were similar to those found across
districts. These findings are discussed below in terms of two research
questions.

Question 1: To What Extent Does Interdistrict Disparity
Exist in the California Public School System,
as Measured by Per-Pupil Expenditures?

Across Schools Across Districts

The results of the school-level analyses are presented in Table 4.2.
The weighted mean per-pupil expenditure across all schools (as
shown in the second column) for the sample was $2,713, with a range
of $1,217 to $5,867 per pupil. The coefficient of variation of 22.6% is
more than double the 10.69% measured across the state's school
districts. The restricted range is $114 per pupil.

The Gini coefficient, which measures the degree to which equal
amounts of an object are distributed to an equally proportioned
number of observations, is 0.127. This indicates that expenditures are
distributed proportionately across 87% of the schools. The McLoone
index is the ratio of the sum of an object distributed across observations below the median to the sum required to provide all observations with the object amount available at the median. As the McLoone
index approaches 1.00, the distribution below the 50th percentile
narrows and approaches the median value. Across schools across
districts, the McLoone index for instructional expenditures is 0.849,
below the 0.9 standard of equity used here. The various equity statis-

Table 4.2. School-Level Per-Pupil Expenditures for Regular Instruction Across and Within California School Districts, 1990-1991

		School Level			
Measure	Study Population	All Schools Across Districts	Elementary Only Across Districts	All Schools Within Districts[a]	Elementary Only Within Districts[a]
Mean ($)	2,651	2,713	2,390	2,435	2,100
Median ($)	2,639	2,618	2,404	2,373	2,059
Standard deviation ($)	196	613	449	448	215
Minimum ($)	2,172	1,217	1,217	1,627	1,217
Maximum ($)	4,016	5,867	4,574	3,184	4,574
Range ($)	1,845	4,650	3,357	1,557	3,357
Restricted range ($)	691	2,000	1,490	1,220	663
Federal range ratio (%)	29.00	114.00	91.02	66.49	36.09
Coefficient of variation (%)	7.40	22.6	18.79	18.47	10.24
Gini coefficient	0.038	0.127	0.102	0.099	0.048
McLoone index	0.951	0.849	0.855	0.879	0.949
Number of districts	190	1,042	791	1042	791
ADA	3,012,498	926,740	543,331	926,740	543,331

NOTE: Variation due to rounding.
a. The statistics listed are the simple averages of across-schools within-district measures.

tics indicate that there was greater disparity in expenditures per pupil across California schools than that measured among these schools' districts in 1990-1991.

Across Schools Within Districts

As shown in the fourth column of Table 4.2, the distribution in expenditures at the school level improves when district boundaries are considered. For the 25 sample districts, the unweighted average spending is $2,435. At the extreme, schools spent on average almost twice as much as schools in the lowest-spending district ($3,184 to $1,627).

Across schools within districts, the average coefficient of variation at 18.47% is lower than that measured across all schools (22.6%), but is substantially higher than the 7.4% calculated across districts in the study population. Nineteen of the 25 districts had coefficients over 15.0%. The Gini coefficient ranges from 0.049 to 0.146, with an unweighted average of 0.099. If the 0.1 or lower standard suggested by Odden and Picus (1992) is used, 12 districts are equitable on this measure, with an additional 7 only 10% above this standard.

The McLoone index ranges from 0.734 to 0.962, with an unweighted district average of 0.879. This is an improvement over the distribution measured across all schools. In a majority of districts, however, spending favored those pupils in the upper half of the distribution.

Summary

These school-level analyses provide some evidence that the distribution pattern of fiscal resources across districts is not a suitable proxy for the variation that exists across schools. On all measures, spending per pupil varied more across schools than across districts. District organization, however, made a difference, as variance across schools was less within districts than across these boundaries. In other words, even in a fairly equitable system, the district in which a child attends school is still an important factor.

These analyses also indicate that variations across schools within districts were, in some cases, substantial. It is possible that these variations are due in part to the range of differences in school type and size within these districts. That is, variance may be greater in districts with a higher percentage of high school pupils or in districts with extreme differences in school size. It is also possible that these variances may be related to other school characteristics, such as the ethnicity of the pupil population. These possibilities are addressed in the next section.

Question 2: Do School Characteristics, Such as Type and Size, or Pupil Characteristics, Such as Ethnicity, Explain the Variation in Per-Pupil Expenditures Between Schools?

Across Schools Across Districts

The analyses indicate that school type (elementary, junior/middle, and high school) was more strongly correlated with per-pupil expenditures than any other school characteristic considered here (r = .52, p = .000). The correlation between expenditures and the size of the school was greater (r = .3, p = .000) than the association between expenditures and the percentage of minority students (r = .138, p = .000). The results of a stepwise multiple regression indicate that over 26% of the variation in expenditures is explained by school type. The addition of the remaining variables to the equation contributes minimally to the explanation of variance (R^2 = .302, F = 149.76, p = .000). This is due to the high correlation between school size and type (r = .682, p = .000) and to the small association between ethnicity and per-pupil expenditures.

When district type is controlled, per-pupil expenditures are not significantly associated with size or ethnicity in high schools. For junior/middle schools, type is moderately associated with both factors: r = .26, p = .001, for school size, and r = .307, p = .000, for ethnicity. Ethnicity is the only significant explanatory variable for the differences in per-pupil expenditures across junior/middle schools, and its contribution is small (R^2 = .094, F = 15.37, p = .0001). For the sampled elementary schools, there is a small negative association between expenditures and size (r = −.141, p = .000) and a small positive relationship with ethnicity (r = .139, p = .000). Combined, these factors explain very little of the variance in expenditures (R^2 = .072, F = 30.63, p = .000).

Considering the relative importance of school type to the variance in expenditures, we recalculated the dispersion measures across schools while controlling for this factor. The third column of Table 4.2 shows that when the across-schools across-district analysis is limited to elementary schools, the measures of variance improve.[3] Given the moderate amount of variance explained by school type (26% for the sample), it is not surprising that all equity measures across elementary schools, though better than when calculated for all school types, indicate substantially less equity than calculated at the district level.

Across Schools Within Districts

When expenditures per pupil by schools in the same district are considered with reference to certain school and pupil characteristics, school type is the important factor. It explains more than 50% of the variance in 22 of the 25 sample districts. In three districts, the percentage of minority pupils was significantly correlated with expenditures, but this factor contributed to the explanation of variance in only two of these districts, in both cases by less than 10%.

When school type is controlled, the factors considered here are not associated significantly with expenditures in the majority of districts. When elementary schools are used—the most numerous schools within each of the districts—size is important in eight of the districts sampled. In three of these districts, ethnicity is a secondary factor. Combined, size and ethnicity explain from 42% to 88% of the variation in per-pupil expenditures in these three districts. In one district, the percentage of minority students is the most strongly associated factor, explaining 23% of the expenditure differences across schools.

Column 5 of Table 4.2 summarizes the results of the analysis across schools within districts when controlling for school type. Not surprisingly, considering the importance of school type, the measures show less variance than when all schools are included in the analysis (second column of Table 4.2). The coefficient of variation, Gini coefficient, and McLoone index are close to or exceed the equity standards used here and approach those measures calculated for between-district expenditures per pupil. Simple averages, however, mask some interesting differences. For example, in three districts the coefficient of variation exceeds 15%, and in two districts the Gini coefficient is larger than 0.1.

Summary

School-level variations, both across and within districts, were strongly associated with school type, only moderately associated with size when type was controlled, and virtually unrelated to the ethnicity of pupils in the majority of sampled districts. The relationship between size and ethnicity was stronger when all schools were considered than when district boundaries were acknowledged, but these variables contributed little to the explanation of expenditure variations in the majority of districts. The exceptions, however, are noteworthy.

District boundaries make a difference: That is, there was less variation in the amount of money spent per pupil at different schools within a given district than was spent at different schools in different districts. But again, a number of provocative exceptions were noted.

Discussion

This study analyzed the degree of disparity in per-pupil expenditures at two levels, district and school. The intent was to evaluate the suitability of district-level equity measures as a proxy for the distribution of money used for educational resources delivered to children in the schools they attend. Judgments on the fairness of the distribution of school funding in California are a matter of perspective. If equity is deemed to be a district-level concern, then California has achieved the goal of most school finance litigation—the equalization of dollars between districts, especially when spending differentials due to the size and type of districts are acknowledged. If, however, the perspective is on children and the fiscal resources spent by their schools, then the findings here suggest that equalizing across districts may not be a sufficient solution to the problem of differential spending. Although this conclusion is mitigated somewhat by the finding that school type is an important factor in explaining the differences measured across schools within their respective districts, there were a number of important exceptions found in the analyses to suggest that some district-level policies unrelated to school type run counter to the distributional patterns established by state funding formulas. The implication of either perspective, district- or school-level, is that money matters in some significant way. Although this input/outcome relationship has been and continues to be debated, it is important to consider that efforts to equalize the distribution of money alone may be as inappropriate in improving an individual pupil's opportunity to learn as this study suggests focusing on district-level rather than school-level equity may be. That is, there is an untested assumption implicit in the efforts to equalize money that the distributional patterns of fiscal resources are related to those of the educational resources money buys.

Relatively little research comparing the equity of the distribution of money with the distribution of other educational resources exists to test this assumption. As discussed earlier, this study included a few such comparisons. Although the focus of this chapter is on the distribution of money, the findings regarding other resources support the results presented here. That is, the distribution of educational resources—teacher-pupil ratios, teacher experience, teacher education, and course offerings in higher-level math and science—was less equitable across schools than was the allocation of money used to buy these resources. Further, the level of equity varied by resource, with teacher-pupil ratios (a relationship partially controlled by state policy) distributed as fairly as educational funding but with course offerings varying widely both across districts and among schools.

Clearly, more research is necessary before the relationship between the allocation of money and the distribution of other educational resources is fully understood. Meanwhile, creating fiscal equity across districts continues to consume a great deal of time, energy, and effort. This study suggests that if equity is to be pursued on behalf of children, these efforts might be more productive if focused on equity across schools, rather than between districts, and on the distribution of the resources that money buys, rather than on money alone.

Notes

1. There are approximately 40 of these "basic aid" districts in California—a small proportion of the 1,012 school districts in the state.

2. The per-pupil expenditures may appear incorrect in comparison with other reported state averages. It is important to remember that throughout this analysis, "per-pupil expenditures" include only those monies intended for all pupils and spent for general education purposes at the school site. In other words, in these analyses, categorical monies, capital expenditures, transportation funds, cafeteria services, and central administration costs are excluded.

3. The analysis is limited to elementary schools because the majority of districts sampled have fewer than five other types of schools, making within-district comparisons unreliable.

References

Berne, R., & Stiefel, L. (1984). *The measurement of equity in school finance: Conceptual, methodological and empirical dimensions.* Baltimore: Johns Hopkins University Press.

Elmore, R., & McLaughlin, M. (1981). *Reform and retrenchment: The politics of California school finance reform.* Santa Monica, CA: RAND Corporation.

Ginsburg, A., Moskowitz, J. H., & Rosenthal, A. S. (1981). A school-based analysis of inter- and intra-district resource allocation. *Journal of Education Finance, 6,* 440-455.

Mitroff, R. C., & Erekson, O. H. (1988). Equity trends in Ohio school finance, 1976-1984. *Economics of Education Review, 7,* 245-250.

Odden, A. R., & Picus, L. O. (1992). *School finance: A policy perspective.* New York: McGraw-Hill.

Owen, J. D. (1974). *School inequality and the welfare state.* Baltimore: Johns Hopkins University Press.

Rodriguez v. Los Angeles Unified School District, No. C611358 (Los Angeles County Sup. Ct. May 5, 1992).

Serrano v. Priest, 5 Cal.3d 584, 487 P.2d 1241 (Super. Ct. for Los Angeles County, CA, 1971).

Verstegen, D. A., & Salmon, R. G. (1989). The conceptualization and measurement of equity in school finance in Virginia. *Journal of Education Finance, 15,* 205-228.

FIVE

Beyond District-Level Expenditures
SCHOOLING RESOURCE ALLOCATION
AND USE IN FLORIDA

YASSER A. NAKIB

Resource allocation in schools has become a generic term used to describe the operational activities required to run our nation's schools. From a broad perspective, resources are all "inputs" (monetary and nonmonetary) used in the educational setting. Inputs are defined as the dollars spent, the resources those dollars buy, and the way these resources are used by educational entities.

Resource allocation analyses provide tools for tracking educational reform. In particular, resource allocation studies can inform research on:

- Educational productivity
- Teacher recruiting and training
- The organizational structure and behavior of schools
- School finance legal concerns as they shift focus from equity to adequacy challenges

AUTHOR'S NOTE: This study was funded in part by the Mellon Foundation and by the U.S. Department of Education's Office of Education Research and Improvement through the Finance Center of the Consortium for Policy Research in Education (CPRE) by Grant #R1178G10039. I thank Dominic Brewer, David Monk, Lawrence Picus, and Christopher Roellke for their comments on an earlier draft. Expressed views are my own and are not necessarily shared by the project sponsors or the reviewers. I also thank the staff at the offices of Financial Management and Management Information System at the Florida Department of Education, Division of Public Schools, for their assistance in providing the data.

Previous research has made advances in resource allocation inquiries. Thomas (1977) and Ryder and Juba (1974) provided some early attempts to delineate resource allocation at the school and classroom levels. Fox (1987), Hayward (1988), Berne and Stiefel (1994), Hughes, Moon, and Barnett (1993), Cooper et al. (1994), Lankford and Wykoff (1995), and Miles (1994) all have provided similar analyses. This earlier work was limited either in its scope, using a sample of a general population; in its object, focusing on state or district levels; or in its approach, by not necessarily analyzing actual resource use. There is a need for more comprehensive analyses at a disaggregated level that include a wider range of the student population in all public education entities in a state. The research reported in this chapter is based on a current study that meets this need (Nakib, 1994). It is part of a series of concurrent studies being conducted in New York (Monk & Roellke, 1994), California (Picus, Hertert, & Tetrault, 1995), and Minnesota (Nakib, in press) by the Finance Center of the Consortium for Policy Research in Education.

This chapter addresses the issue of resource allocation and use, primarily at the school level. The analysis draws on data and findings from Florida, a state that has an advanced data collection system. The first section discusses methods of resource allocation analysis. The second section discusses the study design and data, and includes a brief description of the Florida resource accounting system. The third section describes allocation of funds and staff in Florida's 67 school districts. The fourth section provides resource allocation and analysis of nearly 2,400 schools in Florida. The conclusion suggests implications for contemporary school finance policy and practice.

Analysis of Resource Allocation

There are many directions an analysis of the allocation and use of school resources can take. One approach is descriptive but detailed, accounting for the various components of the allocation process. Such an approach is usually comprehensive, covering a wide range of the population in question and allowing the researcher to draw inferences concerning the process of schooling. Another approach is analytical and is usually based on fairly representative samples of the total population. Still another approach, the most promising, combines descriptive findings with analytical methods.

To be effective, the analysis must be cognizant of certain resource allocation patterns that can be explained only at the school-site level. The analysis must also rely on data that are representative in their scope, readily available, accurate, accessible, and uniformly measured and collected. Current expenditure figures do reflect most of the resources used from all major sources (local, state, and federal).[1] Current per-pupil expenditures are widely used as standard measures that reflect inputs in a school setting (Monk, 1990). Although they are not perfect, they are readily available accounts of most inputs used. An analysis of expenditures is not necessarily a cost analysis, for the former requires unambiguous understanding of the process by which inputs are translated into outputs (Monk, 1994b). As Hanushek (1994) indicated, expenditures at different sites usually yield different outcomes because of varying degrees of efficiency, goals, initial resource endowment, and organizational setups. Nor is the analysis of expenditures necessarily an analysis of accountability, and its usefulness can be obscured when it is so interpreted; especially if the process of evaluating the effectiveness of expenditures is not fully developed (Monk, 1994a).

Analysis of staff allocation patterns at the classroom level complements expenditure analysis and provides it with a contextual perspective. Patterns of staff allocation across curricular areas have received considerable attention in student learning research. Research by Shavelson, McDonnell, Oakes, Carey, and Picus (1987), Porter (1991), Darling-Hammond (1992), and Monk and Haller (1993) stresses the importance of staffing decisions in providing optimal outcomes.

Performing this analysis requires drawing several distinctions. One is the distinction between the disposition and the utilization of resources: *Disposition* refers to the decisions school officials and others make that give the students access to resources, whereas *utilization* refers to the allocation of student time to allow the actual "flow" of these resources (Monk & Roellke, 1994). Further distinctions that become necessary in analyzing pattern variations are random versus systematic, and significant versus arbitrary. Finally, one must establish distinctions among levels of resources used and among proportions dedicated to the various expenditure objects, functions, and programs. Analysis of absolute patterns requires a static format in which "everything else" is held constant.

Study Design and Data

This chapter describes part of a current multistate, multilevel study of resource allocation patterns in Florida, Minnesota, California, and New York being conducted by the CPRE Finance Center. Each individual state study concentrates on three major themes: expenditure patterns, staffing patterns, and resource use. In trying to understand the allocation and use of K-12 education resources at the district and school levels, I review patterns examined in general and as they relate to various contextual factors including district or school capacity, size, and the socioeconomic status of pupils enrolled. Specifically, expenditure and staffing patterns are related to the level of spending, size as defined by enrollment, per-pupil property wealth, percentage of pupils receiving free or reduced-price lunches, and percentage of minority pupils enrolled.

This chapter describes findings from the state of Florida. School finance in Florida is governed by a K-12 funding program that equalizes revenues among its 67 districts. It includes a comprehensive and detailed centralized method of expenditure reporting. The Florida Education Finance Program (FEFP) is the mechanism that drives public school finance in the state and divides responsibilities for public education funding among state and local governments. Each of Florida's 67 counties is a school district. The FEFP adjusts for variations in tax capacity and educational costs among the 67 counties, as well as for various pupil needs and varying district cost. Each district's required local effort, which is almost entirely supported by local property taxes, is determined by the legislature. Millage rates vary among districts due to varying property appraisals.

Florida maintains three major databases at the school and classroom levels to monitor its education system: financial, student, and staff. This analysis is based primarily on 1991-1992 school-year data from all of these databases. The financial base provides current expenditure information for each district and school by each FEFP program, excluding long-term capital, debt services, transfers, and community services. Expenditures are reported as either general revenue or special revenue expenditures. Each record classifies expenditures by function (instruction, instructional support, administration, maintenance, transportation, food, and capital outlay) and object (salaries, benefits, services, material and supply, instructional capital, and other). Funding is extended by program. Excluding adult education programs, the remaining 32 programs were aggregated into 6 major categories: grades K-3, grades 4-8, grades 9-12, at-risk, exceptional, and vocational. Reports of expenditures also identify direct and indirect program expenditures. Direct expenditures are generally associated with direct classroom instructional activities such as teacher salaries, whereas indirect expenditures are generally associated with instructional support activities such as administrative and maintenance services. Because most indirect expenditures cannot be directly attributed to specific program as delineated by the FEFP, they are usually prorated to the various FEFP programs on the basis of the number of students, the number of teachers, or the amount of physical space they occupy. It is important to note that the state uses the Full Time Equivalent (FTE) to represent pupil counts.

In addition to analysis of these three databases, site visits were conducted in a sample of 12 schools in four districts across the state to help understand the factors that influence resource allocation decisions. Districts were selected on the basis of wealth, size, location, and pupil demographic mix. In each district, one elementary, one intermediate, and one high school were visited. Interviews with district officials, principals, department heads, and teachers were conducted following protocols that included the collection and verification of site-level data on spending and resources allocation strategies. Due to space limitations, findings from this portion of the study are not discussed in this chapter.

Allocation at the District Level

Expenditures

Florida's 67 school districts were grouped into quintiles on the basis of five different criteria: (a) level of expenditures per pupil, (b) district enrollment, (c) district property wealth per pupil, (d) percentage of pupils receiving free or reduced-price lunches, and (e) percentage of minority pupils enrolled in the district. Analysis of district expenditures was performed by object, function, and program. Additional analyses of staffing patterns were also performed.

When districts were analyzed by expenditure quintiles, no significant variation in the distribution of funds by object was observed. Table 5.1 shows that when food and transportation expenses are excluded (the top half of the table), about 65% of districts' expenditures

Table 5.1. District-Level Per-Pupil Expenditures by Expenditure-Level Quintiles

	State Average	% of Total	1st Quintile	2nd Quintile	3rd Quintile	4th Quintile	5th Quintile
By Object[a]							
Instructional staff salaries	$1,659	45.5	45.0%	44.1%	45.0%	47.2%	46.2%
Teacher salaries	$1,569	43.1	41.8%	41.7%	43.3%	5.1%	43.4%
Instructional staff benefits	$538	14.8	14.0%	14.5%	14.0%	16.5%	14.8%
Service	$35	1.0	0.9%	0.7%	0.9%	1.4%	0.9%
Materials & supplies	$65	1.8	1.7%	1.7%	2.0%	2.0%	1.6%
Instructional capital	$30	0.8	0.8%	1.3%	0.7%	0.5%	1.0%
Other	$23	0.6	0.9%	0.7%	0.5%	0.2%	1.0%
Direct school expenditures	$2,350	64.5	63.2%	62.9%	63.1%	67.8%	65.5%
Indirect school expenditures	$1,051	28.8	30.8%	30.3%	30.4%	25.9%	26.8%
Total school expenditures	$3,400	93.3	94.0%	93.1%	93.4%	93.7%	92.3%
Indirect district expenditures	$243	6.7	6.0%	6.9%	6.6%	6.3%	7.7%
Total expend. (excluding food & transportation)	$3,644		$3,450	$3,567	$3,649	$3,679	$3,915
By Function							
Instruction	$2,350	58.4	56.4%	56.5%	58.1%	61.7%	59.3%
Instructional support services	$400	9.9	10.9%	10.3%	11.0%	8.6%	8.9%
Pupil personnel	$176	4.4	4.7%	4.3%	4.4%	4.5%	4.1%
Instructional media	$84	2.1	2.3%	2.2%	2.1%	2.0%	2.0%
Curriculum development	$115	2.9	3.4%	3.2%	4.0%	1.3%	2.4%

Insructional staff training	$24	0.6	0.5%	0.6%	0.6%	0.9%	0.5%
Administration	$325	8.1	8.5%	7.8%	8.6%	7.8%	7.7%
School level	$278	6.9	7.1%	6.8%	7.6%	6.6%	6.4%
District level	$47	1.2	1.4%	1.0%	1.0%	1.2%	1.3%
Maintenance & operation	$429	10.7	10.3%	11.3%	11.2%	9.6%	11.0%
Transportation	$167	4.2	5.1%	4.8%	3.1%	3.5%	4.3%
Food services	$211	5.2	5.6%	5.3%	4.8%	5.4%	5.1%
Capital outlay (short-term)	$12	0.3	0.2%	0.4%	0.4%	0.1%	0.3%
Other	$129	3.2	2.9%	3.6%	2.8%	3.3%	3.4%
Fiscal services	$30	0.7	0.7%	1.0%	0.6%	0.6%	1.0%
Central services	$99	2.5	2.3%	2.6%	2.3%	2.8%	2.4%
Total expend. (excluding food & transportation)	$3,644	90.6	89.3%	89.9%	92.1%	91.1%	90.6%
Total expend. (including food & transportation)	$4,022		$3,865	$3,967	$3,963	$4,040	$4,322

a. Breakdown of expenditures by object excludes food and transportation in Florida's accounting method.

was used to fund direct school instruction, including teacher salaries. In fact, on average, 93.3% of the total district budget was spent on school-site operation, and only 6.7% was kept at the district office. An average 45.5% of the district budget was used to pay teachers and other instructional staff members, and 14.8% was used to pay their benefits. When one observes the allocation of direct school funds at the district level, instructional staff salaries and benefits as a percentage of total expenditures were not significantly different in the overall level of spending among districts. Variations across expenditure quintiles were minimal. Only when one observed the allocation of district funds among minor objects (such as service, material and supply, and instructional capital) did significant variations become visible. However, these objects collectively consume no more than 5% of a total district budget.

Grouping districts into quintiles by district size, wealth, percentage of pupils receiving free and reduced-price lunches, and percentage of minority pupils yielded practically the same results as seen in the data presented in Table 5.1. This is not particularly surprising, given that Florida has a highly equalized K-12 district funding program, with strict legislative statutes requiring that at least 80% of revenues be spent on their respective programs. In fact, the analysis of expenditures by the various criteria showed that the widest variation in spending was, not surprisingly, between the highest- and lowest-expenditure quintiles. And even this amounted to only about 13.5% of total expenditures.

Expenditures by function for Florida's school districts were also analyzed by the five criteria described above. Instruction received the lion's share of expenditures, with 58.4% of the total (including transportation and food services). These figures are similar to findings from other states (Odden, Monk, Nakib, & Picus, 1995). Expenses for maintenance and supply were second, at 10.7%. Instructional support services consumed 9.9%, followed by administrative services at 8.1%. District-level administration amounted to only 1.2% of total expenditures. In fact, including food and transportation, functions that directly affect the individual pupil represented 77.8% of total expenditures (see Table 5.1).

When variation in functional expenditures was analyzed by quintiles of per-pupil spending, very little variation was observed. The difference between the lowest- and the highest-spending quintiles amounted to only 11.8% (see the bottom half of Table 5.1). Nor did district size, wealth, or student demographics have a significant impact on resource allocation patterns by function. The variation observed was either at the margin or not systematic. For example, expenditures on instruction increased by about 5% as one moved from smaller to larger districts.

District property wealth had no significant effect on the level of spending, with only a 2% difference in the average level of spending between the lowest- and highest-wealth quintiles. This confirms the earlier contention that Florida's K-12 funding program is equitable at the district level.

As expected, when expenditures by educational levels and special needs programs were analyzed, exceptional education programs showed the highest per-pupil allocation, followed by at-risk and then vocational programs. As constituted by the state funding program, expenditures for Grades 9-12 were the highest among the regular programs, followed by Grades K-3, and then Grades 4-8. On average, expenditures for exceptional student programs consumed about 16% of the overall average district budget, servicing only about 7% of district pupils, for a ratio of 2.3:1. Although regular programs for Grades K-3, 4-8, and 9-12 had the highest percentages of enrollment (31.7%, 31.4% and 19.31%, respectively), they received only 27.6%, 25.8%, and 18.7%, respectively, of total district expenditures, for ratios of 0.87:1, 0.82:1, and 0.97:1. At-risk and vocational programs received a slightly higher proportion of the overall district budget than their enrollment proportions, with ratios of 1.2:1 and 1.1:1, respectively. Except for at-risk programs, these ratios were fairly stable when adjusting for levels of expenditures. There were no consistent and significant patterns of expenditures by program as one moved from the lowest- to the highest-spending quintiles of districts. In general, a higher level of per-pupil expenditure in regular (K-12) and at-risk programs was detected, implying a general tendency to spend more on regular programs as the overall level of spending increased. For Grade 4-12 programs, districts tended to spend less as they increased in size. Ignoring all other possible factors, one could argue that there was a tendency to benefit from economies of scale in these programs.

Staff Allocation

To compare measures of staffing patterns across districts, the ratio of staff per 1,000 pupils enrolled was used. Staff types were divided

Table 5.2. District Staff Per 1,000 Pupils Enrolled by District-Size Quintiles

	State Average	1st Quintile	2nd Quintile	3rd Quintile	4th Quintile	5th Quintile
Elementary teachers	21.4	21.6	20.3	22.4	22.4	19.1
Elementary specialists	16.1	15.6	16.9	17.4	17.1	18.7
Secondary teachers	25.4	26.1	24.2	25.4	22.6	19.7
Secondary specialists	10.3	9.9	11.1	12.1	11.8	11.6
Instructional support	6.1	6.0	6.3	6.9	5.7	6.0
District officials	5.1	6.2	2.9	2.1	2.1	3.3
School officials	3.3	3.3	3.1	3.5	3.6	3.5
Noninstructional support	32.4	33.9	31.2	31.3	24.7	19.7
Aides	14.1	14.8	12.9	12.8	13.9	6.8
Clerical	11.3	11.4	11.1	10.9	10.6	9.6

into the following categories: teachers, instructional support, noninstructional support, district and school officials, aides, and clerical support. Overall, there was no significant variation in staffing patterns across districts when the level of spending, size, wealth, percentage of pupils on free or reduced-price lunch, presence of minority pupils, and the percentage of district expenditure dedicated to instruction were considered. However, some minor differences did exist. As the size of the district grew, there were more elementary specialists and fewer secondary teachers per 1,000 pupils (see Table 5.2). This could illustrate the expected outcome of scale expansion on employment practices. There is a tendency in Florida to have proportionately fewer secondary and more elementary schools as districts get bigger. Similarly, noninstructional support staff substantially decreased as the size of the district increased, suggesting possible economies of scale in this area.

Decisions in allocating teaching staff to various subject areas are crucial to effective educational practice. Table 5.3 shows that Florida high schools have a tendency to allocate more teachers per 1,000 students to language arts (including English) than to any other major subject area. One contributing factor is the increasing need for English as a Second Language classes. For every 1,000 pupils enrolled in high schools, 9.83 language arts teachers were hired, on average. There

Table 5.3. High School Instructional and Other District Staff per 1,000
High School Pupils by Expenditure Quintiles

Staff Category	State Average	1st Quintile	2nd Quintile	3rd Quintile	4th Quintile	5th Quintile
Math	7.23	7.08	6.95	7.09	6.99	7.56
Science	6.65	6.54	6.47	6.40	6.21	6.98
Language arts	9.83	9.76	9.50	10.22	9.44	10.03
Social studies	6.79	6.65	6.60	6.33	6.57	7.16
Foreign language	2.66	2.59	2.89	2.89	2.72	2.50
Humanities	0.14	0.11	0.16	0.09	0.14	0.17
Computer education	0.58	0.42	0.61	0.60	0.80	0.63
Music	1.39	1.12	1.62	1.42	1.15	1.51
Art	1.39	1.29	1.56	1.56	1.25	1.36
Physical education	3.59	3.17	3.67	3.19	3.30	4.01
Dance	0.20	0.18	0.17	0.20	0.13	0.25
Drama	0.55	0.50	0.51	0.69	0.68	0.53
Library/media	0.35	0.33	0.70	0.16	0.21	0.18
Health	1.08	1.13	0.73	0.98	0.82	1.35
Exceptional (ESE)	3.48	3.00	3.48	2.71	3.92	3.94
Vocational	9.83	10.17	9.64	9.25	8.43	10.16
Other[a]	4.11	3.69	3.71	4.29	4.06	4.61
Total H.S. instruction	59.84	57.74	58.97	58.08	56.82	62.93
District-Wide Other Staff						
Instructional support	5.13	4.91	5.25	5.53	5.02	5.15
School administration	3.38	3.35	3.49	3.14	3.45	3.39
District administration	0.30	0.12	0.01	0.04	0.06	0.73
Aides	4.63	4.12	4.11	3.06	3.96	5.92
Noninstructional support	14.99	15.18	14.86	12.26	20.26	14.41
Clerical	7.04	7.39	7.40	6.33	6.84	6.81

a. Includes courses in remedial, research, peer leadership, study hall, temporary placement, community service, ROTC, driver's education, college, exploration, and self-contained.

were fewer teachers per 1,000 high school pupils teaching math, science, social studies, and foreign language. Table 5.3 shows that core subject areas (the first six listed) had 55.6% of the total district high school teaching pool. High school teacher staffing decisions by subject area were practically the same across the various levels of district expenditure. Only computer education and library/media staffing varied significantly across quintiles of expenditure.

Allocations at the School Level

Expenditures

As with the district-level analysis, schools were grouped into quintiles on the basis of their level of per-pupil expenditure, their size, their district's per-pupil property wealth, percentage of pupils being served free or reduced-price lunches, and percentage of minority pupils enrolled in the school. Analysis of school funds was performed by expenditure object, function, and program. Additional analyses of staffing patterns by type of staff and by type of school were also performed.

Expenditures by Object

When schools were grouped by per-pupil-expenditure quintiles, no significant variation in the way schools allocated their funds among various objects was observed. Table 5.4 shows that on average, 64.4% of Florida's school-site expenditures (excluding food and transportation) was used to fund direct school instruction, including teacher salaries. However, variation in the level of expenditures was more disparate at the school than at the district level (a variance of 58% and a coefficient of variation of 0.25).

Although the level of funding varied quite distinctly among schools, the distribution of these funds across objects did not vary significantly regardless of how the data were analyzed. Smaller schools tended to spend significantly more per pupil than larger ones. Schools in the wealthiest districts spent significantly more per pupil, with the bulk of the difference paying for instructional services. At the same time, they spent proportionately less on indirect school activities. Similar patterns existed for schools with the highest concentration of free or reduced-price lunch recipients and minority pupils, although the level of spending among those was practically the same.

Expenditures by Function

Analysis of expenditures by function shows that instruction tended to receive the lion's share, 58.3% of the total. Expenditures for maintenance and supply were second, with 9.9%. District office expenditures prorated to the school amounted to 6.0% of the total. When food and transportation were included, functions that directly affected the individual pupil amounted to about 76% of total school expenditures (see Table 5.4). When analyzed by function, variation among schools occurred mostly in expenditures for central services (mostly debt), transportation, and instructional support services, with coefficients of variation of 0.75, 0.58, and 0.50, respectively. Expenditures for instruction varied the least among schools, with a coefficient of variation of 0.26.

Analysis by school size revealed that except for the smallest quintile, total per-pupil expenditures were practically the same. The manner in which schools distributed their funds across functions indicated that the proportion dedicated to instructional support services (especially curriculum development and staff training) and "other" (mostly central office) decreased with size. It appears that schools tended to benefit marginally from economies of scale in these functions.

Except for schools in the wealthiest districts, the level of spending per pupil was relatively consistent. Aside from food and transportation expenditures, there was a marginally higher level of spending and a higher proportion dedicated to instruction in wealthier districts. Pupil demographics did create a distinctive pattern of allocation by function. Only for schools with the highest enrollment of needy and minority pupils was a distinctively higher proportion dedicated to instruction at the expense of instructional support. The lack of comparable instructional support expenditures in such schools can perhaps provide significant implications for understanding outcomes in schools with high concentrations of needy and minority pupils.

Expenditures by Program

When per-pupil school expenditures were analyzed by grade level and special-need programs, there were no unusual findings. Exceptional education programs showed the highest per-pupil allocation, receiving on average 233% more funds than the highest expenditure

Table 5.4. School-Level Per-Pupil Expenditures by Expenditure Quintiles

	State Average	% of Total	1st Quintile	2nd Quintile	3rd Quintile	4th Quintile	5th Quintile
By Object[a]							
Instructional staff salaries	$1,649	45.5	45.7%	45.7%	45.9%	45.7%	44.9%
Teacher salaries	$1,558	43.0	43.4%	43.3%	43.7%	43.4%	41.6%
Instructional staff benefits	$535	14.8	14.8%	14.8%	15.0%	14.8%	14.6%
Service	$31	0.8	0.6%	0.7%	0.8%	0.8%	1.2%
Materials & suppliers	$65	1.8	1.9%	1.8%	1.8%	1.8%	1.7%
Instructional capital	$30	0.8	0.6%	0.7%	0.7%	0.8%	1.2%
Other	$22	0.6	0.6%	0.6%	0.6%	0.6%	0.6%
Direct school expenditures	$2,332	64.4	64.2%	64.2%	64.8%	64.6%	64.1%
Indirect school expenditures	$1,048	28.9	29.2%	29.0%	28.5%	28.7%	29.2%
Total school expenditures	$3,380	93.3	93.6%	93.3%	93.3%	93.3%	93.3%
Indirect district expenditures	$242	6.7	6.5%	6.7%	6.7%	6.8%	6.7%
Total expenditures (excluding food & transportation)	$3,622		$2,955	$3,257	$3,493	$3,766	$4,670
By Function							
Instruction	$2,332	58.30	57.1%	57.6%	58.4%	58.7%	59.3%
Instructional support services	$328	8.2	8.3%	8.3%	7.9%	8.0%	8.5%
Pupil personnel	$157	3.9	3.7%	3.8%	3.9%	3.9%	4.1%
Instructional media	$81	2.9	2.2%	2.1%	2.1%	2.0%	1.8%
Curriculum development	$73	1.8	2.0%	1.9%	1.5%	1.6%	2.1%

Instructional staff training	$17	0.4	0.4%	0.4%	0.4%	0.4%	0.5%
Administration	$274	6.8	6.5%	6.8%	6.7%	6.9%	7.3%
Maintenance & operation	$394	9.8	9.8%	9.6%	9.7%	9.9%	10.1%
Transportation	$168	4.2	5.2%	4.7%	4.5%	3.8%	3.2%
Food services	$211	5.3	6.0%	4.7%	5.4%	5.3%	4.3%
Capital outlay (short-term)	$7	0.2	0.2%	0.2%	0.2%	0.2%	0.2%
Other (central services)	$45	1.1	1.2%	1.2%	1.2%	1.1%	1.0%
District indirect cost (prorated)	$242	6.1	5.8%	6.0%	6.1%	6.1%	6.2%
Total expend. (excluding food & trans.)	$3,622	90.5	88.8%	89.6%	90.0%	90.9%	92.4%
Total expend. (including food & trans.)	$4,001		$3,326	$3,634	$3,879	$4,144	$5,052

a. Breakdown of expenditures by object excludes food and transportation in Florida's accounting method.

Table 5.5. School-Level Per-Pupil Expenditures by Program by
Expenditure Quintiles

Program	State Average	1st Quintile	2nd Quintile	3rd Quintile	4th Quintile	5th Quintile
Grades K-3	$3,167	$2,754	$3,008	$3,185	$3,459	$3,849
Grades 4-8	$2,984	$2,598	$2,875	$3,054	$3,198	$3,606
Grades 9-12	$3,518	$2,729	$3,026	$3,241	$3,552	$4,057
At-risk	$4,370	$3,897	$3,887	$4,227	$4,283	$4,900
Exceptional	$8,216	$7,095	$7,340	$7,558	$7,845	$9,842
Vocational	$3,978	$3,329	$3,464	$3,625	$3,858	$4,704

regular program (Grades 9-12). At-risk, vocational, Grades 9-12, Grades
K-3, and Grades 4-8 followed respectively (see Table 5.5). A clear
pattern of increasing per-pupil expenditures for all programs was
detected from the lowest- to the highest-spending quintiles. This
indicates that levels of spending were neither proportionally adverse
nor favorable toward a specific program. The data also revealed that
there was a tendency to benefit from economies of scale in all
programs except those for Grades K-3 and at-risk pupils. In general, per-pupil expenditures did decrease significantly with size.
There were no uniform (linear) patterns observable from analysis
of program expenditures by wealth or pupil demographics.
Schools in the wealthiest districts spent on average just as much as
schools in relatively poorer districts.

Staffing Patterns

To make sense of school-level staffing allocations, I analyzed schools
by type: elementary (usually Grades pre-K to 3), middle (Grades 4 to 8),
high (Grades 9 to 12), and combination mix (Grades K to 12). The ratio
of pupils per school staff member was used to assess variations in
staffing patterns across schools. Staff types were divided into the
following categories: elementary teachers, elementary specialists, secondary teachers, secondary specialists, instructional and noninstructional support, district and school officials, aides, and clerical support.
Although expenditures were not significantly different by object,

function, or program among schools in general, staffing patterns showed more significant variations.

High schools tended to have relatively more teachers per pupil than their elementary counterparts. By the same token, elementary schools employed substantially more specialists than did high schools. Schools (regardless of type) tended to increase uniformly all types of staff as they spent more. For elementary schools, substantial increases in specialists, aides, and district officials were visible as the level of per-pupil school spending increased. The ratio of pupils to elementary classroom teachers remained practically the same in all elementary schools regardless of the level of spending. High-spending high schools employed significantly and consistently more classroom teachers. The ratio of pupils to secondary teachers dropped by 22% from the lowest- to the highest-spending high schools. The level of spending showed a consistent and significant increase in employing school officials, noninstructional support, teacher aides, and clerical staff.

Another approach to analyzing staffing patterns is the allocation of teacher time relative to pupil time. Table 5.6 shows the average high school teacher assignment of pupils by subject area for the various levels of expenditure quintiles. Among the core curricular areas, language arts teachers had the least amount of pupils assigned. Science teachers had a considerably heavier load that was close to that of social studies and foreign language. In general, teacher assignments decreased with the level of spending in practically all subject areas.

Overall, variations among high school staffing patterns were greatest in subjects such as drama, library and media, health, exceptional, and maintenance courses (all with a coefficient of variation above 0.32). Among the core areas, math and humanities had the most divergence among schools, with a coefficient of variation at 0.27. When the ratio of a subject area's share of all high school teachers divided by its share of pupils enrolled in the courses out of all school course enrollment was analyzed, fewer variations were observed. Of the six major curricular subjects, only language arts and humanities had a ratio above 1. In these areas, there were proportionally more teachers per pupil assigned. Similar results hold for analysis by the size of the high school, the wealth of the district, and the various student demographics.

Table 5.6. Pupils per Teacher in Subject Areas, and Ratios of Subject Area's Share of All High School Teachers to Subject Area's Share of All School Course Pupil Enrollment, by Expenditure Quintiles

Subject Area	Mean		1st Quintile		2nd Quintile		3rd Quintile		4th Quintile		5th Quintile	
	Pupils per Teacher	Ratio	Pupils per Teacher	Ratio	Pupils per Teacher	Ratio	Pupils per Teacher	Ratio	Pupils per Teacher	Ratio	Pupils per Teacher	Ratio
For entire population	120	1.19	130	1.13	128	1.27	124	1.11	117	1.26	110	1.17
Math	115	0.92	120	0.91	117	0.93	121	0.91	115	0.90	107	0.92
Science	125	0.88	126	0.89	132	0.90	130	0.89	124	0.89	118	0.86
Language arts	102	1.08	103	1.12	106	1.13	101	1.10	101	1.08	99	1.03
Social studies	126	0.86	133	0.85	133	0.88	128	0.86	127	0.86	116	0.84
Foreign language	127	0.91	138	0.89	139	0.89	130	0.91	126	0.90	116	0.93
Humanities	119	1.11	123	1.14	137	0.99	127	1.00	109	1.17	104	1.25
Computer education	118	1.05	135	1.00	127	1.00	120	1.03	117	1.03	107	1.14
Music	142	0.91	159	0.87	152	0.88	145	0.91	135	0.93	134	0.92
Art	131	0.93	143	0.91	141	0.93	129	0.94	124	0.95	127	0.91
Physical education	153	0.78	167	0.75	168	0.76	151	0.79	151	0.78	141	0.78
Dance	147	0.91	177	0.79	154	0.85	148	0.85	138	0.98	124	1.03
Drama	135	0.94	140	0.91	144	0.92	159	0.88	124	0.89	119	0.99
Library/media	89	4.89	103	2.35	104	5.92	99	2.69	56	10.52	72	4.01
Health	128	0.97	142	1.10	124	1.03	131	0.92	133	0.91	121	0.93
Exceptional (ESE)	68	2.22	71	2.40	68	2.51	68	2.12	71	2.04	65	2.20
Vocational	113	1.12	121	1.18	126	1.10	116	1.11	111	1.08	102	1.15
Other[a]	97	1.63	115	1.37	108	1.27	97	1.77	93	1.59	84	1.90

a. Includes courses in remedial, research, peer leadership, study hall, temporary placement, community service, ROTC, driver's education, college exploration, and self-contained.

Conclusion

We have seen that districts, and more importantly schools, behave generally the same way in allocating their funds by object, function and program. Similarities are not confined to the way funds are allocated. This study found that levels of spending overall, and on instruction in particular, did not show much significant difference in Florida. What these expenditures buy of staff might have shown more variation among districts and even more among schools of the same type, but staffing of essential curricular area classes is very similar. To what degree this phenomenon is attributed to the uniform method Florida has established to account for school resource is open for debate. Part of the answers lie in the organizational behavior of the administrative system that might either be against breaking old habits or is faced with environmental forces that inhibit their efforts for change. This chapter has conveyed the results of a major resource allocation study. Although it is more descriptive than analytical, a number of relevant implications can be drawn from it. Analysis of resource allocation patterns at the district and school levels, using a case study in Florida, did not show much significant variation when factors such as the level of expenditures, district and school size, the wealth of the district, the presence of free and reduced-price lunch recipients, and the presence of minority pupils were considered. The lack of significant expenditure variations among Florida's districts and schools is in itself significant. If expenditures do not differ significantly among schools and districts, then what factors contribute to differences in school effectiveness? Answers may lie in the process by which different schools put their resources (funds and staff) into use, serving varying types of pupils in nonuniform communities with divergent organizational structures. Strategic research challenges remain for any resource allocation and even school productivity analyses. Making sense of resource allocation patterns by incorporating school contexts and environments is perhaps the leading venue for many school effectiveness and outcome analyses. Through the systematic effort of combining resource allocation and school context analyses, we may resolve the infamous issue of "whether money matters."

Note

1. Some resources are not accounted for by current expenditure reports but are still used at the district or school site. Examples include donations, private grants, extracurricular-activity fund-raising, and volunteers. However, these resources usually account for no more than 5% of the total operating budget. Sources of funding (federal, state, local, and individual) are not a matter of concern in this study, although they can influence the use of resources.

References

Berne, R., & Stiefel, L. (1994). Measuring equity at the school level: The finance perspective. *Educational Evaluation and Policy Analysis, 16,* 405-421.

Cooper, B., Sarel, R., Darvas, P., Alfano, F., Meier, E., Samuels, J., & Heinbuch, S. (1994). Making money matter in education: A micro-financial model for determining school-level allocations, efficiency, and productivity. *Journal of Education Finance, 20*(1), 66-87.

Darling-Hammond, L. (1992). Educational indicators and enlightened policy. *Educational Policy, 6,* 235-265.

Fox, J. N. (1987). An analysis of classroom spending: Or, where do all the dollars go? *Planning and Changing, 18*(3), 154-162.

Hanushek, E. A. (1994). *Making schools work: Improving performance and controlling cost.* Washington, DC: Brookings Institute.

Hayward, G. C. (1988). *The two million dollar school* (Policy Paper No. PP88-5-5). Berkeley: University of California, Policy Analysis for California Education.

Hughes, J., Moon, C. G., & Barnett, W. S. (1993, November). *Revenue-driven costs: The case of resource allocation in public primary and secondary education.* Paper presented at the annual meeting of the Atlantic Economic Society, Philadelphia.

Lankford, H., & Wykoff, J. (1995). Where has the money gone? An analysis of school spending in New York. *Educational Evaluation and Policy Analysis, 17*(2), 195-218.

Miles, K. H. (1994, April). *Finding time for improving schools: A case study of Boston public schools.* Paper presented at the annual meeting of the American Educational Research Association, New Orleans.

Monk, D. H. (1990). *Education finance: An economic approach.* New York: McGraw-Hill.

Monk, D. H. (1994a). Incorporating outcome equity standards into extant systems of educational finance. In R. Berne & L. O. Picus (Eds.), *Outcome equity in education* (pp. 224-246). Thousand Oaks, CA: Sage.

Monk, D. H. (1994b). Policy challenges surrounding the shift towards outcome-oriented school finance equity standards. *Educational Policy, 8,* 471-488.

Monk, D. H., & Haller, E. J. (1993). Predictors of high school academic course offerings. *American Educational Research Journal, 30*(1), 3-21.

Monk, D., & Roellke, C. (1994). *The origin, disposition and utilization of resources within the New York State public school system.* Paper presented at the annual data conference of the National Center for Education Statistics, Arlington, VA.

Nakib, Y. (1994). *Allocation and use of public K-12 education resources in Florida.* Madison: University of Wisconsin, Wisconsin Center for Education Research, Consortium for Policy Research in Education, The Finance Center.

Nakib, Y. (in press). *Allocation and use of public K-12 education resources in Minnesota.* Madison: University of Wisconsin, Wisconsin Center for Education Research, Consortium for Policy Research in Education, The Finance Center.

Odden, A., Monk, D., Nakib, Y., & Picus, L. (1995). The story of the education dollar: No fiscal academy awards and no fiscal smoking guns. *Phi Delta Kappan, 77*(2).

Picus, L. O., Hertert, L., & Tetrault, D. (1995). *The allocation and use of education dollars at the district and school levels in California.* Madison: University of Wisconsin, Wisconsin Center for Education Research, Consortium for Policy Research in Education, The Finance Center.

Porter, A. C. (1991). Creating a system of school process indicators. *Educational Evaluation and Policy Analysis, 11,* 181-199.

Ryder, K. F., Jr., & Juba, B. M. (1974). *Analysis of the educational personnel system: Staffing patterns in U.S. local public schools* (R-1342-HEW). Santa Monica, CA: RAND Corporation.

Shavelson, R., McDonnell, L., Oakes, J., Carey, N., & Picus, L. (1987). *Indicator systems for monitoring mathematics and science education.* Santa Monica, CA: RAND Corporation.

Thomas, A. J. (1977). *Resource allocation in classrooms.* Chicago: University of Chicago, Department of Education.

SIX

Bringing Money to the Classroom
A SYSTEMIC RESOURCE
ALLOCATIONS MODEL APPLIED TO
THE NEW YORK CITY PUBLIC SCHOOLS

SHEREE T. SPEAKMAN

BRUCE S. COOPER

ROBERT SAMPIERI

JAY MAY

HUNT HOLSOMBACK

BRIAN GLASS

In the haste to restructure America's schools, advocates of systemic school reform—efforts to change the parts to affect the whole—have virtually ignored the use of fiscal resources and thus the all-important question of this volume, "Where does the money go?" This apparent oversight is unexpected because reinventors of schooling place a high premium on the organic relationship among all components of the improvement process—including the use of funds (Malen, 1994; Wohlstetter & Odden, 1992; Wohlstetter, Smyer, & Mohrman, 1994).

The primary emphasis to date has been on the sources and uses of funds in the aggregate at the district level. But the movement of education reform requires that policy analysts revisit issues of funding and resource allocations in the school and classroom as well. For example, Allan Odden, in his groundbreaking essay "Including School Finance in Systemic Reform Strategies: A Commentary" (1994), recognized the importance of developing new fiscal methodologies to parallel the realignment of school goals, expectations, policies, management, and outcomes. He argued in favor of "targeting education policy, including finance policy, more directly on schools, rather than districts" (p. 5). This strategy probably requires, in Odden's words, "an on-line, personal computer-based, interactive system that would provide each school with accurate, up-to-date fiscal information" (p. 7; see also Clune & White, 1988; Cooper et al., 1994; Hartman, 1988; Levin, 1987; Malen, Ogawa, & Kranz, 1990).

Yet an "interactive system" requires serious rethinking of the available models for school fiscal allocations. Many, if not most, school systems use financial paradigms built from the "top down." Thus transferring district-developed financial data onto school-site financial information systems (FISs) may neither promote nor support school needs because such data are not well designed, timely, or configured in ways easily used by school-site decision makers.

Thus, although a determination of "where the money goes" becomes increasingly important as school districts simultaneously cope with revenue pressures and increased site-based management and budgeting, these efforts are undermined by seriously dated information systems. Furthermore, school districts might survive the shortcomings of an inadequate centralized fiscal information system—by centralizing spending authority and limiting the number of individuals who access these same systems. But moving to site-based budgeting, and thus to having 1,000 or more individual users (e.g., one in each of New York City's 1,000-plus public schools), may be more than the centrally managed system could bear.

In New York City, in the absence of well-conceived, widely distributed management information, the constituent parties (school chancellor's office, administrators, city officials, and union) are forced into arguing the "facts of the facts." Time spent on these disagreements sidetracks critical discussions and delays acceptance of mutually acceptable solutions to problems surfaced through rigorous information analysis. Thus the complexity of accounting for the expenditures of a large "central" office and 32 semiautonomous community school districts (each with its own elected board, superintendent, budget, and business function) has made difficult the tasks of rational planning, decision making, and control.

The Process

The answer to the vexing question of how to create information and management systems that support the budgeting and accounting for school allocations may lie in the tenets promoted by "systemic reform" itself. Good school management accounting, we argue, should parallel and illuminate the system being reconfigured. Hence systemic school reform requires a systemic finance model (SFM), one that conforms to the purposes, structure, organization, function, and outcomes of the very reforms being pursued. However, the goals and processes of systemic school reform are currently not well reflected in or supported by the all-important fiscal systems.

Recognizing these shortcomings, this chapter introduces a new SFM developed for the NYC public schools. The usefulness and limitations of the SFM are then tested and demonstrated through the use of the NYC school system budget for school year 1993 to 1994. In the process, we reconfigure the NYC public schools' $8.05-billion adjusted budget into classroom instruction and the indirect resources that support the learning process.

Background

Although school-site management is taking hold in 45 states, school principals and teachers still complain about how little latitude they really enjoy in the management of their schools and classrooms. In theory, their managerial and budgetary discretion should be increasing. But the reality is that "discretionary" resources at the school level are frequently limited in source and application. Funds are so scarce in schools that site-based administrators have little leverage in determining how their schools are staffed, programmed, and operated. This modicum of discretionary money may likewise make it problematic to engage teachers, parents, and community in making joint decisions over such small-dollar resource allocations. When the costs of teachers' salaries, pensions, and fringe benefits, pupils' transportation, food services, special and categorical education, and much more are all already established, discretionary site-based resources may amount to less than 3% of school budgets.

Though school leaders may have some sense of just how few of the district's dollars they can direct to needs inside individual schools, the methodology supporting the financial budgeting and allocations process remains unclear to all but a few top managers and business officials. Budgeting and reporting the "averages of the averages" to districts' schools—say, for "instruction"—may obscure the real needs and the differences among the costs of programs, types or levels of schools, and individual schools.

Rarely, too, is last year's budget reviewed against last year's detailed actual expenditures. This "oversight" allows districts to avoid the measurement and control mechanisms in budgeting that occur only if an organization's actual spending patterns and resource allocations are measured periodically against the individual line-item components of its real year's expenses. We know little in hindsight when total dollars spent are compared only with prior total budgeted dollars, not real with real. High levels of aggregation thus often obscure as much as they tell.

Furthermore, a comparison by administrators of yearly "budget against budget" tends to show "reduced spending," whereas in fact real expenditures in American education have risen 2.2% annually since the 1970s, with an overall increase of 138% (or 48% in real adjusted dollars) during the 1980s. Thus line-item allocations and spending analysis would indicate where resource dollars were placed, how budgeted dollars were spent, and how well or poorly the community is funding its schools.

Moving beyond the detailed review of categories of expenditure, we can review spending patterns among individual schools and programs. Though states and districts have worked hard, as Hertert (1994) reported on California, to equalize resources *across* school districts, these jurisdictions have often failed to recognize and thus to correct the major intradistrict inequalities in money, personnel, and pupil achievement between schools. As the "right-to-learn" and "opportunity-to-learn" movements begin to influence systemic reforms, the need to reevaluate and represent budgetary and financial information becomes even more crucial.

A Case in Point

NYC schools may be the test case of all test cases. In the spring of 1994, a citywide financial crisis challenged the city to cut costs and to live within its means. The new mayor, Rudolph W. Giuliani, had to formulate detailed answers about NYC's spending patterns and looming deficit, estimated now to be $2.6 billion in 1996. Otherwise, under a state law requiring a balanced municipal budget, NYC would face budgetary control by the Financial Control Board if the city's finances (an annual budget of approximately $32 billion) could not be brought into balance.

In 1994, the NYC public school district represented nearly 25% of the city's annual budget and was one of the many city agencies required to support the budget reductions scheduled citywide. But in April, when Mayor Giuliani asked public schools' chancellor Ramon C. Cortines to reduce the district's $8.05-billion budget by approximately $700 million, in part by eliminating at least 2,500 nonschool, administrative positions, Cortines responded by saying that he could not meet the targets without endangering the quality of the system.

In response, the mayor appointed Herman Badillo—former five-term U.S. congressman and Bronx borough president—to be special counsel for fiscal oversight of education. As special counsel, Badillo moved quickly to establish a baseline of information for understanding the system and formulating ideas on cutting noninstructional costs. After several months, it become obvious that neither Badillo nor the mayor could get relatively basic information from the school district on student and employee counts and program spending. In response, Badillo sought out the K-12 Public Education Team at the accounting firm of Coopers & Lybrand L.L.P. to develop comprehensive information on the board's budgeting and spending in NYC schools. To start, Coopers & Lybrand conducted a series of broad interviews with administrative, regulatory oversight, and union officials in the city to understand the needs of the education community. It became rather obvious that these parties themselves could not agree on the facts of school budgeting and allocations.

Thus a detailed analysis of the board's 1993-1994 budget was formulated in three phases: (a) to establish an information baseline, (b) to reconcile budgeted dollars with actual dollars spent, and (c) to relate staff counts to financial costs. This chapter details the results of the initial 12 weeks of analysis, which focused first on the 313,000 line items that made up the district's general ledger. These line items represented the board's 1993-1994 budget allotments for the school year ending June 30, 1994. In analyzing the results of data extracted on July 21, 1994, the exact nature of the budget process and the cloudy, if not misleading, nature of much of school budgetary reporting became clear. Coopers & Lybrand's work focused on aggregate spending at the system level, examining 100% of the operating dollars used in the system. However, the analysis was also designed to describe precisely the location of budget allocations—specifically, which of the dollars were being budgeted to schools and classrooms themselves and which were held at district and central levels for payment. This type of "locational" analysis was a departure from traditional methods.

Traditionally, studies of school finance have concentrated on issues of equity between districts, with much less attention paid to the historical use of resources within the system. Though interdistrict equality may be the right starting point, researchers are now equally concerned with the analysis of what happens to the resources, what percentage reaches children by school and classroom, and how productive the schools themselves are. This study explains the process of analysis, the results, and the framework and design for understanding more exactly "where the money goes" in NYC schools.

A Finance Framework

Exposing the NYC public school costs to systemic analysis requires a new analytical framework, one that helps to conceptualize expenditures in conformity with budget systems and the related structure of expenditures. Because the purpose of this line of research is to marry process to outcomes, education resources were traced through the budgetary system to students in the classroom. Hence each level of analysis brings us a step closer to the students and their instruction, giving a focus and sense of priorities to the process. This mode of analysis also gives a sense of the "additive costs" of operating large school systems with numerous layers of organization, types of schools, and special programs. Several principles underlie the process:

1. *Focus on schools.* Separate "central" from actual "school" budgetary expenses, requiring a structural analysis of school expenditures.

2. *Include 100% of the operating dollars as budgeted*. Distinguish "hidden" and "visible" expenses in the underlying data, both for accuracy and to relieve the nagging concern of some citizens that school leaders are not releasing all the relevant information (pension and debt service, for example).

3. *Use common definitions of systemic functions*, whether for instruction, operations, administrations, facilities, training, or pupil support.

4. *Include program spending*. Note expense differences budgeted for each type of program and level of schooling, including bilingual, special, and categorical education that affects overall costs and averages.

5. *Differentiate by school*. Use the individual school as the unit of analysis to determine what resources are reaching students.

6. *Account for contractual obligations*—regulations affecting teachers' and administrators' use of time and thus costs.

The methodology supporting the work in NYC, starting with the principles detailed above, provides an analytical framework adaptable to the information needs of every school system—urban, rural, or suburban. As such, the method embodies six frameworks: aggregational, structural, functional, typological, programmatic, and contractual—to be defined in the discussion that follows (see Table 6.1). Importantly, though NYC provided a comprehensive test for the usefulness and power of the resultant model, the framework will be more readily applicable in districts smaller and less complex than the NYC public schools.

In the NYC research, these six levels of analysis (aggregational, structural, functional, typological, programmatic, and contractual) are possible because of the use of relational database methodologies. When all six frames are combined, as they are in a dynamic system, budgets, actual expenditures, and programs can be shown separately and interrelatedly. The strength of systemic financial analysis is that it separates costs by operating levels, systemic functions, school types, contractual provisions, and programs delivered. More important, as one works logically through the model from instruction to debt service, this approach demonstrates vividly how much money is needed to support the delivery of instruction—which is considerable in every system but particularly costly in the major urban school districts. When the funds used outside the classroom are layered in analysis, we can see the forms of "structural erosion" of dollars as they make their way from central administration to the classroom.

Methods

It is not possible here to examine the complete process of obtaining, loading, aggregating, reconciling, mapping, configuring, and analyzing the $8.05-billion cost structure of NYC schools. Because the NYC school board and the city of New York rely on separate budgeting and accounting systems, it was first necessary to reconcile the two systems to capture all the dollars as described in the aggregational frame. We mapped and reconciled two major computer files, the Budget File (67,114 records) and the Spending File (277,642 records), each with its own location, unit of appropriation, expenditure, and allocation codes.

With all the data in hand, we then categorized the funds by function, using various levels of coding to describe the budget, locations, and allocations of dollars. It was necessary to perform multiple runs on the $8.05-billion budget to map these dollars against the multitude of uses for structure, function, program, type of school, and location (see "Allocating Money to NYC Schools," 1994).

Results

Tracing funds from central administration to the classroom involved the application of each of the six frames, providing a useful means of determining where the money went in NYC for public education for the school year 1993 to 1994. The first step taken was to ensure that all the relevant resources were included in the analysis.

Frame 1: Aggregational Analysis

NYC presented the 1993 to 1994 education budget as approximately $7.4 billion. This figure leaves out budgeted dollars managed and accounted for elsewhere in the city. To perform accurate systemic analysis, however, it was necessary to present a comprehensive data set, including full pupil enrollment counts and all sources and sums of money. Instead of using a $7.4-billion budget figure, this analysis established a budget total of $8.05 billion, derived from three sources. First, adding the usual federal, state, and local funds, we mapped $6.25 billion into the systemic school allocations model from both local and state "tax levy" sources. We totaled general aid money and

Table 6.1. Six Frameworks for Systemic Analysis of the NYC Public School
Budget, 1993-94

Frame	Focus	Application
1. Aggregational • Budget allocations and spending • Fringe benefits • Pensions • Debt obligations	• Brings together the obvious and hidden costs of education: purpose is to attribute all possible costs to their sources.	• Need to capture all related costs to give a realistic picture of what education is costing taxpayers and other branches of government.
2. Structural • Hierarchy of costs: central, district, school, and classrooms	• Differentiates central, district, and schools on the basis of the structure of the school system. Costs parallel the structure of the system.	• Without a clear sense of the relationship between structure and costs, it is difficult to trace resources to teachers and students.
3. Functional • Management • Operations • Support • Instruction	• Determines the costs of performing various functions in the system; focus is on direct classroom instruction—requiring the isolation of functional expenditures using a model.	• Separating instruction from other related costs. Budget allocations model.
4. Typological • Elementary school • Middle school • High school • Nonschool	• Costs follow the categorization of schools, from elementary through high school. May also show those costs that are not allocated to schools but should be, or that are allocated there but occur elsewhere.	• Costs may be attributable to the particular needs and structures of a category or type of school.

Table 6.1. Continued

Frame	Focus	Application
5. Programmatic • All programs • Special education • Bilingual education • Categorical education • Regular/base education services	• Tracing costs by program because some programs, as mandated, are more expensive than others. Differentiates among federal, state, and local programs.	• Use of average per-pupil cost may obscure the actual resources reaching students, particularly those students without mandated and special services, which are most costly.
6. Contractual • Actual teaching time • Planning time • Supervisory periods • Compensated time (2 or 3 of 8 40-minute work periods)	• Contracts with teachers and other groups stipulate the number of contact hours ("up time") and other administrative, supervisory, planning, and lunch periods.	• Contact minutes per day may not reflect actual time spent with students in conferences, extracurricular activities, etc.

"reimbursable" funds and grants from state and federal programs dedicated to particular categorical programs (e.g., bilingual education, Chapters 1 and 2, special education). Though general and categorical funds have different avowed purposes in NYC, these dollars were tracked by the same budget and accounting system, using predefined "line codes" to identify source, purpose, function, and location of expenditure (see Table 6.2, Item 1). In NYC, the budget and accounting system distinguishes funding sources from application. This analysis focuses not on the sources of funding, but instead exclusively on the applications of fund dollars.

Second, the city of New York pays selected expenses for the board of education, including pensions and fringe benefits, as a result of these dollars' being held and managed in city accounts. These dollars were not mapped among various functional uses as were the dollars in the first category. Rather, this money was "allocated" by formula on the basis of the salary levels of each category of employee. Personnel costs in some districts outside NYC are budgeted for pensions

Table 6.2. Frame 1: Aggregating Total and Per-Pupil Costs by Source and
Means of Allocation—New York City Public Schools, 1993-94

Cost Centers	Subtotals	Pupils	Per-Pupil Cost
1. Direct Budget Allocations			
Allocated:	$6.250 billion	1,016,728	$6,146
2. Amounts Based on District Formulas			
Prorated:			
• Pensions	$0.423 billion	1,016,728	$416
• Fringes	$1.061 billion	1,016,728	$1,043
Subtotal:	$1.484 billion		$1,459
3. City Budget Funds			
Lump Sum Transfer			
• Debt Service	$.318 billion	1,016,728	$313
Total	$8.050 billion	1,016,728	$7,918

along with salaries, usually because these districts are organized as
fiscally "independent." In NYC, the city pays the pension and fringe
benefits of school district staff as well as other NYC public employees:
that is, the police, fire, sanitation, parks, transportation, welfare, health,
and housing (see Item 2, Table 6.2).

Third, the city borrows money on behalf of the board of education
to fund public school construction and renovations. The debt service
obligations on the funds are again held and managed by the city but
are legitimate annual operating obligations of the school system.
Hence we controlled the principal and interest as one lump sum
supporting the general construction costs of the system. These costs
were not allocated to a particular school or program, although one
could consider tracing debt service charges directly to those schools
and facilities that have benefited from construction or reconstruction.
Though traditional analysis of education finance usually excludes
capital carrying costs, we were asked by the mayor to show the $318
million of debt service as part of the city's annual expense for educating students.

As Table 6.2 (Item 1) shows, the allocated budget ran $6.25 billion,
which, when divided by the system's 1,016,728 pupils in 1993 to 1994,
produced a per-student cost of $6,146. When prorated costs (Item 2) of
both fringe benefits ($1.061 billion) and pensions ($0.423 billion) were
also included, they increased the cost of schools by $1,459 per student

or $1.484 billion. The debt service (Item 3), in turn, ran $0.318 billion or $313 per student. Expenditures, as used in this study, went from $6.250 billion to $8.050 billion or $6,146 to $7,918 per student, a considerable difference. Thus the district's allocations, its pension and fringe benefits, and a lump sum transfer for debt service together helped to determine the total 1993 to 1994 operating costs of the NYC public schools.

Frame 2: Structural Analysis

To some degree, the problem of determining the costs of each of the various operating levels within the NYC public schools' organization mirrors the limitations encountered with traditional top-down budgeting. In each instance, relatively few people establish both the content of and access to information, while at the same time they implicate all system employees in their decisions. By focusing "upward" and "outward," districts may fail to look "downward" to their individual schools and classrooms.

Because the purpose of systemic analysis is to follow money to the student in the classroom for direct instruction, Frame 2 (structural analysis) traces resources through the organizational levels in the systems: central to district to schools. Data are thus configured by function, item, and location codes to parallel the structure of the system. Of the total system expenditures of $8.05 billion or $7,918 per student (100% of total district money per pupil spent overall), Frame 2 shows that

- NYC public schools spent $1.5 billion ($1,476 per student) or 18.9%, with $0.801 billion for the central and district office functions, and $0.689 billion for debt service and pass-throughs, which are dollars for contracted services in private and parochial schools.
- 81.4% ($6.55 billion or $6,442 per student) reached the schools in all. The 18.6% for nonschool expenditures can be further differentiated for central and district operations (9.95% or $788 per student), pass-through costs (4.73% or $375 per student), and debt service (3.95% or $313 per student).

Frame 3: Functional Analysis

Knowing that approximately 81% of the 1993 to 1994 operating budget reached the schools is only part of the answer; information is

Table 6.3. Functional Costs for NYC Public Schools, 1993-94

Functions	Total $	$ per Pupil	% to Total
Instruction—Schools			
Instructional teachers	$3,330,148,541	$3,275	41.37%
Substitutes	55,014,643	54	0.68%
Instructional paraprofessionals	419,792,059	413	5.21%
Pupil-use technology	0	0	0.00%
Instructional materials & supplies	45,107,507	44	0.56%
Instruction Subtotal	3,850,062,750	3,787	47.83%
Instructional Support—Schools			
Principals	89,638,381	88	1.11%
Assistant principals	159,114,919	156	1.98%
Guidance & counseling	137,914,478	136	1.71%
Evaluators, social workers,			
therapists, & psychologists	247,172,799	243	3.07%
Instructional Support Subtotal	633,840,577	623	7.87%
Operations—Schools			
Transportation contracts	525,484,502	517	6.53%
Food service delivery	319,950,718	315	3.97%
Safety & health	181,054,631	178	2.25%
Schools—buildings, utilities,			
custodians, & maintenance	600,246,145	590	7.46%
Secretaries, clerical and			
noninstructional aides, &			
paraprofessionals	439,739,660	433	5.46%
Operations—Schools Subtotal	2,066,475,656	2,032	25.67%
Operations—Central & Districts			
Curriculum improvement,			
in-service, & staff development	26,803,036	26	0.33%
Data processing	8,551,225	8	0.11%
Administrative—other	752,404,156	740	9.36%
Chancellor, superintendents,			
community & central boards	13,226,995	13	0.16%
Operations—Central &			
Districts Subtotal	800,985,412	788	9.95%
Pass-Throughs			
Parochial & private schools			
Contracted services	381,069,698	375	4.73%
Pass-Throughs Subtotal	381,069,698	375	4.73%
Debt Service			
Debt service	317,773,000	313	3.95%
Debt Service Subtotals	317,773,000	313	3.95%
Totals	$8,050,207,093	$7,918	100.00%

Table 6.4. NYC Public School Instructional Costs by Subfunction, 1993-94

Subfunctions	Dollars	Per-Pupil Costs	Percentages
Teachers	$3.330 billion	$3,275	41.37
Substitutes	$0.055 billion	$54	0.68
Instruct. paraprof.	$0.420 billion	$413	5.22
Instruct. materials	$0.045 billion	$44	0.56
TOTAL	$3.850 billion	$3,787	47.83

SOURCE: Coopers & Lybrand L.L.P.
NOTE: The total average per pupil does not sum correctly because of rounding off.

also needed about the functions that these resources support in the schools, including instruction at 47.83% ($3,787 per pupil), instructional support at 7.87% or $632 per student, and school-site operations at 25.67% or $2,032 per student (see Table 6.3 for a breakdown of the key functions).

When direct instructional costs, the $3,787 per pupil (totaling $3.850 billion of $8.050 billion), are analyzed for teachers, substitute teachers, instructional paraprofessionals, and instructional materials, the functional frame shows that 41% of the NYC school budget dollars supported teachers' salaries and benefits. Substitute teachers amounted to just $54 per student or 0.68%, and paraprofessionals in the classroom were $413 per pupil or 5.22%. Materials came to $120 budgeted per student, part of which was stipulated by state regulations controlling the distribution of state aid per pupil (see Table 6.4 for "instructional" costs).

Thus, of the 100% budgeted per student, approximately 81% reached the school, on average, and functionally about 48% reached the classroom—the result of the three frames applied thus far. Whereas the national average in the classroom for instruction ranges between 55% and 63% (see Cooper et al., 1994; Cooper & Sarrel, 1993; National Center for Education Statistics, 1994; Robinson & Protheroe, 1994), NYC public schools spent on average about 48% or $3,787 per student.

Frame 4: Typological (Type of School) Analysis

The systemic analysis model permits the breakdown of budgeted costs by school type (grade level) or configurations from prekinder-

Table 6.5. Costs by Type of School and by Function, NYC Public Schools, 1993-94

School Category	Pre-K	Elementary School	Middle School	High School	Nonschool	Total
# of schools	N/A	693	190	179	N/A	1,062
# of students	12,461	498,478	201,536	304,253	N/A	1,016,728 pupils
1. Total						
$ Costs	$.074 billion	$2,304 billion	$.918 billion	$1.308 billion	$3.446 billion	$8.050 billion
Per pupil	$5,964	$4,621	$4,556	$4,299	N/A	$7,918
% of total	75.32	58.36	57.54	54.29	42.51	100
2. Instruction						
Per pupil	$8	$3,900	$3,734	$3,126	N/A	$3,787
% of total	0.1	49.3	47.2	39.5	N/A	47.8
3. Pupil Support						
Per pupil	0	$329	$425	$566	N/A	$623
% of total	0	4.2	5.4	7.2	N/A	7.9
4. Combined Instr. + Suppt.						
Per pupil	$8	$4,229	$4,159	$3,682	N/A	$4,410
% of total	0.1	53.5	52.6	46.7	N/A	55.7

garten through high school. When information is formatted and analyzed by type of school or school category, it becomes possible to determine which resources reach each school type and which funds remain at the 32 community school district offices. Using school-type location codes allows the systemic model to attribute funds to "schools" or "nonschools" or to designate budget dollars as "nonallocated," which indicates budgeted dollars for specific functions centrally contracted and administered but delivered to the school level (e.g., food services, transportation, security, and school maintenance and cleaning).

Tables 6.5 and 6.6 break out costs by type and by function—allowing us to trace funds one step closer to the student in the classroom. Thus elementary schools as a type received the most resources per student, $4,621 per student or 58.36% of the system total average of $7,918 per student (see last column). Middle schools were next at 57.54% ($4,556 per student), and high schools were the lowest, with 54.29% reaching the school. When the instructional function is crosshatched with the

Table 6.6. Costs by Frame and Function, NYC Public Schools, 1993-94

1. Average costs/all students	System spent $7,918 per student (100%) overall.
	Schools spent $6,442 per student (81.4%).
	Classrooms received $3,787 per student (47.8%).
2. Full-time special education	System spent $23,598 per student (298%) overall.
	Schools spent $16,926 per student (213.8%).
	Classrooms received $10,985 per student (134.9%).
3. Special-education-related services	System spent $10,207 per pupil (128.9%) overall.
	Schools spent $8,891 per student (112.3%).
	Classrooms received $4,843 per student (61.2%).
4. Bilingual education	System spent $7,289 per student (92.1%) overall.
	Schools spent $6,220 per student (78.6%).
	Classrooms received $4,185 per student (52.9%).
5. Categorical (Chapter 1)	System spent $7,401 per pupil (93.5%) overall.
	Schools spent $6,097 per student (77.0%).
	Classrooms received $3,525 per student (44.5%).
6. "Regular" Education Students	System spent $5,149 per student (65.0%) overall.
	Schools received $4,287 per student (54.1%).
	Classrooms received $2,308 per student (29.1%).

school type, the data show, again, elementary schools receiving 49.3% ($3,900 per pupil), middle schools receiving 47.2% or $3,734 per student, and high schools receiving the least at 39.5% or only $3,126 per student out of a total district cost of $7,918 per student.

The model also includes instructional support, which averaged $623 per student or 7.9%. When analysis is applied by type of school, the high schools received the most instructional support at 7.2% ($566 per student), middle schools were next at 5.4% or $425 per student, and elementary schools were the lowest at 4.2% or $329 per student. Combining instruction and instructional support, the resources serving students in their schools, we see high schools again the lowest at 46.7% ($3,682 per student), middle schools next at 52.6% ($4,159 per student), and elementary schools the highest at 53.5% or $4,229 per student.

Frame 5: Programmatic Analysis

A major question arises in tracing resources to students in the classroom: How much are the special and categorical program budgets in comparison to budgets for students seen as having no special mandates, needs, or requirements? Frame analysis separated costs by program and by function, including full-time special education students, special education students receiving "related services" (e.g., resource rooms or pull-out programs) part time but not full time, bilingual education students, students in categorical programs (e.g., Chapter 1), and "regular education" students receiving none of the special services mandated for other students by policy and law.

Full-Time Special Education

In the NYC public schools, full-time special education students consisted of 74,089 pupils of the 1,016,728, or just 7.29%. However, the total per-pupil cost for the full-time special education programs ran $23,598 per student or 298% of the NYC system's per-student average of $7,918. This was $2.03 billion of the $8.05-billion total expenditures in 1993-1994. At the classroom instructional level, $10,685 per student was expended, showing that nearly $13,000 was attributed/budgeted to these full-time special students but not to their classrooms. Hence, of the 298% spent on full-time special education students in NYC schools, 134.9% reached the classroom, meaning that NYC spent 163% of the per-pupil costs operating the special education program—including supervision, evaluation, training, and other nonclassroom special education costs.

Special-Education-Related Services

When the part-time special education students, those receiving "related services" or resource room support within regular schools and even the regular classrooms, are subtracted from the $2.03 billion for all special education, we see that these students (numbering 56,445) received a total of $285.5 million, which is $5,059 per student or 63.89%. This per-pupil cost, however, is then added to the "base" or "foundation" expenditures received by all students in the system except those in full-time special education.

This foundation amount is $5,149 per student, the aggregate dollars budgeted to regular education students. Hence part-time special education pupils received an average of $5,149 per student plus program aid of $5,059 per student, for a total of $10,207 per student, or 128.91% of the school system's average of $7,918 per student. But when the instructional costs are removed, we see special-education-related services at $4,843 per student or 61.2%, compared with the system average of 47.8%. The data are informative when we use the various frames for special education pupils. The instructional costs for special-education-related services were 61.2% or $4,843 per student. Thus the "overhead" and management costs of related services for students were much lower at the system level (16.6%, which is the difference between 128.9% district-wide and 11.3% in the school), whereas they were higher within the schools, the difference between 112.3% and 61.2%, or 51.1%.

Bilingual Education

The bilingual education program engaged 154,526 students, full- and part-time, in NYC schools in 1993-1994. The system budgeted $331 million, or $2,141 per student, which is again added on top of the "base" or foundation amount of $5,149 per student because bilingual pupils receive the "regular" education or base program plus additional program instruction. Thus the total was 92.1% of the system average or $7,289 per pupil overall. When the school-site costs are tabulated, bilingual programs spent $6,200 per student (or 78.6%) in the schools and $4,185 per student (or 51.9%) for instruction. Table 6.6 shows the "average" costs for the system for all students ($7,918 per pupil, 81.4% in the school and 47.8% in the classroom) and establishes a baseline for comparing with full-time and part-time special education and bilingual, categorical, and "regular" education.

Chapter 1 and Other Categorical Programs

Chapter 1 and other federal "categorical programs" for children in poverty and falling behind in their work received about the same resources as the bilingual programs. That is, the system spent $7,401 per pupil or 93.5%, $6,097 per student (77.0%) reached the school, and 44.5% or $3,525 was used in the classroom for direct instruction. Chapter 1 students are below the district average of the 47.8% budgeted to instruction, a statistic greatly inflated by the disproportionately high costs of special education. Whereas Chapter 1 students get 44.5% in the classroom for instruction, the "regular" education student with no mandates or special services gets only 29.1% or $2,308 per student for teaching and learning.

Thus, overall, the programmatic frame provides useful information on the costs of the various entitlement and special programs and their effect on the "regular" and "average" education cost data. This information, more than any other, shows the obscuring effects of using averages and "averages of averages" to set budgets and allocate resources. We see that regular education students—those unprotected by federal laws, mandates, and special provisions—received 29.1% of the per-pupil costs in the classroom.

Hence the frames thus far have moved from $7,918 per student, or 100% overall, to 81.4% for the cost of schools as opposed to the cost of central and district operations. Functionally, about 48% overall was spent in the average classroom for instruction, and about 39% reached the high school classroom, using the school-type frame. Again, below we included the "average" and the "regular" student data as a basis of comparison with bilingual and Chapter 1 and other categorical programs.

Then, applying the programmatic frame, we see the difference between full-time special education costs at 298% of average, special-education-related services at 129%, bilingual programs at 92%, and Chapter 1 and other categorical programs at 93.5%. Regular education, meanwhile, came to 65% of total district per-pupil costs. At the classroom instruction level, however, much of the difference disappeared, except for full-time special education, which is 135%. Meanwhile, the cost of special-education-related services dropped to only 61.2% (average, recall, was 48%). Bilingual education in the classroom was 53%, Chapter 1 was 44.5%, and regular education was 29%.

Thus much of the cost of these special programs (special-education-related services, bilingual, and Chapter 1) is budgeted to occur outside the classroom and runs between 45% and 50% of per-pupil costs. Hence a different configuration and a different economy may exist in the special programs, as the regular education budget is 65% overall, and 29% in the classroom. Some 36%, therefore, was used to run a typical students' program, a difference between 65% ($5,149 per pupil) systemwide and 29% ($2,308 per student) in the classroom.

Frame 6: Contractual Analysis

The final frame, contractual analysis, is the cost of working agreements between the board of education and the teachers' union. The contract stipulates how many instructional periods each teacher will instruct versus "administrative periods," "planning periods," "off periods," and lunch. To many, these provisions are supportive of the instructional process. Teachers, like other professionals, need time to think, formulate plans and programs, and muster energy for teaching classes. But in purely systemic financial terms, the system should ultimately reflect the real cost of these contractual provisions on working time and factor in the operating effects of nonteaching periods.

Thus, for purposes of staffing and budget analysis, teachers are in their schools about eight class periods per day or, in some schools, nine. Of that number, teachers work under contract in NYC schools for about five periods, or five eighths or five ninths. In the elementary schools, the ratio of teaching to nonteaching time is about 6:8. Research done in nine schools found that on average, regardless of whether data were drawn from elementary, middle, or high schools, the system required 1.45 teachers to cover one teacher's schedule because the day has eight periods and teachers teach about five. Thus more money does not always mean more "instructional minutes." If more teaching minutes are not possible (perhaps by requiring teachers to teach longer class periods but the same number of periods daily), then more resources may instead translate into smaller classes, better equipment, improved staff development, and enhanced instructional technology.

Hence one can take the 29.1%, which was the average students' resources budgeted to the classroom, and multiply it by either five eighths or six eighths to find that about 21.9% of resources were in the classroom for instruction when six eighths was used and 18.2% when five eighths was used (see Table 6.6 for a breakdown of a typical school, using the schedule).

Summary

Table 6.7 further summarizes the six frames, including the percent, per-pupil, and total dollar amounts that were developed by using this framework. Thus the systemic aggregational, structural, functional, typological (or school-type), programmatic, and contractual perspectives all allow us to examine the use of the nation's largest school budget, the $8.050-billion budget for the NYC public schools in 1993

Table 6.7. "Systemic Erosion" by Frame and Characteristic,
NYC Public Schools, 1993-94

Frame	Percent	Per Pupil	Dollars
1. Aggregation (systemic)	100	$7,918	$8.050 billion
2. Structural (school-site)	81.4	$6,442	$6.550 billion
3. Functional (instruction)	47.8	$3,787	$3.850 billion
4. Typological			
• High school instruction	39.5	$3,126	$0.951 billion
5. Programmatic			
• Regular education (core) for			
classroom instruction	29.2	$2,308	$2.176 billion
6. Contractual (instructional			
periods:total periods)			
• 6:8	21.9	$1,734	$1.763 billion
• 5:8	18.2	$1,441	$1.465 billion

to 1994. Figure 6.1 shows the "walk-down" through the six frames:
from 100% overall at $7,918 per student when all costs are aggregated
(Frame 1), through 81.4% at the schools with the structural frame
(Frame 2), through 47.8% when the resources at the school were sorted
by the functional frame (Frame 3). Hence instruction was on average
about 48%, although if we apply a Frame 3 typological (school-level)
analysis, we see, for example, that high schools received less (39%)
than elementary schools (49%) and middle schools (47%). See Table
6.7 for the distribution of costs by function and frame.

However, as our further analysis shows, the "average" of 48% is
misleading, given the high expenditures on special education ($2.1
billion), both full-time and related services, and the extra costs of
bilingual and Chapter 1 programs. By adding the related services,
bilingual programs, and categorical costs on top of the "base" expenses of $5,149 per pupil, we can ascertain the extra costs of these
additional services. When regular education is separated, we see
about 65% spent overall and 29.2% in the classroom (Programmatic—
Frame 5). When the contractual (Frame 6) is also factored in, we see
that about 20% on average of the dollars spent in NYC public schools
reaches students directly (see Figure 6.1).

Recommendations

Systemic analysis proves a useful tool for tracing the $8.050-billion budget of the NYC schools to students and their instructional and support services. Five major recommendations emerge from the process of mapping and analyzing these funds.

1. *Be inclusive:* The public wants to know what schooling really costs. Efforts to include resources, as was done in the aggregational frame, may reassure citizens that school officials are not "hiding" anything—that education finances are an "open book" for all to see and understand. Using all available costs (pensions, fringe benefits, principal on debt obligations) and common definitions for mapping the funds gives all parties confidence, trust, and a common vocabulary for discussing key funding decisions.

2. *Think "systemic":* Analysis of the funding of schools should follow the structure of the district and be in parallel with reforms and restructuring. This NYC public schools analysis started with general ledger/line-item details and carried through using the structure of the system, as each district is a little different (see the Cooper [1994] study of Hawaii's school finance, for example). Key common elements of "systemic reform" and "systemic financial allocations" are the decentralization of control, information, and decision making, as well as a strong district-wide and school-site commitment to improving school efficiency and classroom instruction. Unless the financial system and the systemic reform effort work in concert, then school-site decision makers will have real problems interpreting costs, making decisions, and improving schools and pupil learning.

3. *Be flexible and interactive:* Our work in the NYC public schools went well beyond the writing and releasing of a report; indeed, we built a computer-based technology system that permits continued analysis, including the ability to query the system for additional information. Although it took 12 weeks to program the $8-billion budget into the SFM, the model now permits us to remap and answer questions received in 2 or 3 hours. Hence flexibility is now possible for the first time in a system that for years had difficulty determining costs, locations, numbers of students, and even the exact definition of what constituted a "school." The SFM is now ready to be used as an interactive system, in which data and questions can be transferred

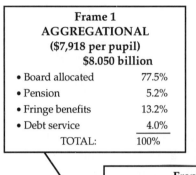

Frame 1
AGGREGATIONAL
($7,918 per pupil)
$8.050 billion

• Board allocated	77.5%
• Pension	5.2%
• Fringe benefits	13.2%
• Debt service	4.0%
TOTAL:	100%

Frame 2
STRUCTURAL
Central/District/City Costs:
$1.5 billion ($1,476 per pupil)

• Central operations	10.0%
• Pass-throughs	4.7%
• Debt service	4.0%
TOTAL:	18.6%
School Site:	**81.4%**

Frame 3
Functional
•School Site (81.4%)
Operations/Support
$2.701 billion ($2,654 per pupil)

•Operations	25.7%
•School support	7.9%
TOTAL	**33.6%**

All Classrooms

•Instruction

•Teachers	41.60%
•Substitutes	0.69%
•Paraprofessionals	5.22%
•Materials	0.56%
TOTAL:	**47.8%**

Figure 6.1. Frame Analysis: Tracking Money to Students, NYC Public Schools, 1993-1994

```
┌─────────────────────────────────────────────┐
│                   Frame 4                     │
│          TYPOLOGICAL (School Type)            │
│  Instruction: $3.850 billion ($3,787 per pupil) │
│            Instruction by type:               │
│  •All schools:          47.8%                 │
│  •Elementary school     49.3%                 │
│  •Middle school         47.2%                 │
│       •High school      39.5%                 │
└─────────────────────────────────────────────┘
```

```
┌──────────────────────────────────────────────────────────────┐
│                          Frame 5                               │
│                       PROGRAMMATIC                             │
│          Classroom: $3.850 billion ($3,787 per pupil)          │
│          (All Students: Total: 100% Instruction: 47.8%)        │
│  • Full-Time Special Education:                                │
│    Total: $23,589 per pupil (298%)    Instruction: $10,985 per pupil (134.9%) │
│  • Special-Education-Related Services                          │
│    Total: $10,207 per pupil (128.9%)  Instruction: $4,843 per pupil (61.2%) │
│  • Bilingual Education:                                        │
│    Total: $7,298 per pupil (92.1%)    Instruction: $4,185 per pupil (52.9%) │
│  • Categorical: e.g., Chapter 1                               │
│    Total: $7,401 per pupil (93.5%)    Instruction: $3,525 per pupil (44.5%) │
│  Regular Education (basic services)                            │
│                      Total: 65%                                │
│       INSTRUCTION:        $2,308 per pupil        29.2%        │
└──────────────────────────────────────────────────────────────┘
```

```
┌──────────────────────────────────────────────────────────────┐
│                          Frame 6                               │
│                       CONTRACTUAL                             │
│  Work Day: 8 periods × 40 minutes = 320 minutes               │
│  Elementary Schools:                                           │
│  •6 out of 8 periods (240 minutes or 75% "direct instructing") │
│                  75.0% × 29.2% = 21.9%                        │
│  High Schools:                                                 │
│  •5 out of 8 periods (200 minutes or 62.5% "direct instructing") │
│                  62.5% × 29.2% = 18.2%                        │
└──────────────────────────────────────────────────────────────┘
```

Figure 6.1. continued

"upward" to the system for analysis and "downward" to schools for improved accountability and decision making.

4. *Pursue results:* Analysis of progress, and even the effects of the expenditure of money, can now be programmed into the system. Perhaps for the first time, leaders can actually "ask" the system how much a school activity or program costs, whether more resources are reaching students, and how much achievement, attendance, and learning are improving as a result. As Greenhalgh (1984) recognized over a decade ago, "In a centrally administered school district, the finalization of a budget is buried deep within a central office accounting complex. In a decentralized school district, the budget [and expenditure record] of each instructional center is developed by building leaders, staff members, parents, students, and the community" (p. 5). But only through a form of systemic finance allocations can resources, activities, and outcomes be interrelated in a restructured system—a real challenge for those reengineering America's schools.

References

Allocating money to NYC schools. (1994, October 8). *New York Times*, p. A1.

Clune, W. H., & White, P. (1988). *School-based management: Institutional variation, implementation and issues for further research.* New Brunswick, NJ: Rutgers University Center for Policy Research in Education.

Cooper, B. S. (1994). *The feasibility of applying the micro-financial analysis model to expenditures for public education in Hawaii: What reaches the classroom. A report to the governor and the legislature of the state of Hawaii.* Honolulu: State of Hawaii, Auditor.

Cooper, B. S., & Sarrel, R. (1993). Managing for school efficiency and effectiveness. *National Forum of Educational Administration and Supervision, 8*(3), 3-38.

Cooper, B. S., Sarrel, R., Darvas, P., Alfano, F., Meier, E., Samuels, J., & Heinbach, S. (1994). Making money matter in education: A micro-financial model for determining school-level allocations, efficiency, and productivity. *Journal of Education Finance, 20,* 66-87.

Greenhalgh, J. (1984). *School-site budgeting.* Lanham, MA: University Press of America.

Hartman, W. T. (1988). District spending: What do the dollars buy? *Journal of Education Finance, 13,* 436-459.

Hertert, L. (1994, April). *Resource allocation patterns at the school level: Equity considerations in California.* Paper presented at the annual meeting of the American Education Research Association, New Orleans.

Levin, H. M. (1987, June). *Finance and governance implications of school-based governance.* Paper presented at the National Advisory Committee of the Work in America Institute, New York.

Malen, B. (1994). Enacting site-based management: A political utilities analysis. *Education Evaluation and Policy Analysis, 16,* 249-267.

Malen, B., Ogawa, R. T., & Kranz, J. (1990). What do we know about school based management? A case study of the literature—a call for research. In W. Clune & J. F. Witte (Eds.), *Choice and control in American education: Vol. 2. The practice of choice, decentralization, and school restructuring* (pp. 289-342). Bristol, PA: Falmer.

National Center for Education Statistics. (1994). *Condition of U.S. education.* Washington, DC: U.S. Department of Education.

Odden, A. R. (1994, April-May). Including school finance in systemic reform strategies: A commentary. *CPRE Finance Briefs,* pp. 1-10.

Robinson, G. E., & Protheroe, N. (1994, September). Local school budget profile study. *School Business Affairs,* pp. 31-40.

Wohlstetter, P., & Odden, A. (1992). Rethinking school-based management and research. *Educational Administration Quarterly, 28,* 529-549.

Wohlstetter, P., Smyer, R., & Mohrman, S. A. (1994). New boundaries for school-based management: The high involvement model. *Education Evaluation and Policy Analysis, 16,* 268-286.

SEVEN

Allocating Resources to Influence Teacher Retention

NEIL D. THEOBALD

R. MARK GRITZ

The goal of the study described in this chapter is to analyze the influence of school district spending priorities on the career decisions of classroom teachers. Specifically, it examines the role that school district expenditures play in setting the occupational context that Lortie (1975) described as crucial in facilitating the retention of teachers in their positions. Although several recent studies question the conventional wisdom that wealthy districts with high expenditures provide a school atmosphere conducive to student learning (Hanushek, 1989, 1994), very little is known about the influence of specific spending patterns on the career decisions of elementary and secondary classroom teachers.

The findings presented in this chapter are drawn from a more comprehensive examination of the early career experiences of beginning elementary and secondary classroom teachers (Theobald & Gritz, 1995). The broader study examines five key dimensions of the career decisions of teachers. First, it investigates the factors that determine how long teachers stay in their first teaching assignment. Second, it analyzes the career choices of teachers who decide to leave their

AUTHORS' NOTE: We thank the Spencer Foundation for their generous support of this research.

first teaching assignment by examining the factors that influence whether teachers transfer to another public school teaching position, transfer to a nonteaching position in the public school system, or leave the public education system. Third, for those teachers who begin another period of teaching in the public school system, it investigates the determinants of the length of time they teach in this new classroom teaching assignment. Fourth, for those individuals leaving the state public school system, it analyzes the factors that affect the likelihood of returning to a classroom teaching position in the public school system after spending at least one year not teaching in the system. Finally, the study integrates all of these components to develop a comprehensive picture describing the total number of years beginning teachers are employed in the state's public education system as classroom teachers in the 10 years following their first teaching assignment.

This chapter focuses on how differences in public school districts' spending priorities influence three of these career decisions:

1. How long beginning teachers continuously teach in their first school district
2. The paths by which beginning teachers leave their initial district
3. How long beginning teachers remain in the profession over the first 10 years after they start teaching

The purpose of this analysis is to provide decision makers with the tools needed to proactively influence the retention behavior of new teachers by targeting expenditures to objects such as salary, classified support staff, and teaching materials.

The research reported here is based on a new longitudinal data set providing information on the career histories of 7,957 Washington teachers. The empirical work uses a generalized variant of a transition probability model and conducts simulations to explore the influence of important policy variables. The model, empirical framework, estimation results, and simulation methods are presented in Theobald and Gritz (1995) and are available from the authors.

Importance of the Study

Educating children is a labor-intensive enterprise. Educational policy makers have come to recognize that efforts to improve elementary and secondary education will critically depend upon their success in attracting and retaining qualified individuals in teaching. Simply put, we cannot have better schools until we have better teachers (Goodlad, 1990).

Despite the crucial role classroom teachers play in school improvement, educational reform efforts in the United States, for the most part, overlook the importance of teacher retention. This oversight is unfortunate because the high percentage of new teachers leaving our classrooms after only a few years (Murnane, Singer, Willett, Kemple, & Olsen, 1991) thwarts efforts to improve the nation's schools by (a) minimizing the influence of teacher education reform, (b) siphoning needed teacher leadership, and (c) staffing classrooms with a large percentage of novice teachers.

Darling-Hammond (1992) argued that strengthened teacher education programs are the most promising avenue to better student learning. The potential effectiveness of current efforts in this direction (Goodlad, 1990; Holmes Group, 1986) is drastically reduced if these better-prepared graduates leave the classroom after only a short time. "Talk of securing and maintaining a stable corps of understanding teachers is empty rhetoric unless serious efforts are made to study and remedy the conditions likely to drive out those already recruited" (Goodlad, 1983, p. 173).

Second, research shows that effective schools are marked by staff stability, continuity, and cohesion (Bryk, Lee, & Smith, 1990; Coleman & Hoffer, 1987). In addition, the ability of less effective schools to continue a successful reform effort crucially depends on the presence of large numbers of teachers who are knowledgeable about and committed to the change (Fullan, 1991). These veteran teachers play a vital role in providing continuing assistance to new teachers and administrators. Several studies point to high turnover in a school's teaching staff as one of the most powerful factors in stifling school improvement efforts (Berman & McLaughlin, 1977; Huberman & Miles, 1984).

Finally, the art of teaching children is a developmental process involving a complex set of abilities, many of which can be sharpened only on the job. Though better preservice teacher education can begin the process of improving teacher quality, research clearly shows that inexperienced teachers continue to refine their talents and become more effective teachers during the first few years in the classroom

(Hedges, Laine, & Greenwald, 1994; Murnane, 1975; Murnane & Phillips, 1981). The continual need for school districts to hire new, inexperienced teachers to replace teachers who leave after a very short teaching spell "can only hinder these districts' efforts to improve the education they provide" (Murnane et al., 1991, p. 65).

Future school improvement efforts, to be successful, must place a renewed emphasis on retaining classroom teachers and recognize that many factors influence the ability of our nation's schools to maintain a highly skilled and motivated teaching force. Historically, educational researchers viewed teacher attrition as reflecting either (a) "life cycle" priorities of young female teachers (Grissmer & Kirby, 1987) or (b) failure by schools to retain their talented teachers (Schlechty & Vance, 1981). Murnane (1987), however, suggested that teacher attrition can be better understood by analyzing the rational decisions teachers make in response to the incentives they face in a labor market.

Teacher salary levels are one set of incentives that have been the focus of recent work examining teacher attrition (Murnane & Olsen, 1989, 1990; Murnane, Singer, & Willett, 1989; Rickman & Parker, 1990). These studies provide compelling evidence that the level of teacher salaries has a marked impact on teacher career choices. Salaries, though, are not the only incentives that influence labor market decisions. With teacher salaries accounting for only 40% of elementary and secondary school spending in the United States (U.S. Department of Commerce, 1993), it seems plausible that the working conditions created by the other 60% of K-12 spending also influence these decisions. The study from which this chapter is drawn extends previous research on teacher attrition by exploring the influence of six school district spending decisions on the career choices of beginning classroom teachers:

1. The annual salary paid to a teacher
2. Expenditures for district-wide administration and supervision of instruction activities
3. Expenditures for classified staff involved in teaching activities
4. Expenditures for teaching materials
5. Expenditures for support activities, such as learning resources; principal's office; guidance and counseling; psychological, speech, and hearing services; health services; and extracurricular activities

6. Total expenditures for regular education, special education, and vocational education

Of course, expenditures are not the only factors that affect the career decisions of beginning teachers. A vast literature describes the influence of personal characteristics (e.g., age, race, gender) and school characteristics (e.g., student demographics) on the career decisions of classroom teachers. Many of these factors are significant determinants of the career paths chosen by beginning classroom teachers. To ensure that our empirical findings do not confound the influence of school district spending priorities with the influence of personal and school district characteristics, our model controls for the influence of these factors. Specifically, in addition to expenditures, the empirical model includes

1. Seven personal characteristics (i.e., age, degree attainment, recency of degree, grade-level assignment, program assignment, and two dummy variables indicating if the teacher is returning to the profession or transferring from another school district)
2. Ten school district characteristics (i.e., enrollment, percentage of students qualifying for a free or reduced lunch, percentage of minority students, average fourth-grade reading/language arts test score on state-mandated exam, expenditures for regular education as a percentage of total expenditures, pupil-teacher ratio, number of teachers, region of the state, proximity to urban area, and a dummy variable indicating if the school district offers K-8 instruction only)
3. One county characteristic (i.e., the unemployment rate)

Apart from several pathbreaking studies that have examined the influence of salaries on teacher retention, very little is known about the extent to which the career decisions of beginning teachers are affected by the resource allocation decisions of school districts. The next two sections briefly describe the data and outline the empirical model and simulation methods used in this study. The last two sections highlight this study's findings concerning the influence of teacher salaries, spending for central office personnel, spending for nonteachers involved in classroom instruction, and expenditures for teaching materials on the career paths of beginning teachers. The discussion does not examine expenditures for support services or total spending levels because our empirical findings indicate that these

Table 7.1. Characteristics of Teachers Beginning Their Careers in
Washington State From 1981 to 1990

Characteristics	Female	Male
Number	5,575	2,382
Average age	29.45	29.49
Percentage with graduate degrees	8.22	6.20
Percentage who are new graduates	41.63	40.93
Average number of years since last degree among non-new graduates	4.76	4.56
Percentage employed in elementary schools	56.16	31.15
Percentage employed across K-12 setting	13.70	7.05
Percentage employed in special education	20.39	8.14
Percentage employed in vocational education	3.89	7.01

aspects of school district spending do not have substantial effects on
the career decisions of new teachers.

Data

The data set used for this study consists of information on 7,957
white teachers who began their teaching careers in Washington State
public schools during the period 1981 to 1990.[1] Table 7.1 presents some
summary statistics of teacher characteristics at the beginning of their
teaching careers. The career of each teacher in the sample is followed
from the year of entry through the 1991-1992 school year. Over this
period, these teachers experience 9,756 spells of consecutive years
teaching in a school district. Table 7.2 presents some summary statistics of these teaching spells.

Empirical Model
and Simulation Methods

The empirical model used to investigate the early career paths of
classroom teachers is a generalized variant of a transition probability
model (TPM), substantially extended beyond that found in applications

Table 7.2. Characteristics of Teaching Spells by Beginning Teachers in Washington State From 1981 to 1992

Characteristics	Female	Male
Number of teaching spells	6,829	2,927
Number of completed teaching spells	3,148	1,310
Average length of completed teaching spells (in years)	2.38	2.35
Percentage who transfer to a teaching position in another Washington school district	30.30	35.27
Percentage who transfer to a nonteaching position in a Washington school district	3.65	4.73
Percentage who leave public education in Washington	66.04	60.00
Number of right-censored (incomplete) teaching spells	3,681	1,617
Average length of right-censored teaching spells (in years)	4.53	4.93

of Markov chains. This empirical framework characterizes five aspects of classroom teachers' career choices that are of central importance in understanding the effect of school district spending decisions on teacher career paths: (a) the number of consecutive years people teach in a public school district; (b) the alternative career paths followed by teachers upon leaving a teaching assignment in a public school district; (c) the number of years individuals remain out of teaching after leaving the public school system; (d) the amount of time spent teaching over an extended period of time, including the number of teaching spells and the cumulative number of years teaching over this horizon; and (e) the extent to which these experiences vary among teachers with various individual characteristics and districts with different teaching environments, including different spending priorities.

The essential elements of the TPM used in this analysis are duration distributions and exit probabilities. The duration distributions describe the number of consecutive years individuals choose to follow a particular career path (i.e., the length of spells). In particular, two duration distributions form the foundation of our empirical model. The first describes the number of uninterrupted years individuals teach in a particular school district; the second describes the number of consecutive years individuals spend outside the public school system between distinct episodes of teaching. The exit probabilities summarize the likely career choices of teachers upon leaving a teaching assignment in a district. Throughout the analysis, we account for the possible effects of differences in individual characteristics, local economic conditions, school district characteristics, and, of course, the spending priorities of school districts on the duration distributions and exit probabilities. Our statistical model provides a flexible alternative to a competing-risks model, with many features incorporated in our specifications that are not found in empirical applications elsewhere in the literature.

The estimates generated by the TPM yield direct evidence only on the very short-term links between continuing to teach in a district and its rewards as compared with the benefits of pursuing other options. To examine issues such as how long an individual will stay in a district, we develop a simulation exercise that captures the experiences of teachers who have just started their first teaching assignment and follows the career choices of these hypothetical teachers for 10 years. The model's estimates are used to calculate predicted transition probabilities (i.e., duration distributions and exit probabilities) that simulate teaching spells, career choices at the end of teaching spells, and periods outside of teaching.

Repeating the above procedure numerous times and recording sequences of annual teaching experiences for a large number of hypothetical teachers provides the basis for characterizing the distribution of teaching activities experienced by new teachers with a given set of personal traits (e.g., age, grade level) and facing particular attributes of alternative career paths (e.g., salary levels). We evaluate these traits and attributes at the average value for male teachers when simulating male teaching experiences and the average value for women when simulating the experiences of female teachers. In most cases, the values of these traits and attributes are set at the beginning of the simulation exercise and held constant over the sequence of years. The variables capturing teaching histories (e.g., the length of the simulated spell that is in progress, salaries at various experience levels) are updated throughout the 10-year simulation to reflect the experiences of the hypothetical teachers.

We examine the relationship between personal traits and teaching experiences by changing three personal characteristics: age, grade level, and teaching program. Previous literature (Murnane & Olsen, 1989, 1990; Murnane, Singer, & Willett, 1988) differentiated between the experiences of teachers who begin teaching before the age of 31 and those who start teaching when they are 31 or older. We also follow this approach. To explore the differences in the experiences of teachers working in specific teaching assignments, we simulate experiences of teachers in elementary and secondary schools and teachers in regular education and special education programs.

Each set of expenditure simulations adjusts the spending for a specific explanatory variable by $3,000 per teacher. For example, when considering changes in salaries, we either add 3,000 to or subtract $3,000 from each cell in a teacher's salary schedule to simulate increases or decreases in salaries. When we evaluate the influence of central office spending changes, we increase or decrease central office spending levels by $3,000 per teacher.

Findings

Although total school district expenditure levels have little or no influence on the career decisions of beginning classroom teachers, the allocation of these funds does affect teacher career paths. This section describes the influence of four categories of district expenditures on the early career decisions of beginning classroom teachers: (a) expenditures for teacher salaries, (b) expenditures for central office supervisory staff, (c) expenditures for nonteachers involved in classroom instruction, and (d) expenditures for teaching materials. Each of the key findings is presented and followed by a discussion of the supporting evidence. Results are presented separately for female and male beginning teachers throughout the discussion.

Teacher Salaries

Overall, the influence of salary levels on teacher career decisions differs by gender. Females respond primarily to local salaries, whereas male retention rates are tied to alternative salaries available in other school districts.

Female beginning teachers remain in their first teaching positions longer when salaries in the district increase relative to teaching salaries in other school districts and earnings in the surrounding community.

An examination of Table 7.3 indicates that the career decisions of female beginning teachers are significantly affected by the relative

Table 7.3. Simulation Results Describing the Influence of Salary Levels on Female Teacher Career Decisions

Part A	*Percentage of Female Teachers Completing More Than n Years in Their First Teaching Position*						
Case	*1*	*2*	*3*	*4*	*5*	*7*	*10*
Base	79.3	66.0	54.8	43.8	35.9	25.9	18.1
All teachers' salaries increased	80.4	67.5	56.1	45.2	37.5	27.7	19.7
Teachers' salaries in own school district increased	82.2	70.0	58.9	46.9	38.3	27.9	19.7
Teachers' salaries in other school districts decreased	81.9	69.7	57.7	45.6	37.1	26.1	18.5
Average annual earnings in community decreased	80.3	67.8	57.1	47.5	40.0	29.6	20.9

Part B	*Percentage of Female Teachers Taking Each Alternative Career Path*		
Case	*% Staying*	*% Transferring*	*% Leaving*
Base	18.1	22.6	59.1
All teachers' salaries increased	19.7	26.2	53.8
Teachers' salaries in own school district increased	19.7	24.8	55.3
Teachers' salaries in other school districts decreased	18.5	21.7	59.3
Average annual earnings in community decreased	20.9	19.6	56.8

Part C	*Percentage of Female Teachers Completing More Than n Years Teaching in State*						
Case	*1*	*2*	*3*	*4*	*5*	*7*	*10*
Base	90.6	83.2	76.9	71.4	66.5	57.1	30.7
All teachers' salaries increased	91.5	84.5	78.1	72.8	68.1	59.1	34.3
Teachers' salaries in own school district increased	92.2	85.3	79.2	73.4	68.6	58.9	33.2
Teachers' salaries in other school districts decreased	92.2	85.7	79.6	74.0	68.6	58.0	29.7
Average annual earnings in community decreased	90.8	83.3	77.1	71.8	67.0	58.0	31.8

differences in teaching salaries between their local district and other districts in the state. For example, the simulation results presented in Part A of Table 7.3, suggest that raising local district teacher salaries by $3,000 increases the proportion of female teachers that remain in their initial teaching positions for each of their first 10 years in teaching. In particular, increased relative salaries have the largest influence in the earlier years of teaching: The proportion of female teachers that remain in their first teaching assignment is 3 to 4 percentage points higher during each of the first 3 years that they are employed in a higher-paying district. After female beginning teachers have remained in their first assignments for more than 3 years, local district salary levels relative to earnings in the surrounding community have a larger influence on their decisions to remain in a district. Increasing all teacher salaries in the state by $3,000 only narrowly increases the percentage of female teachers remaining in their first teaching position.

Male beginning teachers remain in their initial teaching positions longer when the general salary level of all teachers in the state increases.

Changes in salaries have a different influence on the initial career decisions of male beginning teachers when compared to females who are just starting their teaching careers. An examination of Part A in Table 7.4 indicates that raising all teacher salaries in the state by $3,000 significantly increases the percentage of male teachers that remain in their initial teaching positions throughout the first 10 years of their careers, whereas this change has only a minor impact on the career decisions of female beginning teachers. Moreover, decreasing teaching salaries in other districts results in more male teachers leaving their initial teaching assignment. This career behavior is in marked contrast to the career decisions of female beginning teachers facing the same relative salary differences.

Raising teacher salaries in all districts substantially reduces the number of beginning teachers who choose to leave their first teaching position in a public school system and increases the likelihood that beginning teachers will transfer to another school district within the first 10 years.

An examination of Part B in Tables 7.3 and 7.4 indicates that raising all teacher salaries in the state by $3,000 significantly decreases the percentage of teachers choosing to leave the public school system directly from their initial teaching position. For instance, according to Part B in Table 7.3, a $3,000 raise for all teachers decreases the percentage of females leaving their first teaching assignment and not teaching in the public school system in the following year from 59% to 54%, and Part B in Table 7.4 shows the percentage of males choosing this particular career path decreasing from 31% to 23%.

Male beginning teachers are more likely to leave the public school system when teacher salaries are lower in other school districts.

Table 7.4. Simulation Results Describing the Influence of Salary Levels on Male Teacher Career Decisions

	Part A						
	Percentage of Male Teachers Completing More Than n Years in Their First Teaching Position						
Case	1	2	3	4	5	7	10
Base	75.1	60.4	54.0	50.4	47.5	42.1	34.4
All teachers' salaries increased	79.5	66.5	60.6	57.1	53.6	48.0	38.9
Teachers' salaries in own school district increased	77.9	64.2	57.8	53.9	50.5	44.6	36.2
Teachers' salaries in other school districts decreased	73.8	58.8	52.1	48.1	44.8	39.4	31.3
Average annual earnings in community decreased	78.1	64.1	58.2	54.8	51.8	46.2	37.7

	Part B		
	Percentage of Male Teachers Taking Each Alternative Career Path		
Case	% Staying	% Transferring	% Leaving
Base	34.4	32.4	30.6
All teachers' salaries increased	38.9	32.6	22.5
Teachers' salaries in own school district increased	36.2	29.1	30.9
Teachers' salaries in other school districts decreased	31.3	27.8	42.7
Average annual earnings in community decreased	37.7	26.9	30.3

	Part C						
	Percentage of Male Teachers Completing More Than n Years Teaching in State						
Case	1	2	3	4	5	7	10
Base	94.4	89.7	85.8	82.3	78.5	72.3	58.2
All teachers' salaries increased	96.6	93.5	90.3	86.9	83.3	76.9	63.3
Teachers' salaries in own school district increased	95.2	90.6	86.8	83.3	79.5	73.1	57.6
Teachers' salaries in other school districts decreased	92.7	86.6	81.8	77.4	73.1	66.4	48.9
Average annual earnings in community decreased	94.7	89.8	85.7	82.2	78.4	72.3	58.4

Lowering alternative teacher salaries in the state by $3,000 significantly increases the percentage of male teachers choosing to leave the public school system. The percentage of male teachers choosing to leave the profession directly from their first teaching position increases from 31% to 43% when salaries in other school districts are decreased by $3,000 (Table 7.4, Part B).

Males teach for a much longer time when all teacher salaries in the state are increased.

An examination of Part C in Table 7.4 indicates that raising all teacher salaries in the state by $3,000 significantly increases the percentage of male teachers experiencing longer careers in teaching. The percentage of male teachers completing more than 3 years in the state teaching system increases from 86% to 90% when all salaries are increased; the percentage of males completing more than 7 years increases from 72% to 77%; and the percentage completing more than 10 years increases from 58% to 63%.

Expenditures for Central
Office Supervisory Staff

Increased district-wide administration and supervision levels decrease initial retention rates but increase the length of time teachers remain in the profession.

When increases in school district spending are targeted to district-wide administration and supervision, beginning male teachers and female teachers who have remained in their first assignment for more than 2 years are more likely to leave a position within a short period of time.

Employment in a school district with central office supervisory salaries that are $3,000 per teacher above the state average decreases the proportion of male teachers remaining in their first teaching position after 1 year from 75% to 62% (Table 7.5, Part A). Moreover, during their first 3 years, male teachers in these high central administrative cost districts are 13 to 17 percentage points less likely to continue teaching in the district. The negative influence of high central office spending on male retention becomes less important with experience.

The influence of this expenditure category on female teachers is quite different (Table 7.6, Part A). Employment in a school district with central office supervisory salaries that are $3,000 per teacher above the state average has no differential effect on the percentage of female teachers ending their first spell after 1 to 2 years. However, beginning with their third year, female teachers in high central office supervisory salary school districts are 8 to 12 percentage points less likely to remain in their first position than are teachers who have completed 3 years in school districts with average central office supervisory salary spending.

Table 7.5. Simulation Results Describing the Influence of Supervisory Salary Spending on Male Teacher Career Decisions

Part A	Percentage of Male Teachers Completing More Than n Years in Their First Teaching Position						
Case	1	2	3	4	5	7	10
Base	75.1	60.4	54.0	50.4	47.5	42.1	34.4
Supervisory salary expenditures per teacher increased	61.9	43.4	37.5	35.4	33.4	29.8	24.1

Part B	Percentage of Male Teachers Taking Each Alternative Career Path		
Case	% Staying	% Transferring	% Leaving
Base	34.4	32.4	30.6
Supervisory salary expenditures per teacher increased	24.1	53.5	19.6

Part C	Percentage of Male Teachers Completing More Than n Years Teaching in State						
Case	1	2	3	4	5	7	10
Base	94.4	89.7	85.8	82.3	78.5	72.3	58.2
Supervisory salary expenditures per teacher increased	96.9	94.2	90.1	86.5	82.1	74.6	60.7

Increasing expenditures for supervisory salaries substantially increases the likelihood that beginning teachers will transfer to another school district from their first teaching position.

The simulation results presented in Part B of Tables 7.5 and 7.6 suggest that a district's level of expenditures for supervisory personnel significantly affects the early career choices of teachers. For example, the findings in Table 7.6, Part B, indicate that a $3,000-per-teacher increase in spending for supervisory salaries increases the percentage of female teachers transferring to another school district from 23% to 36%. Moreover, the percentage of female teachers remaining in their first teaching position falls from 18% to 10%. Similarly, among male teachers (Table 7.5, Part B), the percentage that transfer increases from 32% to 54% in high supervisory spending districts, whereas the percentage of male teachers staying in their first position for 10 years falls from 34% to 24%.

Table 7.6. Simulation Results Describing the Influence of Supervisory Salary Spending on Female Teacher Career Decisions

Part A							
	Percentage of Female Teachers Completing More Than n Years in Their First Teaching Position						
Case	*1*	*2*	*3*	*4*	*5*	*7*	*10*
Base	79.3	66.0	54.8	43.8	35.9	25.9	18.1
Supervisory salary expenditures per teacher increased	79.3	66.0	50.3	33.2	23.6	14.2	10.2

Part B		
	Percentage of Female Teachers Taking Each Alternative Career Path		
Case	*% Staying*	*% Transferring*	*% Leaving*
Base	18.1	22.6	59.1
Supervisory salary expenditures per teacher increased	10.2	36.1	53.7

Part C							
	Percentage of Female Teachers Completing More Than n Years Teaching in State						
Case	*1*	*2*	*3*	*4*	*5*	*7*	*10*
Base	90.6	83.2	76.9	71.4	66.5	57.1	30.7
Supervisory salary expenditures per teacher increased	92.7	86.9	80.7	74.2	68.5	57.6	28.3

Targeting spending increases to central office supervisory salaries improves the likelihood that teachers will remain in the profession more than 3 years.

When spending in a teacher's first school district is targeted to central office supervision, the percentage of female teachers remaining in the state school system more than 3 years increases from 77% to 81% (Table 7.6, Part C). For males, the percentage who teach in the public school system more than 3 years increases from 86% to 90% (Table 7.5, Part C). However, after 3 years, teachers beginning their careers in districts with high supervisory spending are less likely to remain in teaching.

Expenditures for Classified Teaching Staff

High spending for nonteachers involved in classroom instruction lowers teacher retention rates.

Table 7.7. Simulation Results Describing the Influence of Expenditures for Classified Staff Involved in Teaching on Male Teacher Career Decisions

Part A							
	Percentage of Male Teachers Completing More Than n Years in Their First Teaching Position						
Case	1	2	3	4	5	7	10
Base	75.1	60.4	54.0	50.4	47.5	42.1	34.4
Salaries for classified staff involved in teaching activities as a % of total expenditures increased	68.7	51.6	46.7	44.8	43.3	40.0	32.5

Part B			
	Percentage of Male Teachers Taking Each Alternative Career Path		
Case	% Staying	% Transferring	% Leaving
Base	34.4	32.4	30.6
Salaries for classified staff involved in teaching activities as a % of total expenditures increased	32.5	22.4	43.8

Part C							
	Percentage of Male Teachers Completing More Than n Years Teaching in State						
Case	1	2	3	4	5	7	10
Base	94.4	89.7	85.8	82.3	78.5	72.3	58.2
Salaries for classified staff involved in teaching activities as a % of total expenditures increased	89.7	81.9	77.5	74.2	71.5	66.1	48.9

Beginning teachers continue teaching in a school district for a shorter period of time when spending increases are targeted to classified staff who are involved in teaching activities.

When increases in school district spending are targeted to nonteachers involved in classroom instruction, only 47% of male and female teachers continue working in the school district for more than 3 years, a decrease of 8 percentage points for each gender (Tables 7.7 and 7.8, Part A).

Beginning teachers are more likely to leave their initial teaching position and stop teaching in the public school system when expenditures for classified staff involved in teaching activities are increased.

Spending $3,000 per teacher more on nonteachers involved in classroom instruction increases the percentage of beginning teachers who leave their first teaching position and remain out of the public school

Table 7.8. Simulation Results Describing the Influence of Expenditures for Classified Staff Involved in Teaching on Female Teacher Career Decisions

Part A							
	Percentage of Female Teachers Completing More Than n Years in Their First Teaching Position						
Case	*1*	*2*	*3*	*4*	*5*	*7*	*10*
Base	79.3	66.0	54.8	43.8	35.9	25.9	18.1
Salaries for classified staff involved in teaching activities as a % of total expenditures increased	74.6	59.2	47.4	37.3	29.9	20.9	14.7

Part B			
	Percentage of Female Teachers Taking Each Alternative Career Path		
Case	*% Staying*	*% Transferring*	*% Leaving*
Base	18.1	22.6	59.1
Salaries for classified staff involved in teaching activities as a % of total expenditures increased	14.7	20.8	64.3

Part C							
	Percentage of Female Teachers Completing More Than n Years Teaching in State						
Case	*1*	*2*	*3*	*4*	*5*	*7*	*10*
Base	90.6	83.2	76.9	71.4	66.5	57.1	30.7
Salaries for classified staff involved in teaching activities as a % of total expenditures increased	88.7	80.1	73.6	68.9	64.4	54.2	26.2

system for at least one year. Increases in expenditures for this category of classified staff have a particularly strong influence on the early career choices of male beginning teachers. Specifically, the results presented in Part B of Table 7.7 indicate that the percentage of males who leave their first teaching position and stop teaching in the public school system increases from 31% to 44%. The influence of expenditures for classified staff involved in teaching activities is much smaller for female beginning teachers. The percentage of female teachers leaving their first positions and not teaching the following year increases only from 59% to 64% in districts allocating significant resources to classified teaching staff (Table 7.8, Part B).

Teachers remain in the profession for a much shorter time when spending increases are targeted to classified staff involved in teaching activities.

Targeting spending increases to nonteachers involved in classroom instruction significantly decreases the percentage of teachers who accumulate more teaching experience over the first 10 years after starting their careers in teaching. The percentage of male teachers completing more than 3 years in the state teaching system decreases from 86% to 78% when spending for classified teaching assistants is increased, the percentage of males completing more than 7 years decreases from 72% to 66%, and the percentage completing more than 10 years decreases from 58% to 49% (Table 7.7, Part C). For female teachers, the percentage completing more than 3 years in the state teaching system decreases from 77% to 74%, the percentage completing more than 7 years decreases from 57% to 54%, and the percentage completing more than 10 years decreases from 31% to 26% (Table 7.8, Part C).

Expenditures for Teaching Materials

Spending for teaching materials influences initial male career decisions but has little or no effect over time.

Male teachers continue working in a school district for a longer time when the district targets spending increases for teaching materials. Such spending has little or no influence on the length of time a female teacher continues to teach in the district.

When increased school district spending is targeted solely to teaching materials, male teachers are somewhat more likely to continue working as teachers in the district; similar spending patterns have no significant influence on the retention of female teachers. As shown in Part A of Table 7.9, male teachers are 3 to 4 percentage points more likely to remain in districts when higher spending is targeted to teaching materials. Similar simulations in Part A of Table 7.10 show that such spending does not influence female career behavior. This gender difference may be due to the higher proportion of male teachers employed in the sciences, in which spending for teaching materials strongly influences the range and nature of classroom activities.

Increasing expenditures for teaching materials decreases the likelihood that a male teacher will transfer to another school district from his first teaching position.

Higher program expenditures on teaching materials decrease the likelihood that males in Part B of Table 7.9 will transfer from their first

Table 7.9. Simulation Results Describing the Influence of Teaching Materials Spending on Male Teacher Career Decisions

Part A	Percentage of Male Teachers Completing More Than n Years in Their First Teaching Position						
Case	1	2	3	4	5	7	10
Base	75.1	60.4	54.0	50.4	47.5	42.1	34.4
Teaching materials expenditures as a % of total expenditures increased	77.7	63.9	57.8	53.9	50.6	44.7	36.2

Part B	Percentage of Male Teachers Taking Each Alternative Career Path		
Case	% Staying	% Transferring	% Leaving
Base	34.4	32.4	30.6
Teaching materials expenditures as a % of total expenditures increased	36.2	26.2	35.4

Part C	Percentage of Male Teachers Completing More Than n Years Teaching in State						
Case	1	2	3	4	5	7	10
Base	94.4	89.7	85.8	82.3	78.5	72.3	58.2
Teaching materials expenditures as a % of total expenditures increased	92.5	86.1	81.9	78.0	75.0	68.3	56.0

teaching position from 32% to 26%. Results in Part B of Table 7.10, however, suggest that spending for teaching materials has no influence on the transfer rates of female teachers.

Increasing expenditures for teaching materials has little or no impact on the length of time teachers remain in the profession.

The percentage of males completing more than 10 years in teaching does not change significantly when increased expenditures are targeted to teaching materials (see Table 7.9, Part C).

Policy Implications and Conclusions

The percentage of school district personnel who are classroom teachers fell from 65% in 1960 to 53% in 1988 (National Center for Educational Statistics, 1989). This change has been driven by a diverse

Table 7.10. Simulation Results Describing the Influence of Teaching Materials Spending on Female Teacher Career Decisions

Part A	Percentage of Female Teachers Completing More Than n Years in Their First Teaching Position						
Case	*1*	*2*	*3*	*4*	*5*	*7*	*10*
Base	79.3	66.0	54.8	43.8	35.9	25.9	18.1
Teaching materials expenditures as a % of total expenditures increased	79.7	67.0	56.0	44.9	36.4	26.7	18.6

Part B	Percentage of Female Teachers Taking Each Alternative Career Path		
Case	*% Staying*	*% Transferring*	*% Leaving*
Base	18.1	22.6	59.1
Teaching materials expenditures as a % of total expenditures increased	18.6	21.6	59.5

Part C	Percentage of Female Teachers Completing More Than n Years Teaching in State						
Case	*1*	*2*	*3*	*4*	*5*	*7*	*10*
Base	90.6	83.2	76.9	71.4	66.5	57.1	30.7
Teaching materials expenditures as a % of total expenditures increased	90.8	83.4	77.0	71.0	65.8	56.4	30.3

set of factors, including an increasing number of students who are deemed "at risk" for failure in the conventional classroom setting, changing societal expectations of the role of schools in providing noninstructional services, and evolving service delivery models (e.g., mainstreaming special education students) that depend increasingly upon other types of instructional personnel, such as instructional assistants. Our findings suggest that this shift of resources away from teachers toward other school personnel significantly increases turnover among beginning teachers.

Findings outlined in the previous section indicate that higher teacher salaries may help to mitigate the negative influence of higher spending for central office and other classified staff. Yet our findings suggest that district-level policy makers may not be able to increase teacher retention in their districts simply by keeping salaries above those prevailing in neighboring districts. Female teachers in their first 3 years are influenced to remain in a district primarily by such relative salary levels. However, females with more than 3 years of experience are influenced to remain with the district more by the relationship of their own salary to wages prevailing in other employment opportunities in the local county. Male teachers of all experience levels remain in their positions when the general level of teacher salaries compares favorably with nonteaching salaries in the state.

Our findings also suggest that school districts should carefully consider the impact on beginning teachers of efforts to include large numbers of classified staff in the regular education classroom. Beginning teachers stay in their initial teaching assignment for a shorter period of time when they are employed by a school district with high spending for classified instructional staff. Three possible explanations exist for this somewhat surprising result:

1. Novice teachers often struggle in developing their own classroom organizational skills, and the additional responsibilities of supervising another adult in these circumstances may influence their decision to continue in this type of position.
2. High spending for classified staff in regular education classrooms may reflect a district's decision to mainstream large numbers of special education students, and the additional complexity of classrooms in these districts could influence a beginning teacher's decision to leave.
3. A school district must reallocate funds away from other priorities of beginning teachers (e.g., teacher salaries, professional development) to fund these higher classified staff costs.

The first explanation appears to be the most reasonable. The relationship between novice teachers and classified staff could parallel that of recently commissioned officers and career subordinates in the military. Although novice teachers are officially in control of a classroom situation, this does not ensure that experienced classified staff members will follow their directions.

Beginning teachers who are leaving their first teaching assignment are less likely to transfer to another position within the public school system when they exit from a school district with high spending for classified instructional staff. The decision to leave the state system when classified spending is increased could reflect state funding policy during this period. Increases in state aid were linked to increased adult-student ratios. As large numbers of school districts increased their classified staff expenditures to receive additional state funding, teachers leaving these districts were likely to find fewer openings available with low classified staff spending.

This result has important policy ramifications as federal mandates spur schools to move increasingly toward the inclusion of large numbers of special education students into the regular education classroom. This inclusion movement is creating teaching situations unlike any seen previously. If such programs are not to increase turnover among beginning teachers, school districts must consider the extent to which novice teachers are prepared for these unique settings and devise strategies to help them cope with the added complexity of their classrooms.

Finally, our findings support the notion that districts can better influence teacher retention by looking for ways to lower spending for central administration and channel these funds toward teacher salaries and classroom materials. The context created by high central office spending increases the likelihood that teachers will leave a district. Funds allocated to teacher salaries and to teaching materials, on the other hand, create an environment that increases the probability that teachers will stay in the district.

The influence of central office and classified instructional staff spending on teacher turnover warrants further investigation. For example, studies need to examine the extent to which differences in geographic mobility explain the differential impact by gender of high central office spending. Work is also needed on the relationship between high classified instructional staff spending and the length of time beginning teachers stay in their initial teaching assignment. For instance, in-depth studies should be conducted to investigate any difficulties that novices face in supervising another adult in their classroom. Another issue that needs further examination involves the extent to which school districts reallocate funds away from other priorities of beginning teachers (e.g., teacher salaries, professional development) to fund higher classified staff costs. The particular policy implication that should be investigated is the role that state mandates linking funding to increased adult-student ratios play in the reallocation of funds, with an emphasis on the influence of these mandates on career decisions of classroom teachers.

This study's focus on teacher retention is only a first step in rebuilding and renewing our schools. Additional research, especially work that leads to greater understanding of college students' decisions to enter teaching, will contribute substantially to our ability to help policy makers more efficiently and effectively shape teacher personnel policies.

Notes

1. Minority teachers are not included because (a) previous research (Dworkin, 1980; Kemple, 1989; Murnane et al., 1991) suggests that the determinants of minority teachers' first spell lengths are different from those of white teachers, and (b) minority teachers starting their careers during this period accounted for only 579 teaching spells, limiting the validity of any study of minority teacher career path behavior.

References

Berman, P., & McLaughlin, M. (1977). *Federal programs supporting educational change: Vol. 7. Factors affecting implementation and continuation* (Rep. No. R-1589/7-HEW). Santa Monica, CA: RAND Corporation.

Bryk, A. S., Lee, V. E., & Smith, J. B. (1990). High school organization and its effect on teachers and students: An interpretive summary of the research. In W. J. Clune & J. F. Witte (Eds.), *Choice and control in American education: Vol. 1. The theory of choice and control in American education* (pp. 135-226). Philadelphia: Falmer.

Coleman, J. S., & Hoffer, T. (1987). *Public and private high schools: The impact of communities.* New York: Basic Books.

Darling-Hammond, L. (1992). *Excellence in teacher education: Helping teachers develop learner-centered schools.* Washington, DC: National Education Association.

Dworkin, A. G. (1980). The changing demography of public school teachers: Some implications for faculty turnover in urban areas. *Sociology of Education, 53,* 65-73.

Fullan, M. G. (1991). *The new meaning of educational change.* New York: Teachers College Press.

Goodlad, J. I. (1983). *A place called school.* New York: McGraw-Hill.

Goodlad, J. I. (1990). *Teachers for our nation's schools.* San Francisco: Jossey-Bass.

Grissmer, D. W., & Kirby, S. N. (1987). *Teacher attrition: The uphill climb to staff the nation's schools* (Rep. No. R-3512-CSTP). Santa Monica, CA: RAND Corporation.

Hanushek, E. A. (1989). The impact of differential expenditures on school performance. *Educational Researcher, 18*(4), 45-51.

Hanushek, E. A. (1994). *Making schools work: Improving performance and controlling costs.* Washington, DC: Brookings Institution.

Hedges, L. V., Laine, R. D., & Greenwald, R. (1994). Does money matter? A meta-analysis of studies of the effects of differential school inputs on students' outcomes. *Educational Researcher, 23*(3), 5-14.

Holmes Group. (1986). *Tomorrow's teachers: A report of the Holmes Group.* East Lansing, MI: Author.

Huberman, M., & Miles, M. (1984). *Innovation up close.* New York: Plenum.

Kemple, J. J. (1989, March). *The career paths of black teachers: Evidence from North Carolina.* Paper presented at the annual conference of the American Educational Research Association, San Francisco.

Lortie, D. C. (1975). *Schoolteacher: A sociological study.* Chicago: University of Chicago Press.

Murnane, R. J. (1975). *The impact of school resources on the learning of inner city children.* Cambridge, MA: Harvard University Press.

Murnane, R. J. (1987). Understanding teacher attrition. *Harvard Educational Review, 57,* 177-182.

Murnane, R. J., & Olsen, R. J. (1989). The effects of salaries and opportunity costs on duration in teaching: Evidence from Michigan. *Review of Economics and Statistics, 71,* 347-352.

Murnane, R. J., & Olsen, R. J. (1990). The effects of salaries and opportunity costs on length of stay in teaching: Evidence from North Carolina. *Journal of Human Resources, 25,* 106-124.

Murnane, R. J., & Phillips, B. R. (1981). What do effective teachers of inner city children have in common? *Social Science Research, 10,* 83-100.

Murnane, R. J., Singer, J. D., & Willett, J. B. (1988). The career paths of teachers: Implications for teacher supply and methodological lessons for research. *Educational Researcher, 18,* 22-30.

Murnane, R. J., Singer, J. D., & Willett, J. B. (1989). The influences of salaries and "opportunity costs" on teachers' career choices: Evidence from North Carolina. *Harvard Educational Review, 59,* 325-346.

Murnane, R. J., Singer, J. D., Willett, J. B., Kemple, J. J., & Olsen, R. J. (1991). *Who will teach? Policies that matter.* Cambridge, MA: Harvard University Press.

National Center for Educational Statistics. (1989). *The condition of education: Elementary and secondary education.* Washington, DC: U.S. Department of Education.

Rickman, B. D., & Parker, C. D. (1990). Alternative wages and teacher mobility: A human capital approach. *Economics of Education Review, 9,* 73-79.

Schlechty, P. C., & Vance, V. S. (1981). Do academically able teachers leave education? The North Carolina case. *Phi Delta Kappan, 63,* 106-112.

Theobald, N. D., & Gritz, R. M. (1995). *An economic model of teacher turnover: An analysis of public school teachers in Washington State.* (Available from Neil D. Theobald, Associate Professor, Indiana University, School of Education, Room 4228, Bloomington, IN 47405.)

U.S. Department of Commerce. (1993). *Public education finances: 1990-91.* Washington, DC: Author.

EIGHT

Stretching the Tax Dollar
INCREASING EFFICIENCY IN
URBAN AND RURAL SCHOOLS

DAVID M. ANDERSON

The Need for a
Measure of Efficiency

Although equity concerns dominated the educational community during the 1960s and 1970s, quality and excellence concerns have become increasingly important in the past 15 years. Even though most state finance reforms continue primarily to address the issue of funding inequities among school districts, the public is becoming increasingly concerned about quality in the schools. Such a concern for quality combined with a concern for effective use of funds represents a clear call for an understanding of efficiency in education.

Another clear mandate for a better understanding of efficiency comes from the judicial system. Many courts have based their school finance reform decisions on the "thorough and efficient" clauses in their state constitutions. Although these clauses have often been interpreted as requiring an equitable distribution of resources, they have also been interpreted as addressing the issues of quality and effectiveness in schools.[1]

Measuring Efficiency
for School Reform

In general, the most effective reform proposals in any field depend upon clearly defined goals and expectations. In education, many important values have emerged over the years as the focus for educational goals and the subsequent efforts at school improvement and reform. These values include such concepts as adequacy, equality, equity, efficiency, quality, empowerment, excellence, effectiveness, and choice. Unfortunately, these concepts do not have commonly accepted operational definitions or standards associated with them. However, an effective reform effort requires a stable and useful definition of the focus of the reform. If efficiency is an important objective of school finance reform, then we need to examine and adopt an operational definition of efficiency. Measuring efficiency in education is much more difficult than in private industry. In the private sector, companies respond to periods of fiscal strain and inadequate output by increasing their efficiency. In other words, they attempt to find a better use and distribution of their scarce resources in order to improve their productivity. Unfortunately, in education, resource use and its relationship with educational "products" are much more complex. There are no precise formulas that describe how any one student can most effectively learn. Because of this complexity and the lack of widespread measures of relevant school characteristics, there have been few attempts at addressing school efficiency. This chapter presents one possible approach to developing an operational definition of educational efficiency.

The Focus on
Urban and Rural Schools

Urban and rural schools are especially important in studies of efficiency because these schools are typically those that face the most severe budget constraints and resource shortages.[2] However, urban and rural schools represent, for many researchers, separate ends of a spectrum that is related to population density and community complexity. In many respects, these two types of schools are very different: The strengths of one are often seen as the weaknesses of the other and vice versa. Thus, even though both types of schools face issues of efficiency, a comparison of the two should illustrate some interesting contrasts. Urban schools, although they often have relatively high per-pupil expenditures, face serious problems. They face issues surrounding student diversity (in terms of both ethnicity and special-needs students), large school size, urban deterioration, poverty, violence, drugs, teen pregnancy, teen suicide, and poor attendance. Rural schools also face serious difficulties characterized by homogeneous student populations, close community-school relationships, small schools, poverty (albeit slightly different from that of urban schools), and professional isolation.

For both school types, efficiency has become a serious issue for educators, policy makers, and the public. This research should help (a) to illuminate one possible approach to developing an operational definition of educational efficiency for both rural and urban schools, and (b) to characterize those aspects of urban and rural schools and districts that influence efficiency in education.

Developing a New Measure of Efficiency: The Modified Quadriform

The difficulties with many studies on efficiency are that (a) most of these studies mix district, school, and individual levels of analysis in ways that tend to underestimate effects of the aggregated levels—that is, districts and schools (Burstein & Miller, 1981); (b) the studies fail to adequately address the contextual differences of schools; and (c) the studies do not begin with a clear definition of efficiency around which a study of optimization can revolve.

To address this latter need for a consistent definition of efficiency, Alan Hickrod and his colleagues in their work at the Center for the Study of Educational Finance (CSEF) (Hickrod et al., 1989) recognized that instead of simply identifying the factors that relate educational inputs to outcomes, improving efficiency depends on optimizing the relationship between inputs and outputs. In classical economic theory, this is accomplished by maximizing the input-output ratio (or maximizing the output given a certain input level).

However, because the relationship between educational inputs and outcomes is extremely complex, the CSEF researchers developed an alternative (and potentially more useful) way of approaching this input-output relationship, called the *quadriform* approach. In school finance, the input is typically school expenditures, and the output is some measure of student or school achievement (e.g., test scores, dropout rates, graduation rates).

This analysis uses a "modified quadriform," which is essentially similar to the CSEF approach. It is a two-stage model. Stage 1 captures the input-output relationship in two separate linear regressions. For the input regression, current operating expenditures per pupil (COEpp) is regressed against a group of unalterable school characteristics. For the output regression, an appropriate school outcome is regressed against a similar set of unalterable school characteristics. These two regression equations are of the form

$$Z_i = b_0 + b_1 W_{1i} + b_2 W_{2i}$$

where Z is the expected value for each school (either expenditure or outcome) and the W variables are the unalterable values for each school (the unit of analysis is the school). Once these regressions have been calculated, residual values can be found for each school. The residuals are the difference between the actual school expenditure or outcome values and the predicted values from the two regressions. The two regressions are illustrated in Figure 8.1, along with an example of a relatively efficient and a relatively inefficient school.

On the basis of the residuals of these two regressions, schools are categorized into the following four quadrants (the quadriform):

1. *Efficient* schools are those that have higher than expected outcomes with lower than expected expenditures (i.e., positive residuals with respect to outcomes and negative residuals with respect to expenditures).
2. *Inefficient* schools are those that have lower than expected outcomes and higher than expected expenditures.
3. *Lighthouse* schools are those that have higher than expected outcomes and higher than expected expenditures.
4. *Frugal* schools are those that have lower than expected scores and lower than expected expenditures.

Once the relatively efficient and inefficient schools have been identified, the analysis for Stage 2 follows. In Stage 2, a discriminant analysis is conducted to identify the "alterable" school characteristics that distinguish relatively efficient schools from relatively inefficient schools.

This approach to defining and analyzing efficiency in education is an improvement for at least two primary reasons. First, because inputs

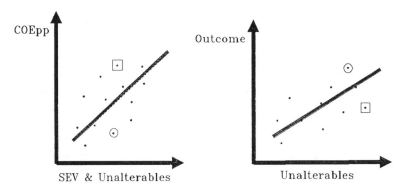

○⊙ Relatively Efficient: Low COEpp, High Outcome

⊡ Relatively Inefficient: High COEpp, Low Outcome

Figure 8.1. Quadriform Regressions for a Relatively Efficient and a Relatively Inefficient School.

and outputs are separated into two distinct regressions, this approach is sufficiently flexible to account for the complex relationship between inputs and outputs in education. For example, this approach allows different sets of unalterable predictors for the inputs (expenditures) as compared to the outputs (school outcomes). This is important because the unalterable determinants of these school variables could be quite different. Second, the two stages of the quadriform approach separate the effects of unalterable and alterable characteristics. This is important because the focus should be on the effects of alterable school characteristics (such as the level of education of the teacher or the class size). However, past research has shown that these effects are often overwhelmed by the effects of the unalterable school characteristics (like poverty). The quadriform removes the variance due to the unalterable characteristics, which then allows more stable analysis of the alterable characteristics.

Additional Analysis Features

Some additional features of this particular analysis are important. First, because the significance of any results would be diluted when comparing schools that are slightly above or below the regression lines with schools that vary significantly from the predicted regression lines, schools falling within a 0.1 standard error band around the regression lines were dropped from the analysis.

Second, on the basis of earlier research work on the relationships between community types (such as urban and rural) and student outcomes using the quadriform approach, it was clear that there were significant interaction effects with respect to different community types.

Such interaction effects could not be controlled by (a) including dummy-coded versions of community-type variables in the initial quadriform regressions or (b) including unalterable school characteristics in the initial regressions that might account for the effects of the various community types. So separate quadriform analyses were done for urban school districts (predominantly working-class communities of more than 50,000) and rural school districts (communities under 2,500). These separate analyses are described below along with comparisons between the two analyses.

Finally, all expenditure values were normalized using a cost-of-doing-business index derived from a method similar to the one suggested by Berne and Stiefel (1984). This index was found by regressing average district salary against a set of community characteristics suggested by Berne and Stiefel: the logarithm of the number of pupils, dummy-coded variables representing community and region, proportion of students in special education, percentage of minority students, and a poverty measure consisting of the percentage of students receiving free and reduced-price lunches. The predicted salaries were then divided by the state average to give a district-level price index. Once these index values were calculated, all the expenditure values were divided by these cost-of-doing-business index values.

The Quadriform Analysis: Stage 1

Choosing Outcome Variables

One strength of the quadriform approach is that multiple outcomes can be considered so that patterns across different outcomes can be examined. This analysis focuses on Michigan schools. ACT scores, the reading and math scores from the Michigan Educational Assessment Program (MEAP), and the percentage of students taking the ACT (a surrogate for intent to attend college) for the entire population of rural and urban schools in Michigan were used. The MEAP tests were used because they are much more widely taken within Michigan (in fact, almost all students are required to take the test) than is the ACT. The ACT is taken only by those students planning on attending college and thus is not as indicative of the achievement of all students. On the other hand, an important drawback of using the MEAP scores is that they are taken only in the 10th grade and thus do not fully represent the effect of the high school experience. Thus these four achievement outcomes complemented each other very well.

Choosing Unalterable School Characteristics

A review of the current research on efficiency and resource allocation was conducted in order to identify the alterable characteristics that might differentiate between efficient and inefficient schools as well as the unalterable school characteristics that would have to be included in the input and output regressions in identifying efficient and inefficient schools. Most current research on efficiency falls into three categories: (a) resource allocation studies, (b) cost-effectiveness and cost-benefit studies, and (c) production function analyses. An overview of the studies conducted at these levels, including empirical and hypothetical relationships, suggested an appropriate set of variables for inclusion in this analysis (MacPhail, Wilcox, & King, 1986).

Most research indicates that the poverty level of school district is one of the principal determinants of both expenditures and outcomes. In this analysis, the percentage of students receiving free and reduced-price lunches was used as the "poverty impaction" factor. Free and reduced-price lunches were combined by taking twice the percentage of students receiving free lunches plus the percentage of students receiving reduced-price lunches in the district.

In addition to poverty and community type, the review of research indicated that several additional unalterable school characteristics needed to be included in the analysis: the size of the school, the percentage of special education students in the district, the percentage of minority students in the school, and the region in the state (Detroit Metropolitan Area, Southern Lower Peninsula, Northern Lower Peninsula,

Table 8.1. Unalterable School Characteristics and Outcomes
(Urban Schools)

Variable	Mean	SD
School Size	1168.86	755.36
% Minority	51.20	36.70
SEVPP	55,406.44	32,712.16
% Special Ed	4.93	2.48
% Free Lunch	36.56	17.16
% Reduced Lunch	3.81	1.44
Cost Index	1.06	0.07
COEPP	4,042.14	462.29
ACT COMPOSITE	15.54	3.57
MEAP READ	67.48	15.70
MEAP MATH	52.56	20.13
% Taking ACT	35.24	26.34

and Upper Peninsula). Descriptive statistics for these variables are included in Tables 8.1 and 8.2, for urban and rural schools, respectively.[3]

Table 8.2. Unalterable School Characteristics and Outcomes
(Rural Schools)

Variable	Mean	SD
School Size	333.59	221.59
% Minority	5.30	9.06
SEVPP	78,009.88	66,020.31
% Special Ed	1.86	1.21
% Free Lunch	20.62	11.61
% Reduced Lunch	5.01	3.04
Cost Index	0.83	0.06
COEPP	3,276.27	700.84
ACT COMPOSITE	18.21	1.65
MEAP READ	83.66	11.64
MEAP MATH	70.63	13.75
% Taking ACT	55.66	13.31

Table 8.3. Unalterable Predictors for COEPP (Urban Schools)

Variable	FACTOR1	FACTOR2
Poverty	+.90	+.19
Special	+.29	+.75
Lnsize	+.17	-.83
Minority	+.93	+.09
Property	-.79	+.12

Combining Unalterable Predictors for the Input Regression

To prepare for the input regression of the expenditures (current operating expenditures per pupil—COEPP), a principal components analysis was used to combine all of the unalterable school characteristics (except region) into a set of two orthogonal factors that were included in the initial regressions. This allowed a much more stable regression line to be established.

As an example, the results of these factor analyses for the urban schools are presented in Table 8.3. The *Poverty* variable is a transformed version of the combination of free and reduced-price lunches, and the variables *Special, Lnsize, Minority,* and *Property* are transformed versions of the percentage of special education students in the district, the enrollment of the school, the percentage of minority students in the school, and the SEVPP of the district, respectively. Notice that the first factor, FACTOR1, principally contains the contributions of poverty, minority, and property (with the last one inversely related to the first two). The second factor principally represents the effects of school size and the percentage of special education students in the district.

Thus the regression equation for COEPP is

$$Y_i = b_0 + b_1 X_{1i} + b_2 X_{2i}$$

where Y_i = the predicted current operating expenditures for the ith school, X_{1i} = the value of FACTOR1 for the ith school, and X_{2i} = the value of FACTOR2 for the ith school.

Table 8.4. Unalterable Predictors for Outcomes (Urban Schools)

Variable	BACK1	BACK2
Poverty	+.95	−.10
Special	+.37	−.70
Lnsize	+.15	+.87
Minority	+.96	−.01

As mentioned earlier, separate analyses were done for rural schools. Thus the actual form and effects of FACTOR1 and FACTOR2 are different (as would be expected for the two different community types).

Combining Unalterable Predictors
for the Output Regression

Because the property values in a school district are not directly related to student outcomes, a separate principal components analysis was conducted to combine the unalterable school characteristics for the output regression by removing the *Property* variable. Table 8.4 contains the results of this analysis. The addition of these factors, along with region in the state, made it possible to remove the effects of unalterables and isolate the variance due to alterable school characteristics. This aspect of the analysis, as well as the differential treatment of the inputs and outcomes at this level, represents the strengths of this two-stage model. Once again, notice that the first factor, BACK1, represents poverty and minority, whereas the·second factor represents school size and the percentage of special education students in the district.

Thus the regression equation for the outcomes is

$$Z_i = b_0 + b_1 W_{1i} + b_2 W_{2i}$$

where Z_i = the predicted current operating expenditures for the *i*th school, W_{1i} = the value of BACK1 for the *i*th school, and W_{2i} = the value of BACK2 for the *i*th school.

Table 8.5. COEPP Quadriform Regressions: Standardized Beta Coefficients

	Urban	*Rural*
FACTOR1	+.01	–.73
FACTOR2	+.23	+.30
STHLOW	+.24	
NTHLOW		–.19
UPPER	–.16	+.17
R-SQU	+.18	+.68

Again, separate analyses were done for rural schools. Thus the actual form and effects of BACK1 and BACK2 are different (as would be expected for the two different community types).

The Input-Output Regressions: Forming the Quadriform

Once the unalterable independent variables had been constructed, the quadriform regressions were calculated and residuals established for all schools in the population. So in order to establish the initial quadriform prediction equations for current operating expenditures per pupil (COEPP) and the first outcome variable, ACT composite scores (ACT COMPOSITE) for 1988 to 1989, these two variables were regressed against the set of unalterable school characteristics described in the previous section, along with dummy-coded variables representing regions in Michigan (STHLOW = Southern Lower Peninsula excluding the Detroit Metropolitan Area, NTHLOW = Northern Lower Peninsula, and UPPER = Upper Peninsula).

As can be seen from Table 8.5, effects of the unalterables for rural schools are sufficiently different from urban schools to warrant separate analyses. Specifically, for COEPP, FACTOR1 (poverty, minority, and property) is a strong negative predictor for rural schools, whereas it is close to zero for urban schools. Finally, the unalterables account for a much larger percentage of the variance of COEPP for rural schools than urban schools (68% as opposed to 18%).

In contrast to the results for COEPP, for ACT composite scores, the second factor, BACK2 (school size and percentage of special education students), is a positive predictor for rural schools but a negative predictor for urban schools, whereas BACK1 is a negative predictor for both rural and urban schools. These unalterable variables account for a much smaller percentage of the variance in ACT composite scores for rural schools than urban schools (12% as opposed to 51%). Although these are interesting intermediate results (consistent with other research findings), the focus of this analysis is to examine the relationships between efficiency and alterable school characteristics. This is done in the next and final stage of the quadriform analysis.

The Quadriform Analysis: Stage 2

Choosing Alterable School Characteristics

The second stage of the analysis for any given outcome variable is to identify the variables that discriminate between the relatively efficient and relatively inefficient schools. Tables 8.6 and 8.7 provide the descriptive statistics for the variables chosen. These variables were chosen on the basis of the thorough review of the research literature described in the previous section.

Overall, the variables can be grouped into three categories: (a) fiscal resource allocations, (b) staff characteristics, and (c) school characteristics.

The fiscal resource variables included in the analysis were (a) percentage of COE spent on basic instruction (% BASIC INST., consisting of classroom costs of the basic instructional program within a school); (b) percentage of COE spent on added instruction (% ADDED INST., consisting of the classroom costs of the added-needs instructional programs, such as special education, compensatory education, vocational education, and other programs designed to improve or address special physical, mental, social, and/or emotional circumstances or to provide learning experiences preparing an individual for specific occupations); (c) percentage of COE spent on general administrative services (% GEN. ADM., consisting of the costs of those district-level activities of the superintendent and school board concerned with establishing policy, operating schools and the school system, and providing facilities and services for staff and pupils); (d) percentage of COE spent on school administration (% SCHOOL ADM., consisting of the costs of those activities concerned with the overall admini-

Table 8.6. Alterable School Characteristics (Urban Schools)

Variable	Mean	SD	Min.	Max.
% BASIC INST.	31.51	4.14	28.24	41.56
% ADDED INST.	13.83	3.47	5.76	17.88
% GEN. ADM.	21.58	2.70	15.06	26.28
% SCHOOL ADM.	5.48	1.02	3.64	6.52
% PUPIL SUPP.	5.07	1.54	2.31	8.86
% STAFF SUPP.	4.32	2.15	2.39	8.59
SALARY	33,152.42	3,066.96	26,455.56	38,074.29
STF. YRS. CLASS	17.72	2.66	13.00	23.00
% MASTERS/DOC	69.26	10.18	36.00	83.00
PRINC. YRS. CLASS	8.74	3.87	3.00	19.00
LIB. PERS/STU	1.15	0.45	0.74	3.13
BOOK/STU	13.16	5.50	5.95	26.85
LIB. EXP/STU	2.15	0.28	1.68	3.08
% MATH & SCI.	20.04	5.92	0.00	31.91
% LANG & SOC.	35.70	8.76	21.49	69.01
TEACHERS/STU	46.25	5.77	39.35	58.93
GUIDANCE/STU	3.54	0.71	2.22	5.08
CLASSTIME	1,147.30	114.83	1,080.00	1,456.00

stration of a single school); (e) percentage of COE spent on pupil support (% PUPIL SUPP., consisting of the costs of those activities designed to assess and improve the well-being of pupils, including attendance services, guidance services, health services, and social work services); and (f) percentage of COE spent on staff support (% STAFF SUPP., consisting of those costs associated with assisting instructional staff with the content and process of providing learning experiences for pupils, such as teacher in-service, curriculum development, and audiovisual services). Because of high intercorrelations among these variables, this set of six variables was collapsed to three: (a) the percentage of COE spent on instruction (% INSTRUCT)—a sum of basic and added instruction, (b) the percentage of COE spent on support (PCTSUPP)—a sum of staff and pupil support, and (c) the percentage of COE spent on administration (PCTADMIN)—a sum of general and school administration.

Table 8.7. Alterable School Characteristics (Rural Schools)

Variable	Mean	SD	Min.	Max.
% BASIC INST.	44.86	4.62	25.89	55.81
% ADDED INST.	7.64	2.79	1.66	16.37
% GEN. ADM.	24.14	3.71	16.66	40.96
% SCHOOL ADM.	5.10	1.31	0.01	8.40
% PUPIL SUPP.	2.34	1.18	0.00	7.31
% STAFF SUPP.	1.72	0.83	0.00	4.94
SALARY	28,270.27	3,179.62	20,078.00	35,271.00
STF. YRS. CLASS	14.16	2.57	8.00	20.00
% MASTERS/DOC	43.14	12.85	10.00	68.00
PRINC. YRS. CLASS	9.03	4.97	2.00	28.00
LIB. PERS/STU	2.49	1.38	0.00	10.31
BOOK/STU	23.83	13.48	7.59	83.99
LIB. EXP/STU	2.93	0.66	1.67	4.96
% MATH & SCI.	24.85	4.19	13.85	36.36
% LANG & SOC.	31.59	5.40	17.32	46.27
TEACHERS/STU	54.94	13.08	25.91	113.40
GUIDANCE/STU	3.45	1.27	0.00	9.71
CLASSTIME	1,093.54	53.43	900.00	1,260.00

The staff characteristics consisted of the following variables: (a) the average salaries of the instructional staff (SALARY); (b) the average number of years of classroom experience of the staff (STF. YRS. CLASS); (c) the percentage of staff members holding master's degrees, specialists' degrees, or doctoral degrees (% MASTERS/DOC); and (d) the number of years of classroom experience of the principal (PRINC. YRS. CLASS).

The school resource variables consisted of (a) a factor that measured the quality of the library, combining the number of media specialists per pupil, the number of books in the library per pupil, and the library expenditures per pupil (LIBRARY); (b) the percentage of courses offered in math and science (% MATH & SCI); (c) the percentage of courses offered in language arts and social studies (% LANG & SOC.); (d) the teacher-student ratio (TEACHERS/STU, consisting of the number of full-time-equivalent teachers in the school divided by the number of students); (e) the guidance counselor-student ratio (GUIDANCE/STU, consisting of the number of full-time-equivalent

Table 8.8. Urban Schools: Standardized Canonical Discriminant Function
Coefficients

	ACT	MATH	READ	% TAKE ACT
% INSTRUCT.	–0.24	–3.08	–2.02	–1.58
% SUPPORT	–1.41	–4.29	–2.59	–2.13
% ADMIN.	–1.56	–2.28	–1.96	–2.60
SALARY	–0.33	–0.23	–0.49	–1.78
STF. YRS. CLASS	–0.59	–1.29	–1.03	–0.25
% MASTERS/DOC	+1.55	+1.41	+1.19	+1.73
PRINC. YRS. CLASS	+0.46	–0.16	–0.09	–1.13
LIBRARY	–0.04	+0.76	+0.73	–0.47
% MATH & SCI	–0.18	–0.72	–0.66	+0.55
% LANG & SOC	–0.69	+0.02	–0.60	–0.45
GUIDANCE/STU	–0.47	–0.26	–0.86	–0.39
TEACHERS/STU	–0.47	–0.88	–0.75	+0.18
CLASSTIME	+0.59	–0.76	+0.06	+0.93
#INEFFIC	9	10	15	8
#EFFIC	18	17	18	13
TOTAL	27	27	33	21
#MISSED	0	1	0	0
% CORRECT	100.0	96.3	100.0	100.0

guidance counselors divided by the number of students in the school);
and (f) the total amount of instructional time offered by the school in
a year as measured in hours (CLASSTIME).

These sets of variables were then included in a discriminant analysis, and the analysis was repeated for the additional outcomes variables:
MEAP reading and math scores (READ and MATH, respectively) and
the percentage of students planning to attend college (% TAKE ACT),
measured by the number of students taking the ACT test divided by
the total enrollment in Grade 12.

Discriminant Analysis

The results of the discriminant analyses for all the outcome variables are presented for the urban schools in Table 8.8 and for the rural
schools in Table 8.9.

Table 8.9. Rural Schools: Standardized Canonical Discriminant Function Coefficients

	ACT	MATH	READ	% TAKE ACT
% INSTRUCT.	+0.46	+0.14	–0.14	+0.78
% SUPPORT	–0.35	–0.48	–0.44	–0.18
% ADMIN.	–0.59	–0.28	–0.23	–0.05
SALARY	–0.93	–0.91	–0.67	–0.88
STF. YRS. CLASS	–0.19	+0.54	+0.45	+0.11
% MASTERS/DOC	–0.13	–0.32	–0.55	–0.10
PRINC. YRS. CLASS	+0.05	+0.06	+0.02	–0.24
LIBRARY	+0.53	+0.27	+0.16	+0.69
% MATH & SCI	+0.28	–0.16	+0.18	–0.16
% LANG & SOC	+0.11	–0.08	–0.26	+0.38
GUIDANCE/STU	+0.67	+0.42	+0.69	+0.07
TEACHERS/STU	–1.06	–0.35	–0.52	–0.45
CLASSTIME	–0.23	+0.40	+0.36	–0.05
#INEFFIC	37	34	36	39
#EFFIC	50	55	54	43
TOTAL	87	84	90	82
#MISSED	13	28	22	27
% CORRECT	71.3	68.5	75.6	67.1

It is important to point out that this analysis is more descriptive than causal. The intent is to identify patterns and relationships that can inform further research. The intent is not to provide direct policy recommendations for all schools.

Discussion

Interpretation of Results

An interpretation of the results of the discriminant analysis can be divided into three parts. First, we can focus upon the consistent effects that emerged across all outcomes for both rural and urban schools. Second, we can examine the consistent differences between the rural and urban contexts. Third, we can examine those characteristics that did not exhibit consistent effects for rural or urban schools.

Urban and Rural Similarities

First, salary is negatively related to efficiency. This is probably due to the fact that higher salaries will lead to relative inefficiency because the higher salaries will not necessarily attract better teachers in an already constrained job market, but will lead to higher costs. Of course, this does not mean that improving salary levels in the teacher profession as a whole will not improve the quality of education. Rather, it means that given the existing salary structure, the supply of teachers, and the limited mobility of many teachers, an individual school will probably not affect its quality by offering higher salaries than its neighboring school. This result is supported by other research, including a study of rural schools in Kansas by Horn (1988) and results for urban schools reported by Lomotey and Swanson (1989).

Second, class size is positively related to efficiency (teacher-student ratio is negatively related to efficiency). This is also supported by much current research because many studies have shown that for class sizes greater than 15 (where individual instruction, or even small-group instruction, is less likely to occur), there is little loss of teaching effectiveness with larger class size, but considerable reduction in instructional cost (Caillods & Postlewaite, 1989). Because the average class size for both rural and urban schools is greater than 15 (or, equivalently, less than 70 teachers per 1,000 students), this result is not surprising.[4]

Urban and Rural Differences

For the urban schools, the coefficients of the resource allocation variables are all negative, whereas for rural schools, they are also negative except for the coefficient for instructional expenditures.[5] For urban schools, the fact that there are no differential patterns among the different resource variables is significant because it addresses frequently heard anecdotal statements that urban schools spend too much on administration and not enough on instruction. If this were true, we should see consistently more positive (or at least less negative) coefficients for the instruction variables and more negative coefficients for the administration categories. In fact, this is not the case for urban schools, but it is the case for rural schools. This can be explained by the fact that administrative leadership has very different characteristics in the urban and rural contexts.

Effective-schools research has found that "effective urban schools are characterized by strong leadership, manifested primarily by principals who have assumed control whether or not they have been granted formal authority" (Lomotey & Swanson, 1989, p. 443). For these urban schools, there is not often a close working relationship between the school board and the principal, or between the community and the principal. Thus effective leadership depends on developing and maintaining an experienced administrative staff.

On the other hand, rural schools are often the training grounds for administrators in small cities and suburbs; "professional leadership often has a fleeting quality and tends to be inexperienced. Program continuity is frequently provided by the lay and teaching personnel rather than the administrators" (Lomotey & Swanson, 1989. p. 443). Thus most rural schools have adapted to higher administrator turnover and less experienced administrators. For this reason, a more supportive administration, maintained by higher administrative expenditures, would be critical for urban schools, but possibly not as cost-effective for rùral schools. This is certainly supported by these results.

Next, for urban schools, more years of teachers' classroom experience contributes negatively to efficiency. This is perhaps explained by many factors inherent in the urban job that teachers feel are beyond their control and that they recognize only through experience: isolation, lack of student interest, overcrowded classes, lack of parent interest, inadequate resources, and the relative "flatness" of the salary scale. As Goodlad (1984) pointed out, it is often not realistic to expect teachers to teach enthusiastically year after year when they are forced to make 200 or more decisions per hour of instruction within an environment that often lacks a sense of community.

On the other hand, because of the stronger sense of community within rural schools, teachers are able to establish much closer relationships with their students (as well as parents, community members, and administrators) (Goodlad, 1984). This might well mitigate the tendency for teacher "burnout."

For urban schools, the level of education of the teachers is positively related to efficiency. This should not be a surprising result because after controlling for years of experience and salary, better educated teachers should have greater professional awareness and effectiveness in their teaching, and this should affect student achievement.

However, the fact that the level of education of teachers is negatively related to efficiency for rural schools is much less intuitively apparent. One plausible explanation is that most schools of education focus their advanced curriculum upon current social issues and research that has been dominated by urban issues and urban environments (Hobbs, 1987).

Next, for urban schools, the quality of the library was not consistently related to efficiency, whereas for rural schools it was positively related to efficiency. A possible explanation for this relationship is that because rural schools play a much more central role in their community and because they are more isolated from other service and information centers, a strong library is much more critical to the effectiveness of a rural school than it is for an urban school. This result is supported by a recent study by Kohr (1989).

Finally, efficient urban schools seem to have fewer guidance counselors per student, whereas efficient rural schools tend to have more guidance counselors per student. This is probably an artifact of the set of outcomes examined. Often, especially in an urban environment, guidance counselors typically must concentrate more on issues that are not related to student achievement—familial problems, suicide, attendance, drugs, violence, and so forth (Clark, 1987).

Thus greater reliance on guidance counseling might not have a relatively positive influence on student test achievement, but it would have an influence on student satisfaction and attendance. On the other hand, because of the closer sense of community in rural schools, guidance counselors are able to concentrate more directly on student achievement; thus higher numbers of guidance counselors will have a much more positive effect on achievement in rural schools than in urban schools (Gothberg, 1990). Also, because there are fewer counselors (in absolute number) in any given rural school, any addition to the counseling staff would have a relatively large per-student effect (represented by large variance).

The remaining characteristics did not have consistent effects over the outcomes examined: principal's years of classroom experience, curriculum distribution (math/science versus language arts/social studies), and amount of time spent in the classroom.

Evaluation of the Model

An earlier study found that in general, the effects of the unalterable school characteristics were very consistent from year to year (Anderson, Kearney, & Mora, 1991). This lends validity to the assumption that schools are not moving randomly from quadrant to quadrant in different years. Moreover, significantly more schools were consistently found in each quadrant than would be expected by chance alone. Given the 550 schools of the total school population, one would expect that about 9 schools would appear consistently in each quadrant over 3 years by chance alone. In this earlier analysis, 50 to 70 schools were consistently appearing in each quadrant. This means that the identification of schools by the model is not simply an artifact of the regressions. Certainly, some shifting of schools from quadrant to quadrant is expected because schools do change their patterns of resource allocation and, in so doing, will change quadrants as predicted by the model.

In order to assess the effectiveness of removing the variance due to the unalterable characteristics, the analysis was repeated using a model similar to the original CSEF model, with only poverty impaction and SEVPP used in the initial regressions. This led to a less stable model, with fewer alterable school characteristics significantly discriminating between the efficient and inefficient schools. Thus the improvements over the original form of the model do seem statistically justified.

Conclusion

Overall, there is very little research available to use for comparison purposes in a discussion of the results. There are several reasons: (a) very little research makes direct comparisons of urban and rural schools, (b) very little research has extensive data available on such a wide group of schools (necessary for strong statistical analysis), and (c) very little research uses multivariate methods of quantitative data analysis. Although there is some quantitative research available, no other study combines the richness of data with a multivariate analysis that simultaneously controls for diverse school characteristics (in the regression sense). This particular method combines many strengths and has provided intriguing results that are supported in the general literature.

Analyses such as this one are important first steps in developing an understanding of the usefulness and adequacy of certain research directions. It is hoped that this work will initiate further discussion and analysis and will provide an additional foundation for more clear-sighted research endeavors within the very nebulous field of educational efficiency.

Notes

1. For example, in the case *Somerset County Board of Education v. Hombeck* (1981), a Maryland court ruled that *efficient* meant "using the least wasteful means" (see Mullin, 1982).

2. The data set used for this analysis consisted of information for the approximately 550 Michigan public high schools that were accredited through the Bureau of Accreditation and School Improvement Studies (BASIS). The data were drawn from eight principal sources: (a) the Michigan High School Accreditation data, (b) the School Aid Instant Data Exhibits (SAIDE), (c) Form B data source, (d) the Michigan Racial and Ethnic Census data, (e) the Professional Personnel Register data, (f) the Michigan Educational Assessment Program (MEAP), (g) the American College Testing (ACT) program, and (h) the free/reduced-price lunch data set.

3. It is also important to remember that the results reported in these tables (and subsequent tables) represent analyses on a population (i.e., all the public accredited schools), not a sample. Thus there are no reported inferential statistics. All effects and effect sizes are the actual effect sizes.

4. Of course, this is not to say that reducing class size (preferably to 12 or less) would not be beneficial to educational quality, but rather that marginal reductions in class size *within the constraints that most schools operate* may have greater influences on raising costs than improving instructional effectiveness.

5. The fact that these coefficients are negative is partly an artifact of this particular analysis because schools that spend more money on any of the resource categories (including teacher salaries) will appear to be less efficient (controlling for the other covariates). In comparing different categories, however, we hope to see consistent patterns within these budget areas.

References

Anderson, D. M., Kearney, C. P., & Mora, C. E. (1991). *Technical efficiency in Michigan school districts*. Ann Arbor, MI: Bureau of Accreditation and School Improvement Studies.

Berne, R. & Stiefel, L. (1984). *The measurement of equity in school finance*. Baltimore: Johns Hopkins University Press.

Burstein, L., & Miller, M. D. (1981). Regression-based analyses of multilevel educational data. In R. F. Boruch, P. M. Wortman, & Associates (Eds.), *Reanalyzing program evaluations*. San Francisco: Jossey-Bass.

Caillods, F., & Postlewaite, T. N. (1989). Teaching/learning conditions in developing countries. *Prospects, 19*(2), 169-190.

Clark, R. M. (1987). *Guidance and counseling in urban schools*. (ERIC Document Research Service No. ED286081)

Goodlad, J. I. (1984). *A place called school*. New York: McGraw-Hill.

Gothberg, E. J. (1990). *The joys and challenges of school counseling professionals in rural communities: A qualitative study*. (ERIC Document Research Service No. ED326791)

Hickrod, G. A., et al. (1989). *The biggest bang for the buck: An initial report on technical economic efficiency in Illinois K-12 schools with a comment on* Rose v. The Council. Normal, IL: Center for the Study of Educational Finance.

Hobbs, D. (1987). The school in the rural community: Issues of costs, education, and values. *Small School Forum, 2*(3), 10-13.

Horn, J. (1988). *A study of the perceived effectiveness of Kansas small schools.* Manhattan: Kansas State University, Center for Rural Education and Small Schools.

Kohr, R. L. (1989). *An examination of community type differences in the educational quality assessment data.* Harrisburg: Pennsylvania State Department of Education, Bureau of Educational Quality Assessment.

Lomotey, K., & Swanson, A. D. (1989). Urban and rural schools research. *Education and Urban Society, 24,* 436-454.

MacPhail-Wilcox, B., & King, R. A. (1986). Resource allocation studies: Implications for school improvement and school finance research. *Journal of Education Finance, 11,* 416-432.

Mullin, S. (1982). The budget crunch: Educational production functions as a resource allocation tool. In A. A. Summers (Ed.), *Productivity assessment in education.* San Francisco: Jossey-Bass.

NINE

The Allocation of
Educational Resources and
School Finance Equity in Ohio

THOMAS B. TIMAR

In July 1994 a trial court in New Lexington, Ohio, declared the state's school finance system unconstitutional. The current school finance system violated not only the state constitution's equal-protection principle but also its "thorough and efficient" provision.[1] The court reached this conclusion after a 30-day trial. The total record of testimony that brought the court to its decision in *De Rolph v. State of Ohio* (1994) comprised nearly 11,000 pages. Over 500 exhibits were reviewed and admitted into evidence. Thirty-eight witnesses testified at the trial, and another 33 testified by deposition. The court spent 123 hours reviewing the various findings, posttrial briefs, and conclusions of law. In his findings, Judge Lewis, Jr., rejected the Ohio Supreme Court's standard for school finance equity that it had established in 1979 in *Board of Education of the City of Cincinnati v. Walter*. The decision, and the conclusions of law upon which it is based, is of particular interest to policy makers for two important reasons. First, it redefines standards of school finance equity. Unlike the case *Serrano v. Priest* (1971) in California, which defines the limits of absolute deprivation but tolerates relative deprivation, the standard established by the trial court in Ohio is one of absolute deprivation. The court redefines the meaning of both *equal protection* and *adequacy*. Second, unlike other school finance equity cases in which there is no clear delineation between taxpayer and student equity, the decision in *De Rolph* lands squarely in the corner of educational entitlement and equal opportunity. This chapter examines spending and resource allocation patterns at the district level, with specific focus on the equity of that distribution. I integrate these findings into a discussion of school finance equity in Ohio, using the standards established by the court in *De Rolph*. In assessing the equity of resource allocation among districts, I examine two lines of argument, the defendants' and the plaintiffs'. Defendants in the case, the state of Ohio, took as their legal touchstone the Supreme Court's *Walter* decision. Their arguments focused on two factual issues: Had relative funding disparities across districts improved or worsened between 1979 and 1992, and what was the state's role in either ameliorating or exacerbating existing disparities? Plaintiffs simply compared the 50 highest-property-wealth districts with the 50 poorest (and in some instances the 5 wealthiest and 5 poorest) and argued that the resulting disparity in resource allocation and student outcomes at the extremes was constitutionally intolerable.

Resource Allocation Provisions
Under the *Walter* Standard

The school finance system upheld by the Ohio Supreme Court in 1979 has its roots in a foundation program begun in 1935. Like other foundation programs, it is based on a principle of local control, with property as the mainstay for school funding. The state finance system in *Walter* was based upon an equal-yield formula. To qualify for state aid, districts were required to levy at least 20 mills. The finance scheme also rewarded districts that levied more than 20 operating mills commensurate with their millage up to 30 mills. The latter was regarded as "reward for effort." Power-equalizing formulas such as Ohio's are familiar to policy makers as ways of equalizing the property tax base across districts under the principle of equal yield for equal effort.

By 1978, the equal-yield scheme was replaced by the current funding formula at issue in *De Rolph*. Unlike the old power-equalizing formula, the current formula does not reward districts that levy above 20 mills. Instead, low-wealth districts have had to rely on ad hoc infusions of "equity funds" from the state. The state allocated $150 in such funds between 1991 and 1993 and an additional $75 million in

1994. In addition to local and state foundation grant funds, called *state basic aid*, the state provides additional categorical program funding for special needs. Basic aid includes Disadvantaged Pupil Impact Aid (DPIA), which allocates funds to districts based on the concentration of children whose families receive Aid to Dependent Children (ADC). In the 1993 fiscal year, the per-pupil amount of such grants ranged from $103 to $1,092.

Categorical programs include funds for vocational education, special education, and student transportation. Finally, there are various supplemental grants for special-purpose programs as well as fiscal relief to school districts for homeowner property tax exemption allowances (Ohio Department of Education, 1993).

Attorneys for the state endeavored to show that despite a new funding system, the state had sufficiently and systematically provided additional funding for poor districts that made them better off, and certainly no worse off, than they were in 1975. A principal finding of the trial court, on the other hand, was that the state had abrogated its constitutional responsibility to provide a state system of education that was both "thorough and efficient" because per-pupil funding was left to the vagaries of local property tax wealth. The question, then, is whether the court is correct: Has the state failed to provide adequately for its schools? Has state policy allowed poor school districts to wither financially while other, wealthy districts prosper? Table 9.1 displays distributional data.

It should be noted that for purposes of this analysis, only local and state basic aid revenues are considered. This is because it is assumed that the two revenue sources not only make up the majority of district funds (over 80%) but also represent unrestricted dollars that are neither designated for special purposes nor used to offset excess costs. It should be noted also that outliers at the top of the distribution are excluded from the data. The reason for the exclusion is that the 5% of students in the highest-wealth districts are anomalous and would simply skew the distribution.[2]

It is evident from Table 9.1 that considerable differences existed between the lowest- and highest-wealth districts (even after excluding the top 5% of students in the wealthiest districts). The range between the highest and lowest in 1979 was $1,577, whereas in 1991 it was $1,458. Although the reduction in revenue disparity may seem insignificant, it is worth noting where within the distribution the greatest

Table 9.1. Ohio Education Finance Distribution Descriptors (Local Revenues and Basic Aid Revenues per Pupil, Selected Years) (in Constant, 1979 Dollars)

Year	Mean $/PP	Median $/PP	High $/PP	Low $/PP	1st Quartile $/PP[a]	4th Quartile $/PP[a]
1979	1,137	1,085	2,076	499	888	1,470
1981	1,324	1,243	2,285	729	995	1,777
1985	1,462	1,417	2,292	980	1,223	1,770
1988	1,464	1,415	2,283	805	1,220	1,795
1991	1,593	1,550	2,401	943	1,317	1,946

SOURCE: Raw data provided by the Ohio Department of Education.
NOTE: The data exclude outliers at the top of the distribution. Thus 5% of students in the highest-wealth districts are excluded.
a. First- and fourth-quartile figures are interquartile means.

change occurred. Per-pupil funding in districts in the lowest quartile increased by 43% in constant dollars, whereas funding in the top quartile increased by 32%. Median and mean funding per pupil increased by 43% and 40%, respectively. Though such increases are clearly the result of multiple factors, the issue here is to determine how much of that increase is due to state intervention. Thus, if we isolate increases in state basic aid support from local revenues, we get a better understanding of the state's role. Between 1979 and 1991, mean per-pupil state basic aid in the highest-revenue-quartile district increased 37%, after adjusting for inflation. Mean per-pupil state basic aid revenue (inflation adjusted) in the lowest-quartile district increased 62% over the same period of time. Mean per-pupil revenues in the lowest-quartile district increased by an average amount of slightly more than 4% each year (after adjusting for inflation). Per-pupil revenues in the highest-quartile district have increased (after adjusting for inflation) by an average of approximately 2.7% per year. Between 1979 and 1991, the lowest-revenue district in Ohio increased per-pupil revenue by 89%—7.4% annually (in constant dollars), whereas the wealthiest district, after adjusting for inflation, increased per-pupil revenue by 16%, an annual average of 1.3%.

Another way of looking at the policy effects of state basic aid is to consider the relationship between basic aid and assessed valuation.

Table 9.2. Basic Aid and Assessed Valuation per ADM (BAID/AVADM),
           1979 and 1991

Decile	BAID/ AVADM 1979	BAID/ AVADM 1991
1st	5%	7%
2nd	4%	5%
3rd	3%	4%
4th	2%	3%
5th	2%	3%
6th	2%	3%
7th	1%	2%
8th	1%	2%
9th	1%	1%
10th	0%	0%

SOURCE: Raw data provided by the Ohio Department of Education.

In both 1979 and 1991, districts with the lowest per-pupil assessed valuation received a higher share of state basic aid support, and as assessed valuation increased, state basic aid support decreased. Indeed, state policy intervention attempted to counter the disequalizing effects of property wealth by providing relatively greater support to low-wealth districts. The simple correlation between foundation aid and per-pupil assessed valuation was −.52 in 1979 and −.65 in 1991. Thus, in 1979, 27% of the variation in basic aid is explained by differences in assessed valuation (as per-pupil assessed valuation increases, basic aid decreases), whereas in 1991 42% of the variation is explained. On the basis of these results, we can conclude that state policy has indeed moved toward attenuating the relationship between property wealth and state foundation support. Similarly, if we examine the relationship between combined basic aid and local revenues on the one hand and per-pupil assessed valuation on the other, we find a similar decline over time in the significance of property wealth in determining school revenues. In 1979, the simple correlation between per-pupil revenue (basic aid) and local assessed value per pupil was .72, which means that 52% of the variation in revenue can be explained by differences in assessed valuation. By 1991, the correlation had dropped to .60, thereby reducing the explained variance in revenue associated with differences in wealth to 36%.

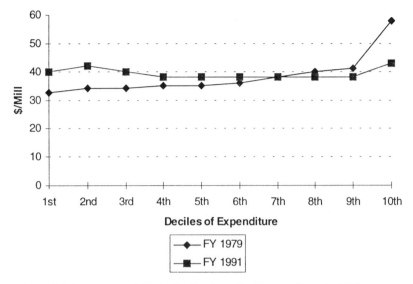

Figure 9.1. Revenues per Mill by Decile of Per-Pupil Expenditure (in 1979 Dollars)

Yet another way of assessing the relationship between property values, tax effort, and revenues is to look at per-pupil revenues by deciles of tax effort. Figure 9.1 shows the relationship between per-pupil state basic aid and local revenues and tax effort. If, at each decile of per-pupil expenditure, equal effort resulted in equal revenues, the line going across deciles of effort would be straight. The degree to which the line is not straight indicates levels of inequality of effort and shows, moreover, where in the distribution inequality occurs. As the figure shows, effort and yield are fairly equal between the 1st and 9th deciles: One mill of effort generates approximately $40 in revenue in 1991—increasing its value from about $32 per mill in 1979. It is not until the 10th decile of effort that the value of one mill of effort increases to about $43 in 1991. The kink in the line at the 10th decile indicates that state equalization efforts have not successfully neutralized the effects of property wealth at the 10th decile of student per-pupil funding. However, this fact raises again the issue of whether state policy should focus on leveling the slope of the line at the 10th decile or whether it should endeavor to straighten the line between the 1st and 10th deciles.

Table 9.3. Technical Equality Statistical Measures Compared (1979 and 1991), Local and State Basic Aid Revenues

Measure	1979	1991
Coefficient of variation	0.22	0.16
McCloone index	0.90	0.91
Gini coefficient	0.11	0.09
Federal range ratio	3.16	1.55
High/low ratio	4.16	2.55

SOURCE: Raw data provided by the Ohio Department of Education.

By the standard statistical measures of school finance equity, it can also be argued that the distribution of funding in Ohio school districts has improved somewhat but certainly has not worsened since the *Walter* decision in 1979. Table 9.3 displays the usual measures of equality.

On the basis of the 1979-1991 comparative data, it is reasonable to argue that state policy intervention did ameliorate fiscal conditions in low-wealth school districts. By increasing foundation support, the state was successful in reducing some of the fiscal disparities connected to differences in property wealth. Even so, disparities do exist. According to the McLoone index, in 1991 it would have taken 9% more money (about $270 million in basic aid) to bring districts that were below the median up to the state median. Similarly, although funding to the poorest districts grew at a faster rate than funding to the wealthiest districts, the disparity between mean per-pupil revenues in the first and fourth quartiles increased from $582 in 1979 to $629 in 1991. However, by relative measures, funding equity did not deteriorate over time, and, thus, by the standard imposed by the Supreme Court in *Walter*, it can be argued that the current school finance system in Ohio is constitutional.

Resource Allocation and Relative Deprivation

Whereas defendants focused on changes in the allocation of school resources in relationship to overall distribution over time, plaintiffs focused on disparities in resources between the poorest 50 and the richest 50 districts in the state.[3] Much of their testimony focused on the differences in revenues and resulting resource allocation between the 50 "low-capacity" and 50 "high-capacity" districts. According to the analysis for the plaintiffs, for 1980-1981, the 50 high-fiscal-capacity districts showed a mean per-pupil local revenue of $2,493, whereas the 50 low-fiscal-capacity districts raised only $597 per pupil. "By 1988 to 1989, the 50 high fiscal capacity school districts had increased their mean per-pupil revenue to $4,287 and the 50 low fiscal capacity school districts had increased their mean per-pupil local revenue to $617" (Alexander & Salmon, 1990, p. 16; it should be noted that these figures are unadjusted for inflation). Moreover, for the state as a whole, the mean per-pupil revenue was $1,255 for 1980-1981 and $1,660 for 1988-1989, an increase of $405 or 32.3%. Although the plaintiffs' analysis accurately points out that property values in low-assessed-valuation districts grow at a much slower rate than property values in high-assessed-valuation districts, it ignores the role of state policy in equalizing such differences. During the same period, state support of low-wealth districts increased by just over 88% in unadjusted dollars or 37% if adjusted to 1979 dollars. Over the same period, state support to the 50 high-wealth districts rose from $639 to $982. This represents a 54% increase in current dollars and a 12% increase in 1979 dollars. On the basis of the testimony of the plaintiffs' expert witnesses, the mean per-pupil difference in state and local funding in 1980-1981 was $1,063 when measured in 1979 dollars and $1,383 in 1988-1989, an increase of $320. The comparable figure for the high-wealth districts was $551, with $493 of that amount attributed to changes in local revenue, and $231 for the 50 low-wealth districts, of which $120 was attributable to local revenues.[4]

Focusing on the best and worst cases may be an effective legal strategy if for no other reason than its drama. However, such an approach may not be the best for fashioning state policy. In 1991, the 50 highest-wealth districts enrolled 5 percent of the state's students. In most analyses, and certainly as common practice in federal policy, the top 5% are excluded because they represent outliers in the distribution. A more reasonable and stable measure is to focus on the 90% of the distribution that contains the majority of students, rather than on the 5% at each end. Thus, if we look at the interquartile means for 1990-1991, the mean per-pupil state basic aid and local revenue in the highest-quartile assessed-valuation districts is $3,972 ($2,105 in 1979 dollars) and $3,042 for the lowest quartile ($1,612 in 1979 dollars)—a difference of $931, or $493 when adjusted for inflation. For 1979, those figures were $1,037 and $1,296—a difference of $259. Thus in real dollars the disparity between high- and low-wealth districts has increased by $234. Moreover, bringing all districts in the state to the average of the 50 high-wealth districts would cost an additional $3 billion. In 1991, that would have necessitated increasing basic aid allocation from about $2 billion to $5 billion, a 150% increase—not a likely scenario in today's political world.

District Effort and Fiscal Capacity

Plaintiffs' and defendants' arguments stayed the course in the debate over fiscal capacity and effort. Attorneys for the state focused their arguments on the five plaintiff districts that had benefited from state policy through the basic aid program and claimed that differences in revenues between plaintiff districts and the state average were the result of lower fiscal effort by plaintiff districts. Specifically, expert testimony for the state argued that plaintiff districts' tax effort generally lagged behind the state average and that the discrepancy between their effective tax rates and the state average local district tax rate had intensified over time. Two of the plaintiff districts taxed themselves less than the state effective millage mean in 1979. In 1992, four of five plaintiff districts taxed themselves less than the state effective mean millage rate. The dates are shown in Table 9.4. Expert witnesses also argued that all plaintiff districts had received revenue increases during the period from 1979 to 1992 that exceeded both Consumer Price Index (CPI) and School Price Index (SPI) growth. As the data in Table 9.4 indicate, the lowest 1992 per-pupil revenue plaintiff district (Northern Local) received sufficient added revenues between 1979 and 1992 to outdistance SPI-measured inflation by $486 per pupil. Youngstown City outdistanced inflation, as measured by SPI, by more than $1,000. (Gains in excess of SPI are expressed in 1992 dollars.)

Plaintiffs' experts continued their line of argument, which focused on differences between the state's 50 low- and 50 high-capacity districts. They offered as explanation for the plaintiff districts' below-state-average effort the fact that increased effort yielded so little additional revenues that they were simply discouraged from even trying. Again, plaintiffs argued principally on the basis of assessed

Table 9.4 Plaintiff District Comparisons With Ohio Revenue and Tax Effort Trends

Plaintiffs	Mean $/Pupil (State and Local)		% Change in 1979 Dollars	% Growth Above SPI[a]	$ Gain Above SPI[b]	Effective Mean Millage		$ Change Per Pupil at State Mean Millage Rate, 1992[c]
	1979	*1992*				*1979*	*1992*	
Dawson-Bryant	1121	1649	47	25	781	19.85	22.04	98
Southern Local	1195	1737	45	26	883	27.88	25.91	40
Northern Local	1034	1586	53	28	846	19.78	25.92	77
Lima City	1331	1983	49	26	975	30.05	24.93	67
Youngstown City	1684	2391	42	22	1008	32.0	41.92	240
State Mean						26.26	28.81	

SOURCE: Raw data provided by the Ohio Department of Education.
NOTE: All dollars are 1979 dollars unless noted otherwise. School Price Index deflator to convert 1992 to 1979 dollars is 0.469.
a. Plaintiff district's revenue growth in excess of SPI.
b. Revenue increase in excess of SPI in 1992 dollars.
c. Added property tax revenue is in 1992 dollars.

valuation and how those differences were manifested between the 59 poorest and wealthiest schools. Again, plaintiffs ignored or discounted the effects of state equalization efforts. They pointed out that in 1989 to 1989, one mill levied by the 50 high-fiscal-capacity school districts resulted in over $140 per pupil, whereas a similar levy for the 50 low-fiscal-capacity school districts raised less than $26 per pupil. At the extremes of the wealth continuum, they argued, the disparities were even greater. In the case of Huntington Local School District in Ross County, the poorest school district in Ohio, one mill of tax effort raised less than $15 per pupil, whereas the same tax effort for Cuyahoga Heights Local School District in Cuyahoga County, one of the wealthiest school districts, yielded $488 per pupil. These facts are accurate, but they ignore the fact that although in 1990-1991 Huntington generated only $483 of local revenues at a 31.7-mill tax rate (the state average millage rate for the year was 40), state basic aid was $1,939. In the same year, Cuyahoga generated $9,819 in local revenue at a 19.5-mill tax rate and received $43 per pupil in state basic aid. Huntington has a per-pupil assessed valuation of $24,000, whereas Cuyahoga's is $528,003.

There is no doubt that disparities in wealth exist across districts and that these disparities are caused by differences in property values. The real issue is how one is to think about the state's role in equalizing such disparities and what levels of inequality are tolerable. As in their earlier arguments, plaintiffs make their case at the extremes of the distribution. Cuyahoga is not the average district. It enrolls 763 students out of the state's 1.77 million—0.04%. Should state policy be fashioned around less than one tenth of 1% of students?

In areas of curriculum, also, plaintiffs focused on the differences between low- and high-wealth districts. Measuring in terms of advanced-placement courses, plaintiffs chose to look only at the five poorest districts and the five wealthiest districts. Predictably, the poor districts suffered by the comparison. The same was true for elective and prehonors courses in math, English, biology, and chemistry. By all comparisons, the five low-wealth districts did not match the high-wealth districts in advanced course offerings in foreign languages, mathematics, science, history, and social science. Not surprisingly, the number of students planning to attend college differed by district wealth. The trouble with these data is that the conclusions toward which they aim are misleading. As an abundance of social science research has shown, a number of intervening variables influence college attendance rates. The facts, as they are presented by plaintiffs' experts, ignore the effects of family socioeconomic status and peer group. By implication, plaintiffs argue that the complex factors that shape culture and different preferences for learning and attainment— professional, material, and cultural—would be obviated if differences in assessed valuation were equalized between rich and poor districts.

By less extreme measures, the wealth differences do not spur the same types of differences in resource allocation. Again, if districts in the bottom quartile of wealth are compared with districts in the top quartile of wealth, the disparities are attenuated to a more policy-amenable range. Table 9.5 displays the differences among first- and fourth-quartile districts as well as state averages on several variables.

Although disparities exist among high- and low-wealth districts, the quartile means do not suggest the levels of gross inequality portrayed by the plaintiffs. Differences among teacher salaries exist, but beginning salaries for teachers with bachelor's and master's

Table 9.5. Selected District Characteristics by District Assessed Valuation

District Expenditure	State Mean	First Quartile	Fourth Quartile
Beginning teacher salary with B.A.	$18,452	$17,946	$19,118
Beginning teacher salary with M.A.	$20,329	$19,667	$21,141
Median teacher salary	$31,030	$29,243	$33,357
Professional staff-pupil ratio	17	17	17
Pupil-teacher ratio	18	19	18
Teacher-administrator ratio	10	10	11
% of budget to salary	89	90	90
% of budget on materials	4	4	4
Median income	$23,407	$21,615	$25,925

SOURCE: Raw data provided by the Ohio Department of Education.
NOTE: Quartile values are interquartile means.

degrees are well within a standard deviation of the state mean and just under a standard deviation from the fourth-quartile salaries.

Finally, plaintiffs argued that the academic achievement of students in low-wealth districts was below that of students in high-wealth districts and attributed these differences to funding disparities (Conclusions of Law and Mem. at 468 [Fortune Tr. 3493; Pl. Ex. 306, 306A, 305]). Witnesses for the defense argued that no such relationship exists and, moreover, that social science research generally has been unable to find unambiguous linkages between educational expenditures and student achievement. Once students' socioeconomic status and school peer group and social composition are taken into account, district mean revenue differences do not explain differences in student achievement. Indeed, if one looks at the results of the state ninth-grade math and writing achievement tests, the mean scores of students across low- and high-wealth districts do not vary significantly. The scores easily fall within one standard deviation of one another.[5] Moreover, the relationship between student achievement in math and writing and a set of independent variables that measure school social composition, family socioeconomic status (SES), and school resource variables (including mean per-pupil expenditure) shows that the most significant determinants of student achievement are SES, peer group, and school social composition.[6] These findings hold, generally, for the state as a whole as well as for high- and low-wealth (first- and fourth-quartile) districts. Among districts in the first quartile of wealth, the only significant determinant (at the 95% confidence level) of writing achievement is the district dropout rate. For high-wealth districts, the percentage of AFDC families and median family income are significant, as is class size. For the state as a whole, AFDC, dropout rate, median family income, and median teacher salary are significant. Per-pupil revenue, however, is insignificant for all groups. Similarly, math achievement among first-quartile-wealth districts is influenced by the percentage of families in a district receiving AFDC and median family income. For high-wealth districts it is also AFDC, median family income, and dropout rate. When all districts are included in the analysis, math achievement is influenced by AFDC, the percentage of minorities in a district, the dropout rate, and the pupil-teacher ratio.

On the basis of the state's data, it is impossible to conclude that there is any systematic relationship between mean per-pupil expenditure and student achievement in math and writing. The district charac-teristics variables that are positively related to achievement are dis-tributed differently according to district wealth. As the data above indicate, there is little difference in class size between low- and high-wealth districts. Nor is there a consistent relationship between median teacher salary and achievement. Indeed, the only consistent indicators are those of SES and school composition. The purpose of the discus-sion here is not to argue that resources do not matter or that there is not some mix of resources in which various district characteristics conflate to shape student achievement. Rather, it is to question the plaintiffs' and subsequently the court's blanket assertions that "based upon a reasonable degree of statistical probability and certainty, regu-lar instructional expenditures are associated with school perform-ance, as defined by a percent of students passing the ninth grade proficiency tests" (Conclusions of Law and Mem. at 468). When expert witnesses for the plaintiffs argue that "school districts in the State of Ohio with expenditures in the top 30% have, by subject matter, higher levels of students succeeding or passing the proficiency tests and scoring satisfactorily on achievement scores" (Conclusions of Law and Mem. at 460), they are correct in their statement of the facts. However, their argument is fundamentally specious. If their conclu-sions are correct, they have succeeded in establishing a relationship between school resource allocation and student achievement that has eluded a generation of social scientists.

School Finance in Ohio
in the Shadow of *De Rolph*

The court uncritically accepted the plaintiffs' expert witnesses' testimony. "Can a system that has nearly 17,000 seniors who have not as yet passed the ninth-grade proficiency test consider itself thorough and efficient?" asked Judge Lewis, the trial judge in *De Rolph* (Conclusions of Law and Mem. at 468). It is a rhetorical question, and asking it unleashes a rush of evidence to support the plaintiffs' claims that the system of school funding in Ohio fails to live up to its constitutional mandate. According to the findings of the court, the equality of Ohio's system of funding ranks third worst in the nation behind Missouri and Alaska. Due to poor test scores, 48 districts qualified for intervention from the state education department staff. According to a state survey, school districts needed an additional $328 million for asbestos removal as well as $153 million for handicapped access. The court found that in one district some students were educated in former coal bins. In another, students had no restrooms in the school building itself. In one county, "The only library is an abandoned library truck; the band practices in the kitchen and plays in the cafeteria during lunch" (Conclusions of Law and Mem. at 474). Some buildings lacked running water. One local trustee opined that his animals were housed better than the district's children. Conditions in plaintiffs' schools are such that they cannot hire teachers, buy paper, repair buildings, or purchase equipment.

> While some of the plaintiff school districts must ration paper, paper clips and use out of date textbooks, our wealthier districts are able to provide violin cases [with or without violins, one wonders] in the second grade and have contests through computer networking, allowing their students to compete directly against children from Finland, Germany and other American cities. (Conclusions of Law and Mem. at 475)

According to Judge Lewis, "This Court saw grown men and women cry as they explained the conditions and situations in which some of the youth of this State are educated" (Conclusions of Law and Mem. at 473).

The emotional charge of such an argument is difficult to counter. Perhaps that explains the popularity of Kozol's *Savage Inequalities*

(1991). Evidence presented during the trial and in pretrial depositions argues emotionally and persuasively for children in the worst funded Ohio school districts. The court, like Kozol, chose to look at the best and worst of districts, and such comparisons inevitably lead to dismal conclusions regarding school funding disparities and the differences in educational resources available to students. Even in a state like California, which has putatively the most equitable school funding system, a compelling case could be made for inequality if one were to turn the analytic spotlight on the state's richest and poorest districts.

For state policy makers, the court's conclusions are troubling. The court, in basing its Conclusions of Law on plaintiffs' testimony, affirmed a definition of school finance equity that was based on shaky evidence and questionable social science research. In reaching its conclusions, the court saw a glass that was half-empty rather than half-full. In doing so, the court accepted evidence of resource disparity among districts that was based on conditions at the extremes of the distribution. Finance distribution data, as noted earlier, compared the 50 poorest and 50 wealthiest (in terms of their assessed valuation) districts. Evidence on curriculum and program offerings was based on the five poorest and five wealthiest districts.

In his Conclusions of Law, Judge Lewis listed 24 findings of harm to plaintiffs. Among them were the conclusions that the system of funding did not provide sufficient revenue to afford an adequate education program, that state funds were insufficient to cover the actual costs of providing an education in any school district (presumably this included the wealthiest districts whose per-pupil expenditures exceeded $9,000), and that the system relied on local property wealth as a determinant of revenues. He concluded also that teachers were unable to carry out their duties and responsibilities as teachers, thus denying students in their charge the educational opportunity to which they were entitled. On the basis of expert testimony, the judge concluded that fiscal disparity among districts was attributable to differences in property wealth. In its findings, the court ignored the fact that statewide only 16% of the variation in per-pupil expenditure was attributable to differences in assessed valuation of property. For districts in the first quartile of property wealth, the explained variation was 1%, whereas for districts in the fourth quartile, it was 16%. Generally, the court found that the system of funding public education in Ohio was neither "thorough nor efficient" and therefore deprived children of their fundamental rights in violation of its constitutional mandate.

Judge Lewis went on to define the components of a constitutionally acceptable system of school funding. It is one in which the state takes ultimate responsibility for the system of public schools and ensures that it is thorough and efficient throughout the geographic area of the state. It is also the responsibility of the state to ensure that children, regardless of where they live, are provided with "free schools on an equal basis, which includes equitable and adequate educational opportunities, educational materials, equipment and supplies to all children" (Conclusions of Law and Mem. at 460). The court then defined *adequate educational opportunities* as a long list of academic, personal, vocational, physical, and extracurricular desiderata. Among the outcomes was the mandate for "sufficient facilities, supplies and instruction to enable both female and male students to compete equally within their own schools as well as schools across the State of Ohio and worldwide in both academic and extracurricular activities" (Conclusions of Law and Mem. at 460).

In reaching its decision, the court rejected the relevance of the Supreme Court's *Walter* decision, and with it defense arguments that *Walter* was binding upon the court in *De Rolph*. The court noted that numerous changes had come about since that decision and argued that the doctrine of *stare decisis* was not binding in the present case inasmuch as the *Walter* decision was confined to the facts before the Supreme Court at the time of its decision, and that because the facts had changed, they were not binding upon the trial court. It can be argued, however, that the facts in *Walter* and the legal precedent they established were precisely what the trial court should have addressed rather than rejected. The facts are particularly important *because* provisions of law have changed since *Walter*, and therefore, how those changes in law have reshaped the current system in relation to the facts in the prior case becomes significant.

As noted above, the court rejected defense arguments that emphasized the lessening of fiscal disparities among districts since 1979 and, most important, the state's systematic role in attenuating those disparities. Instead, the court based its findings on evidence that was partly anecdotal and partly reliant on weak social science methodology.

State Policy Implications of De Rolph

If the state were to take the trial court at its word, Ohio would have to revamp its entire system of elementary and secondary public education. Policy makers, like the court, would have to redefine *educational opportunity* in terms of educational outcomes. Such redefinition carries implications for new standards of accountability that include statewide standards for curriculum, instruction, extracurricular activities, equipment, and facilities, and assessments to measure how well schools attain prescribed standards. The court stated that local control without discretionary funds was a myth and affirmed that the state's school system was not made up of a number of local districts but was a single state system.[7] As such, *De Rolph* can be construed as a mandate for a state system of funding much like California's. An important difference between the *De Rolph* standard and California's *Serrano* standard is that the latter ignores the issue of adequacy. The size of the school finance pie is unimportant as a constitutional matter so long as the pie is distributed equally. The trial court in *De Rolph* specified not only the size of the pie but its contents. By joining student outcomes with finance, the Ohio court adopted a standard similar to the one articulated by courts in Alabama and Kentucky. In both of those states, the entire system of education was found to be inadequate because of disparities not just in funding but also in student attainment.

At the current stage of litigation in *De Rolph,* the state has several options. One is to appeal the trial court's decision. Given the different political context of appellate court and ultimately the Supreme Court, from the trial court in Perry County, one of the plaintiff districts, the trial court's decision could be overturned. Another option, one that does not preclude the former, is for state policy makers to effect remedies to *De Rolph*. A solution to that end, and one that might require the least modification of the current system, would be to address the issue of adequacy in terms of student proficiency by using the ninth-grade proficiency exams as the standard of adequacy. Policy makers might then establish a 70% pass rate on the proficiency test as a minimum standard of attainment and then determine what level of resources districts require to meet that minimum standard.

The larger question that looms over the trial court decision is the level of state funding that would be required to comply with the various provisions in *De Rolph*. In 1991, Ohio spent about $6.7 billion on K-12 education. Of that, roughly $3.7 billion came from local revenues. It would take a 9%—approximately $270 million—increase in state support to bring all students up to the state per-pupil median.[8] How much new money would be required to raise all students to a specified level of proficiency and how willing state residents would be to pay higher taxes to accomplish that are questions that will most likely be answered in the political arena.

Notes

1. Section 2, Article 6, of the Ohio Constitution states that "the General Assembly shall make such provisions, by taxation, or otherwise, as, with the income arising from the school trust fund, will secure a thorough and efficient system of common school throughout the state."

2. Rather than using the federal range, which is often used in school finance analyses, the defense used what it called the "modified federal range." This excluded the top 5% of students in the highest-wealth districts or highest-revenue districts, depending upon the analysis. The range included districts at the bottom of the distribution. The rationale for using such a range is that although districts at the bottom may be statistical outliers, policy should address their conditions. Moreover, the fiscal problems associated with districts at the bottom of the distribution are amenable to policy intervention. Funding issues associated with districts at the top of the scale are not, at least not in any way that is politically realistic.

3. Expert witnesses for the plaintiffs also looked at two periods, 1980-1981 and 1988-1989, but it is not clear why these two academic years were chosen. If the point of the exercise was to assess change from the *Walter* decision, 1979 would have been a more logical choice because it would approximate conditions more accurately (Alexander & Salmon, 1990).

4. It is unclear from the Alexander & Salmon (1990) analysis (noted above) what measures of state support plaintiffs are using, whether only basic aid or other state funding sources as well.

5. On the state-developed achievement test for ninth-grade math, the state mean is 59.5 ($SD = 14.1$); for schools in the first quartile of property wealth, the mean is 56 ($SD = 13.7$); and for schools in the fourth quartile of property wealth, the mean is 63.4 ($SD = 14.2$). For writing, the state mean is 69.7 ($SD = 14.6$); for the first quartile of property wealth, the mean is 66.6 ($SD = 13.0$); and for the fourth quartile of property wealth, the mean is 73.1 ($SD = 13$).

6. Data used in this analysis were raw data provided by the Ohio State Department of Education. They are district aggregate data and therefore mask school-level differences. The purpose in using them is not social science research, but policy. Therefore, the principal inference is that no positive relationship between student achievement and resource inputs can be posited on the basis of these data. The student composition variables are the district-wide percentage of students whose families receive AFDC, district dropout rate, and percentage of district-wide enrollment made up of minority

students. School characteristics variables are district-wide mean class size, district mean teacher salary, and district mean per-pupil local and state basic aid revenues. Family socioeconomic variable is school district family median income.

7. According to the court, "Local control without discretionary funds is a myth and does not justify the vast disparities in educational funding and educational opportunity throughout this State. There is only one system of education in this State and that is a state system" (Conclusions of Law and Mem. at 470).

8. The calculation is based on the McLoone index. Because the index measures the disparity between actual funding and funding if all students were at the median, it can be expressed as a percent difference between current and median funding levels.

References

Alexander, K., & Salmon, R. (1990). *Fiscal equity of the Ohio system of public schools: A report of the Coalition of Rural and Appalachian Schools.* Unpublished manuscript, Virginia Technical Institute.

Board of Education of the City of Cincinnati v. Walter, 390 N.E.2d 813, 58 Ohio St.2d 368 (1979).

De Rolph v. State of Ohio (C. P. Perry County 1994).

Kozol, J. (1991). *Savage inequalities: Children in America's schools.* New York: Crown.

Ohio Department of Education. (1993). *The Ohio law for state support of public schools: Biennium 1992-1993.* Columbus, OH: Author.

Serrano v. Priest, 5 Cal.3d 584, 487 P.2d 1241 (Super. Ct. Los Angeles County, CA, 1971).

TEN

Resource Allocation Patterns Within School Finance Litigation Strategies

R. CRAIG WOOD

JEFFREY MAIDEN

Education finance litigation has traditionally been the arena of competing political and social interests and pressures. It represents a significant area of education finance in terms of both scholarly endeavor and public policy. Although few education finance researchers specialize in this area, their impact on the distribution of scarce state and local moneys for public education has been overwhelming.

During the past several years, education finance litigation has focused on traditional measures of equity as well as how educational dollars were spent within school districts. Generally successful litigation reflects sound legal strategies, knowledge of education finance research, and expert data analysis (Wood, 1992a, 1992b). School finance analyses address the effects of the distribution of revenues among districts and individual schools, rather than issues related to the simple distribution of monetary resources. The questions surrounding these issues are complex and multifaceted. The most basic questions concern whether revenues are distributed equitably among schools or, more specifically, classrooms or programs.

Present Education Finance Dilemmas

Historically, within-district equity issues were highly interwoven with the issues of desegregation and the presence of suspect classes of schoolchildren (Camp, Thompson, & Crain, 1990). Early cases such as *Hobson v. Hansen* (1966) have perhaps always provided a methodology applicable to certain education finance equity cases. Although these issues are outside the confines of this discussion, the methodology of examining resources, professional staffs, programmatic opportunities, and other resource allocation decisions is still important.

Plaintiffs must demonstrate that a general aid formula is inequitable in order to show that it fails at the school/classroom level. If they cannot demonstrate this, then the court must accept that the formula is equitable. If it is equitable, any inequities that may exist at the school/classroom level are not a function of the aid distribution formula, and the state can argue that such inadequacies and inequities are largely a local function.

In effect, plaintiffs must make a twofold argument: (a) The general aid formula is inequitable, and (b) as a result, the formula creates unequal educational opportunities across the state. If the first argument is lost, then the second cannot follow without admission that the local school districts are at fault. If the general state aid distributional formula were judged as acceptable, then the disparate results are essentially self-created by the plaintiff school districts, and serious questions must be raised as to why these differences exist.

To date, limited research has been conducted on the question of within-district equity. Within-district student needs appear to be a function of a number of variables, including the size of the schools; the number of students eligible for limited resources; student aptitude, achievement, socioeconomic background, and transience; and the number of mainstreamed students. Schroeder's (1987) research indicated that in the one school district studied, four of five of the neediest schools received the lowest fiscal resources. This research raises basic questions regarding the allocation of resources at the local school district level.

When school districts allege, as they generally do in filing complaints, that the lack of educational opportunity is a direct and attributable result of the state aid distribution formula, states must be prepared to examine what is identified in the effective-schools research as the "enacted curriculum"—that is, the actual curriculum delivered in the classroom. They must also consider the allocation of curriculum-related resources by each school district and examine measures of teaching strategies actually used in each school (Porter, 1993).

Plaintiffs demonstrate disparity by comparing expenditure patterns of the highest-spending school district with those of the lowest-spending school district. Such disparity, from the plaintiffs' point of view, demonstrates an unacceptable state aid distributional formula. But if the formula were operationalized equitably for the vast majority of school districts, it is acceptable. The plaintiffs constantly search for outliers to demonstrate their position. From the state's point of view, the solution is to deal with the outliers and not to declare the entire distribution system as unacceptable. Often the few outliers are districts that are atypical of the distribution pattern.

Although the plaintiffs constantly address disparity, they seldom mention the vertical equity adjustments found in various state aid distributional formulas. In discussing greater equity, they present methodologies that are focused solely on horizontal equity issues. Plaintiffs have great difficulty accepting the concept that equity can be achieved only when legitimate needs are met within a given state general aid plan. The simple fact that disparity of expenditures (or revenues) exists does not demonstrate that a state distribution system is inequitable. Not to acknowledge legitimate variables that lead to vertical equity adjustments is to dismiss all vertical equity issues.

Plaintiffs have presented many theories before the courts. Although these have varied greatly, they nonetheless have certain common features. In fact, many of the complaints are remarkably similar. For example, from these complaints one could assume that minimum foundation and resource accessibility programs (Thompson, Wood, & Honeyman, 1994) are so similar as to suffer from the same flaws. Often the complaints compare horizontal equity issues without mention of the legitimate variations that do exist among school districts. In states with a high level of state fiscal assistance, plaintiffs' arguments are either that the general aid formula does not reflect variations due to much-needed vertical equity adjustments or that the overall state aid is inadequate. Thus it becomes apparent that there are no definitive standards by which formulas are acceptable to those who question the distribution of moneys within a given state.

Plaintiffs' arguments concerning the adequacy of a general state aid distribution formula raise a fundamental question concerning the role of the state. An evaluation of a state aid distribution formula must examine the structure of the formula without regard to the amounts of money being appropriated. This effectively says that if the analysis demonstrates that the formula operates correctly so that differences are not, as plaintiffs always claim, an undue function of adverse formula design, the discussion concerning differences in expenditure on pupils is fundamentally irrelevant because these differences will not be a function of the formula itself (Thompson, Wood, & Honeyman, 1994). This is a most powerful methodology in that the differences that may appear must be largely those that are created by local school districts.

Of course, it can be argued that the role of a formula should be to prevent certain local school districts from spending beyond what other school districts spend. There is no more fundamental question before the courts. Operationally, the plaintiffs' arguments can only be engaged only by lowering the expenditures of a minority of districts and redistributing the relatively minuscule fiscal resources obtained to the remaining school districts. Such remedies are fiscally irresponsible and pander to the lowest common political denominator within a state. They yield no discernable results other than harming public education. In many areas of the United States, curtailing expenditures of high-spending school districts will only drive the more affluent from supporting public education. Evidence is very clear that no new significant moneys can be generated from such plans. Thus the overall adequacy of state support for education will be reduced, less support for public schools will be generated, and the public schools increasingly will be educating only the poorest within our society.

It is all too popular to claim that the pattern of state aid distribution is seriously flawed because of the heavy reliance on the property tax and the uneven distribution of the wealth of the state. But it is a basic concept of American society that property tax wealth, like all other forms of wealth, is unevenly distributed within a given state. If the formula were designed properly, the relative wealth of a given community should have little, if any, effect. The fact that local taxes are based on a property tax system is not a flaw. Nonetheless, one must wonder whether the plaintiffs are questioning the formula or the property tax system itself. In reality, many complainants would do better to focus on proper and uniform distribution assessment of real property. If property wealth were not assessed properly, the issue is one of property tax administration, not the school finance distribution formula.

Table 10.1. Analysis of Expenditures per Pupil and Mill Values per Pupil (in Dollars) for a Matched Set of Plaintiff and Nonplaintiff Districts

Group	Mean	SD	Minimum	Maximum	Range	Restricted Range
All Districts						
Exp./pupil	4,537.31	2,178.50	1,832.78	16,570.70	14,737.00	6,570.50
Mill value/pupil	44.84	67.80	0.26	911.45	911.20	129.50
Plaintiffs						
Exp./pupil	5,407.50	2,426.50	2,562.31	14,014.90	11,452.70	6,820.00
Mill value/pupil	52.36	44.58	6.912	230.62	223.70	150.00
Nonplaintiffs						
Exp./pupil	4,388.40	2,100.20	1,832.78	16,750.69	14,737.91	6,625.00
Mill value/pupil	43.56	70.94	0.264	911.45	911.20	129.45
Matched Nonplaintiffs						
Exp./pupil	5,440.02	2,691.00	2,020.35	14,344.35	12,324.00	8,960.00
Mill value/pupil	45.77	36.93	0.26	183.58	183.32	190.50

SOURCE: Wood, Thompson, Honeyman, & Miller, 1992; see also Honeyman, Miller, Wood, & Thompson, 1992, p. 16.

Remedy for faulty property tax administration is relatively easy. A number of methodologies are available, from simply requiring and monitoring the assessed valuation practices in every property tax jurisdiction to designing and utilizing an adjusted assessed valuation system that simply indexes the property tax rates or valuations. A number of states have used these methodologies for many years.

Notwithstanding plaintiffs' arguments, the reliance on the property tax system for state aid distribution may be judged acceptable on the basis of an in-depth analysis. For example, a selected part of such an analysis of expenditure data appears in Table 10.1, which reflects results and correlation analysis on a matched set of plaintiff and nonplaintiff districts. Further analyses would test the assumptions stemming from the resource accessibility data and thus the examination of wealth neutrality. A complete analysis is beyond the limits of this chapter, although it does indicate that the overall state education finance formula is wealth and tax neutral (Thompson et al., 1994).

Thus plaintiffs' arguments about lack of wealth neutrality in state education finance formulas may well be misdirected. Plaintiffs, in many instances, would be better advised to address the perceived problems of assessed valuations to include such issues as the reduction of the assessment levels by the state, the exemption of certain classes of property from taxation, fundamentally inequitable tax assessments among tax jurisdictions, and problems related to agricultural use valuations. All of these issues may compound the disparity of local education revenue inequities among school districts. In one current complaint, the plaintiffs allege that revenue disparities are based on disparate levels of wealth among school districts. However, in this instance, school districts have unlimited authority to increase local taxes for the purposes of the general fund. In addition, both parties have acknowledged that the property tax assessment system is not uniform.

In many complaints, the plaintiffs allege that the state aid distribution formula is unconstitutional because of heavy reliance on local wealth to support education. It would follow from this view that in states that do not heavily rely on local property taxes, distribution formulas are, by definition, acceptable, but certain states are engaged in litigation concerning the formula despite the absence of property tax reliance.

It is clear that the trend of challenging state education finance distribution systems will continue. Regardless of the nature of the formula, the percentage of state aid, or the distributional pattern, the lawsuits commonly involve challenges to the state aid distributional systems based on alleged violations of the state's education clause and the equal-protection clause.

Because data may generally not be available on the school level, the state's defense often centers on the following comparisons:

1. Comparisons between plaintiff and nonplaintiff districts
2. Comparisons of plaintiffs to the state as a whole
3. Comparisons of plaintiff to nonplaintiff districts by selected variables

Strategies of Plaintiffs

The most common strategies employed by the plaintiffs are arguments involving the fundamentality of education as dictated by the language of the state constitution, the lack of wealth neutrality in the distribution of funding, the insufficiency of funding from the state to ensure compliance with certain educational criteria, the lack of equalization of funding beyond the general formula, the lack of a dimension for vertical equity, the lack of taxpayer equity, and in some instances the alleged variations in education program quality resulting from funding variations. In almost every case, plaintiffs examine the distributional formula on a school-district-by-school-district basis.

The state is in partnership with legislatively created school districts, and school funding distribution formulas are designed to aid school districts. The partnerships will vary greatly, from highly state-centered programs to highly locally centered programs, and each presents a unique set of variables, operations, and philosophies. Regardless, state aid distribution formulas are generally not designed to aid individual schools, although such is certainly implied by the nature of the formulas.

Thus, when the parties examine how moneys are being spent in the individual schools, several questions must be addressed and sufficiently answered to the satisfaction of the court:

- How are revenues being distributed to individual schools?
- Are revenues that are distributed to local schools distributed in such a manner as to maximize the efficiency of the educational system within each school district?
- On what basis have central school offices made decisions to distribute revenues?
- What is the basis for offering programmatic opportunities in each school?

Overriding these previous questions are questions concerning

- How the distribution formula causes these inequities
- How plaintiff districts are disenfranchised by the distributional formula

The fundamental question is that of resources and expenditures at the school level, placing the burden on the plaintiffs to demonstrate that the state distribution formula is the root cause of these disparities and that district funds are distributed and allocated equitably to each school building.

The availability of data determines much of the nature of the discussion. If data are not readily available on a school-by-school basis, the plaintiffs tend to rely heavily on anecdotal testimony by school practitioners. Such testimony, though on occasion offering

helpful insights, is largely nonreplicative. Local school superintendents often explain the dire needs of their district, yet have great
difficulty in presenting any evidence of how specific programs have
suffered and under cross-examination are unable to say to the court
that any child is receiving an inadequate education by their professional standards.

Overall, several questions, on both a district level and a school level,
may be presented to investigate the claims of the plaintiffs (Wood &
Thompson, 1993a):

- What are the distributional characteristics of the state aid formula
  concerning plaintiffs' grievances regarding the equality of educational
  dollars?
- What are the distributional characteristics of the state aid formula
  concerning the plaintiffs' grievances regarding equality of taxation for
  education?
- On the basis of the results of the first two questions, what is finally the
  determination of the actual merits of plaintiffs' grievances in the context
  of measurable equity within the state school aid formula?

Often plaintiffs raise issues based on various state constitutional
provisions requiring uniform taxation. Generally, plaintiffs allege that
legislatures created school districts that have a wide variance of
wealth subject to taxation. The plaintiffs' claims follow a national
pattern of school finance litigation by attacking the uniform and equal
taxation provision commonly found in state constitutions. Plaintiffs
claim that any differences in tax rates have both de facto and de jure
negative effects on children's educational opportunity because taxpayers in different school tax jurisdictions will pay taxes at different
levels with no assurance of exactly equal educational opportunities
for unequal tax dollars levied. Generally, plaintiffs claim, in effect, that
the state aid distributional formula violates the provisions of these
applicable constitutional requirements because school districts do not
levy identical tax rates and because tax yields on each mill of tax effort
differ among the various school districts in a given state (Wood &
Thompson, 1993a).

These claims present an interesting dilemma for the parties involved. If educational opportunity were judged to be equal, would
the then-nonuniform tax rates be determined to be acceptable? For
example, if a state distributional system were equitable, under a

normal foundation plan, the state would be assuming much greater fiscal responsibility in the poorest school district than in the wealthiest school district, but the tax rates would be significantly different. Significant tax effort in the wealthiest school district could not be achieved without a form of recapture. This would be true even in the face of a very high level of state fiscal support. Only a statewide uniform tax rate could generate the remedy to satisfy the plaintiffs' demands, and only a tax rate levied or enforced by the state with a recapture provision could generate a uniform tax rate. The fact that there are unequal tax bases that vary from school district to school district would always generate nonuniform levels of effort.

Although the argument is straightforward, the only remedy is to completely redesign the manner of generating local taxes in support of education. In reality, the alternatives are limited either to having a single tax jurisdiction or to setting every local tax rate at a given point, as dictated by the state, with all excess moneys reverting to the state for redistribution.

Although wealth neutrality is given attention in many of the complaints, another issue addressed is the insufficiency of revenues provided by the state. Generally, the allegation is that state funding is insufficient to enable some or all districts to meet accreditation standards or educational mandates established at the state level.

As an overall concept, the issue before the court is whether the plaintiff districts are significantly different from the nonplaintiff districts. That is, the plaintiff districts must be able to demonstrate harm—specifically, via the state aid distribution formula. But a careful analysis of education finance data often reveals that the school districts that may be negatively affected are quite few and are statistical outliers. If that were the case, the state should deal with such outliers by making special adjustments or allowing them to function in a different financial capacity—that is, making a separate state aid support tier given the unique circumstances of the affected school district.

Nonequalization of Areas
Outside the Basic Program

Plaintiffs in some instances argue the lack of equalization of funding areas outside the basic support program. This argument typically holds that although the basic formula may be equalizing, many categorical or special areas are not equalized by the state, allegedly adding to constitutional deficiencies. One complaint contests the lack of equalization of categorical funding, which further widens interdistrict funding disparities. Another cites several areas not equalized by the state, including capital facilities, teacher retirement, social security, and unemployment costs.

Vertical Equity

Some state funding systems are accused of failing to recognize the vertical equity principles of unequal treatment of unequals. These systems allegedly did not make provisions for additional levels of funding in the face of greater needs.

One complainant claimed that higher levels of expenditures were needed in the large urban schools because of the higher costs associated with urban areas. Although this argument may be valid, it is interesting to note that in another state the complainant alleged that rural districts needed higher levels of expenditures because of higher costs associated with rural areas. Although diseconomies of scale have been demonstrated within the research literature and are applicable to both groups of school districts, it is interesting that the plaintiffs did not suggest the other side of the equation (Thompson et al., 1994). In one state, a complainant requested the court to include cost-of-living differences in the formula as well as student differences. Yet in another state, a highly equitable distributional formula with significant adjustments to allow for cost-of-living issues and sparsity-of-population issues, as well as a highly sophisticated weighted pupil mechanism, was still attacked as inadequate. Thus the evidence again indicates that regardless of the attributes of state distributional formulas, they will continue to come under attack.

Increasing Funding Variations

Some complainants claim that funding variations have increased in recent years or that a formula has not been fully funded by the legislature. In many states, the overall state support for all governmental services has declined due to the recession as well as tax restriction movements. State aid to support public education in many states is somewhat elastic due to the reliance on income and sales taxes. Thus, in periods of economic recession, the state's overall financial resources decline, along with state support to all governmental services. Given this reality, the only remedy would be a court-ordered judgment that the state could not reduce state aid to public education regardless of the overall economy or other exogenous fiscal variables. This hardly appears to be a wise public policy, and its success appears unlikely even in the most activist of courts.

Disparity of Resources

Although the aforementioned strategies are employed to challenge state education finance distribution systems, by far the most important strategy focuses on the effects of an allegedly inequitable distribution. Virtually all recent complaints include a discussion of programmatic variations that are said to result from a constitutionally deficient funding system. These variations include both variations in school input variables, such as student-teacher ratios and advanced-placement course offerings, and variations in outcomes, such as results on standardized test scores.

Complainants discuss, for example, variations in the quality of teaching staffs, in the delivery of education services, in equipment, and in facilities. Other complainants provide descriptions of differences in student-teacher ratios, variations in teacher turnover rates, differences in the levels of teacher experience and levels of training, and differences in computer facilities. In addition, they claim more restricted curricula among districts with lower property values. They cite the existence of inferior facilities, textbooks, and library facilities, as well as higher staff turnover in poorer districts. Although there are certainly differences in a variety of measurements among school districts, the analysis is often anecdotal in nature, testimonial in presentation, and difficult to examine, replicate, or verify beyond individual professional views.

For example, often complainants assert that lower-wealth districts are prone to have lower average teacher salaries. However, careful statistical examination may yield insightful explanations that are perfectly consistent with vertical equity adjustments. In other cases, complaints allege that urban areas have higher per-pupil costs. If the state allows higher state aid as an adjustment for the cost of living, either implicitly or explicitly, then teacher salaries, as a reflection of the higher costs of education, should be higher. This issue is further exacerbated in those states that have allowed the collective bargaining process to exist in local school districts. Thus to allow collective bargaining will tend to create a degree of disparity by virtue of the inherent process. Generally, urban areas have more sophisticated teacher bargaining units, and thus higher salaries and fringe benefits tend to follow. The issue is whether the distributional formula created this disparity. Again, careful and sophisticated analysis of education finance data tends to demolish these simplistic arguments.

Effective-Schools Research

Recent complaints have examined spending education dollars at the building level. Plaintiffs focus on programmatic opportunities and the resultant expenditure pattern. They argue that all failures of the public educational system are directly linked to the distributional formula, by virtue of the fact that any remedy will ultimately be formula driven or derived.

Thus state defendants examine disparities and analyze whether these are the result of the general aid distribution formula. When the plaintiffs present their anecdotal evidence, as described and discussed here, the state defendants need to pursue an in-depth analysis of what actually occurs in the school districts and in particular in the schools in question.

Effective-schools research offers a useful approach to examining the relationship between inputs and results. Unlike the classical productivity analysis, it generally does not focus on dollar inputs as part of the investigation. Rather, it identifies, on the basis of qualitative methods, certain organizational features that characterize effective schools (Thompson et al., 1994).

In the majority of effective-schools studies, the schools identified as effective were those that demonstrated a high degree of educational output given limited inputs. These schools served largely urban, minority, and lower socioeconomic communities, meaning that a high level of fiscal resources was not available to support education relative to wealthier areas. Yet they were noteworthy for possessing extraordinary student achievement, as demonstrated by the results of standardized achievement tests.

On the basis of the results of these studies, characteristics possessed by effective schools may be enumerated. According to a summary by Edmonds (1979), effective schools have a climate in which all instructional personnel are instructionally effective for all pupils. Further, good administrative leadership is common and can be identified. These schools are quite concerned that students not be allowed to "fall between the cracks." In addition, they possess an atmosphere that is orderly, but not rigid. Their overall goal is to ensure that students acquire basic skills. Fiscal resources at the district level are focused on expenditures directly connected to teaching and learning. Finally, effective schools frequently monitor student progress.

These issues may be demonstrated in several ways—for example, comparing class sizes of the plaintiff districts to class sizes in the nonplaintiff districts. If observations on class size can be coupled with the number and distribution of demographic variables related to disadvantaged children in individual schools, then the implications become apparent. If, in fact, the plaintiff school districts are able to show to the court's satisfaction that many factors are beyond the direct control of the plaintiffs, then another picture may emerge.

When these issues become compounded by other disadvantages children may face due to the demographics of economic and social ills, the challenge in providing an equal and excellent education becomes formidable. In rich and poor districts alike, the only means by which districts can hope to offset any of these conditions, external to the school, is to structure the learning environment carefully via various artificial mechanisms (Thompson, Wood, & Honeyman, 1992). For school districts with higher percentages of disadvantaged children, the importance of reducing class size and providing additional academic and social assistance and other fiscal resources becomes critical (Wood & Honeyman, 1991).

Other characteristics of effective schools have been attributed to the presence of (a) principals who possess a unitary vision with regard to the improvement of student learning and (b) teachers who possess similar goals (Rosenholtz, 1985). Effective schools reflect "tight coupling" rather than "loose coupling" in terms of the administrative structure. In addition, principals in identified effective schools convey the concept that teachers can positively affect student achievement. Effective schools have teachers who demonstrate a large degree of commitment, and these teacher efforts are linked to specific outcomes.

Researchers note greater "professional" interaction among teachers in effective schools and more frequent principal-staff interactions specifically addressing increased achievement. Effective schools also have fewer interruptions to the "flow of teaching" and fewer situations extraneous to the teaching and learning process. They reflect a sense of ownership and participation in decision making throughout the school. Finally, they encourage ongoing skill acquisition by classroom teachers and reflect norms of continuous improvement for all professional staff.

Effective-schools research can be a powerful tool of those defending the state distribution formulas against generalized litigation. Certainly, it may be pointed out that poor urban schools facing extraordinarily poor economic conditions may nevertheless produce quality educational programs.

Conclusions

Education finance litigation has historically focused on the distribution of state aid to school districts. This focus will continue and, in many instances, be joined by a focus on exactly how school districts spend money within individual schools. Such data may help or harm plaintiffs' position, depending on the quality and robustness of those data. Much of the discussion will be a function of what data are available from the state as a whole, as well as from individual schools. In the absence of quantitative data, discussion will depend primarily on qualitative case studies that are largely nonreplicative and unscientific. It is reasonable to project that individual school data will add to both the complexity and the clarity of the issues before the courts concerning the effects of systems of financing public education.

References

Camp, W. E., Thompson, D. C., & Crain, J. A. (1990). Within-district equity: Desegregation and microeconomic analysis. In J. Underwood (Ed.), *The impacts of litigation and legislation on public school finance* (pp. 273-292). New York: Ballinger.

Edmonds, R. (1979). Effective schools for the urban poor. *Educational Leadership, 37*(1), 15-24.

Hobson v. Hansen, 252 F. Supp. 4 (1966).

Honeyman, D. S., Miller, M. D., Wood, R. C., and Thompson, D. C. (1992). *The study of resource accessibility, wealth neutrality, and state yield in* Montana Rural Education Association v. State. Gainesville, FL: Wood, Thompson & Associates, Inc.

Porter, A. C. (1993). *Defining and measuring opportunity to learn: The debate on opportunity-to-learn standards.* Washington, DC: National Governors' Association.

Rosenholtz, S. J. (1985). Effective schools: Interpreting the evidence. *American Journal of Education, 93,* 352-388.

Schroeder, J. (1987). *Equal educational opportunity: Examining resource distribution and relative need characteristics at schools within a school system.* Unpublished doctoral dissertation, North Carolina State University.

Thompson, D. C., Wood, R. C., & Honeyman, D. S. (1992). *Adequacy of educational revenues in Oklahoma school districts: Expert analysis on behalf of plaintiff in* Fair School Finance Council, Inc. v. State of Oklahoma. Manhattan, KS: Wood, Thompson & Associates, Inc.

Thompson, D. C., Wood, R. C., & Honeyman, D. S. (1994). *Fiscal leadership for schools: Concepts and practices.* White Plains, NY: Longman.

Wood, R. C. (1992a, February). *School finance in the 1990s.* Paper presented at the National Symposium on Education Finance, National Conference of State Legislatures, San Antonio, TX.

Wood, R. C. (1992b, November). *School finance litigation in America.* Paper presented at the annual meeting of the National Organization on Legal Problems of Education, Phoenix, AZ.

Wood, R. C., & Honeyman, D. S. (1991). Rapid growth and unfulfilled expectations: Problems for school finance in Florida. In J. G. Ward (Ed.), *Who pays for student diversity? Population changes and educational policy* (pp. 160-179). Newbury Park, CA: Sage.

Wood, R. C., & Thompson, D. C. (1993a). *Education finance law: Constitutional challenges to state aid plans: An analysis of strategies.* Topeka, KS: National Organization of Legal Problems in Education.

Wood, R. C., & Thompson, D. C. (1993b). *Findings of fact and opinion on the equity and fiscal neutrality of South Dakota's state aid formula to public schools: Expert analysis on behalf of the state in* Bezdichek et al. v. State of South Dakota (Vol. 1). Gainesville, FL: Wood, Thompson & Associates, Inc.

Wood, R. C., Thompson, D. C., Honeyman, D. S., & Miller, M. D. (1992). *Funding public education in Montana: Based on the concept of cost of living indices in* Montana Rural Education Association v. State. Gainesville, FL: Wood, Thompson & Associates, Inc.

ELEVEN

Redefining School-Based Budgeting for High-Involvement

PRISCILLA WOHLSTETTER

AMY VAN KIRK

School-based management has become an increasingly popular strategy to reform education. Within this current trend to decentralize management to schools, budget authority is usually the most common responsibility delegated to the site (Clune & White, 1988; David, 1990; Hatry, Morley, Ashford, & Wyatt, 1993). It is thought that devolution of budgeting to individual schools will encourage innovation and change (Raywid, 1990). States and even local school districts are considering school-based budgeting as a potential tool for achieving financial equity among schools (Bradley, 1994; Odden, 1994). In addition, advocates have argued that school-based budgeting will enhance organizational effectiveness and productivity by placing decisions closest to students (Levin, 1987) and by directing accountability toward

AUTHORS' NOTE: In preparing this chapter, the authors benefited in significant ways from Allan Odden's wisdom and policy sense. The research we present is part of the Studies of Education Reform program supported by the U.S. Department of Education, Office of Educational Research and Improvement (OERI), Office of Research. This research has also received generous support from the Carnegie Corporation of New York and the Finance Center of the Consortium for Policy Research in Education (CPRE). The opinions expressed in this chapter do not necessarily reflect the position or policy of the U.S. Department of Education, the University of Southern California, the Carnegie Corporation, or CPRE, and no official endorsement should be inferred.

individual schools instead of the central office and board of education (Ornstein, 1974).

Although the literature is slowly growing, there is still a need for more information about how to structure school-based budgeting as part of effective school-based management. Recent research has analyzed district and state policy related to school-based budgeting (Wohlstetter & Buffett, 1992), but there continues to be a deficit of information about how to carry out budgeting at the school site and about the support structures needed for implementation. This chapter adds to the knowledge base by exploring effective school-based budgeting practices within effective school-based management contexts.

Early research on school-based management focused on how much power was devolved to schools. Recent research has examined a broader set of conditions for school-based management, including the professional development activities, information, and rewards needed to create high-performing school organizations. In the first section of this chapter, we explore the implications of an expanded notion of school-based management as a context for examining the budgeting process. In the second section, we analyze exemplary school-based budgeting practices in several school-based managed districts to learn more about how schools effectively redesigned themselves to accommodate their new budgeting responsibilities.

The High-Involvement Framework: Strategies for School-Based Budgeting

High-involvement, or decentralized, management, has become a prevalent strategy in the private sector to enhance organizational effectiveness and productivity (Lawler, 1992; Lawler & Mohrman, 1993). Studies conducted in the private sector have indicated that decentralized management works best in organizational settings where the work is complex, is most effectively done collegially or in teams, and involves a great deal of uncertainty (Mohrman, Lawler, & Mohrman, 1992). Therefore, although the high-involvement framework is not appropriate for all types of organizations, it is applicable to schools due to the intellectual complexity and uncertainty of teaching and the fact that teaching is best done collegially (Mohrman et al., 1992; Wohlstetter & Odden, 1992).

Research based on Lawler's (1986) work has found that organizational effectiveness and productivity improves when four key resources are decentralized within the organization: power, information, knowledge, and rewards. In the context of school-based budgeting, the high-involvement framework implies that schools need "real" power over the budget to make allocation and expenditure decisions, fiscal and performance data for making informed budget decisions, professional development and training for the budget process so that people at the school site will have technical knowledge to do the job, and control over the compensation system to reward performance. In this section, we review previous research on decentralized management and school-based budgeting by applying the high-involvement framework. Our analysis, therefore, is structured around the following four questions:

1. Who should be empowered and what types of powers are needed for school-based budgeting?
2. What types of information are needed for school-based budgeting?
3. What training is needed for school-based budgeting?
4. What changes in the reward structures are needed for school-based budgeting?

Who Should Be Empowered and What Types of Powers Are Needed for School-Based Budgeting?

In the private sector, several levels of the organization, including departments or divisions and work teams, may be empowered to make budgeting decisions. Operating in a high-involvement framework, these groups function almost as "small businesses" or as "mini-enterprises" (Lawler, 1992). Their responsibilities include hiring and firing, scheduling, setting standards, managing inventory, and dealing with customers. Although many private sector organizations have devolved these tasks to the department or division level, there are now examples of these duties being delegated to work teams as well.

Lawler's (1986) work suggests that school-based budgeting would entail allocating most of the budget to schools in a lump sum and then empowering key stakeholders at the site—the school-site council, the principal, and teachers—to make budget decisions (Wohlstetter & Mohrman, 1993). Research in schools further indicates that sites need flexibility with the budget so that school-level participants can make changes to the instructional program, such as the ability to decide the mix of personnel. In Hannaway's (1993) research of two school-based managed districts, principals cited budget flexibility as a critical ingredient for effectively addressing school-specific problems. Research conducted by Brown (1990) also supports the importance of budget flexibility. In his study of centralized districts, one of the primary complaints of principals was that they did not have the flexibility to acquire the resources they felt they needed to do their job competently. A report by the U.S. General Accounting Office (1994) found that schools were able to meet needs as they arose when they had the flexibility to make changes in their budgets.

The literature on school-based budgeting suggests four major areas of authority that need to be shifted from the central office to the school site in order to provide school-level participants with the power and flexibility to improve school performance (Hentschke, 1988; Wohlstetter & Buffett, 1992):

1. Authority over the mix of professionals at the school site
2. Ability to control expenses related to substitute teachers and utilities (Hentschke, 1988)
3. Control over the source of supply (Hentschke, 1988; Murphy, 1991)
4. The ability of individual schools to carry over unspent money from one year to the next (Hentschke, 1988; Murphy, 1991)

What Types of Information Are
Needed for School-Based Budgeting?

In the private sector, Lawler (1992) found that information needs to accompany power in order for departments and work teams to be able to make good decisions. Indeed, according to Lawler (1992), "Effective communication of financial and strategic information is a primary responsibility of senior management" (p. 208). This information might include revenues and costs disaggregated to the department and unit levels, time lines, production reports, and customer satisfaction results. Lawler (1992) suggested the use of technology, particularly electronic mail, as one way to speed up the collection and dispersal of this information.

Similarly, schools need to receive the information necessary for making decisions about how to create and plan a budget, how to allocate dollars, and how to monitor the budget. Brown (1991) recommended that schools be provided with a district handbook to guide staff members through the budget-planning process. This handbook might include district goals to guide the budget process; a planning timetable for the upcoming year; district allocation processes used; costs, such as personnel and services, to be incurred at the site; and the budget format to be followed. In addition, ongoing monitoring of the budget needs to occur throughout the year. School personnel need continuous access to the status of their accounts, including monthly information about revenues and expenditures relevant to the budget by object, function, and program, so that they can participate in budgeting decisions effectively (Prasch, 1990). An on-line, interactive computer network would give schools ready access to such fiscal information (Wohlstetter & Mohrman, 1993) and could provide an electronic invoice and purchase-ordering system. Knight (1993) found that information technology also can be utilized to model the financial costs of alternatives.

Other types of information that would be useful to schools with school-based budgeting include comparative data about other schools' budgeting activities/processes, survey data from parents and other community members about school priorities and performance, and student achievement and personnel data. Such information could be used to inform the budget development process by clarifying student needs and by providing useful school-based budgeting models (Brown, 1990; Wohlstetter, Smyer, & Mohrman, 1994).

What Training Is Needed
for School-Based Budgeting?

The high-involvement approach suggests that power and information combined with a lack of knowledge of how to do the tasks assigned produces inefficiencies in organizational performance. Lawler (1992) described two types of training activities that are needed to build this knowledge base in the private sector. The first type is technical training so that members of the department or work team have the skills to take on the tasks that are required of them. According to Lawler (1992), this training may need to be provided for as long as 6 to 10 years depending on the complexity of the tasks. Interpersonal and team skills, or process skills, are the second type of training. This training, which may be provided by a supervisor, should be continued until the team has reached maturity, and can last as long as 2 to 4 years.

On the basis of the high-involvement framework, implementation of school-based budgeting would include two types of knowledge development. First, participants need technical training designed to build managerial knowledge, such as training in program budgeting and fiscal accounting (Wohlstetter & Mohrman, 1993). Second, school-based budgeting participants need to be provided with process training in teamwork skills and the like because work groups are often created at the school to handle financial decisions.

Not only must participants be trained for their new roles and responsibilities, but the acquisition of knowledge needs to be an ongoing, continuous activity (Wohlstetter & Briggs, 1994; Wohlstetter & Mohrman, 1993). Little (1989) found that staff development was often fragmented in content, form, and continuity. A school's financial environment is highly complex and often unstable, and membership on the school-site council is likely to change. Therefore, participants in the budgeting process need to be provided with continuous professional development activities so that they can effectively adapt to changes in the environment and in school performance. According to Lawler (1992), these activities may need to last as long as 10 years depending on the complexity of the budget process and how long it takes the budget team to reach maturity.

What Changes in the Reward Structures Are Needed for School-Based Budgeting?

Finally, Lawler (1992) stated that employees in the private sector need to be rewarded for demonstrated skills and performance in order for an organization to achieve and maintain high performance. Budgeting may be one skill block in a skill-based pay system that rewards individual employees for the number and types of budgeting tasks they can perform. Employees may also be awarded bonuses for group performance. These pay-for-performance programs include gain sharing and profit sharing (Lawler, 1992) that require control over budget allocations and expenditures.

In terms of school-based budgeting, schools need the authority to control faculty and staff compensation. With a high-involvement approach, teachers would be paid on an individual basis for what they know and can do, and as a group for improved performance (Wohlstetter & Mohrman, 1993). On an individual level, as teachers took on the new tasks required of them in a decentralized management system, they would be compensated for demonstrated acquisition of the knowledge and skills needed to discharge these responsibilities, such as budget management and scheduling (Firestone, 1994). Groups within the school would also be compensated for improved performance. Schools, for example, might reward members on a budget task force for balancing the budget or accruing savings. Firestone (1994) cautioned, however, that this process would have to be designed to ensure that savings were not realized by undermining the educational programs of the school, such as through underordering supplies.

In sum, staff could be compensated on an individual basis, particularly if one person was charged with the responsibility for monitoring the budget, and on a group basis for budget development and planning. Such an approach entails moving away from the current policy of rewarding teachers for years of education and experience.

What Are the Budgeting Practices in Effective Site-Based Managed Schools?

The study reported here used the high-involvement framework to explore effective school-based management reforms and, within them, exemplary school-based budgeting practices. This research, which is part of a larger study of school-based management, is based on data collected from nine school districts: Bellevue, Washington; Chicago, Illinois; Denver, Colorado; Edmonton, Alberta, Canada; Jefferson County, Kentucky; Milwaukee, Wisconsin; Prince William County, Virginia; Rochester, New York; and Victoria, Australia. In each of the nine districts, an elementary school and a high school were studied. These schools were not typical schools. We went to districts that had delegated real budgeting and personnel responsibility to the school. Within these districts, we went to schools that had been identified as actively restructuring by either the superintendent or the associate superintendent for curriculum and instruction. Actively restructuring schools were defined as schools that had active school-based management governance activities in place and had made concrete, observable changes in their instructional approaches. Thus our sample included schools that had used school-based management to improve school performance. Each district was visited by a team of two or three researchers for 2 to 4 days. During this period, budget documents were collected and extensive interviews were conducted. At the district office, the superintendent, four assistant superintendents (for school-based management/restructuring, curriculum/instruction, personnel and finance), selected school board members, and the union president were usually interviewed. School-site visits included interviews with the principal, the vice principal, members of the school-site council, the union chair, resource specialists or selected department chairs, and several other faculty members. In addition, a follow-up interview was conducted by telephone with each district's budget specialist, usually the associate superintendent for finance.

How Is Money Allocated to Schools?

Among the districts in our sample, all had an allocation formula that was either wholly or partially based on various categories of student needs and/or grade levels. Prince William County allocated money to schools based on 10 different categorizations of students (by grade level, special needs, program type, etc.). Jefferson County varied the per-pupil allocation according to grade level and student need by providing, for example, an extra $16 for a 3rd-grade student on a reduced-lunch program and an extra $25 for an 11th-grade student on a reduced-lunch program. Sometimes other conditions, such as the size and condition of the school building, were taken into account in the allocation formula as well. Schools in Chicago received money on the basis of enrollment, special needs of students, operation and maintenance of the site building, special programs of the school board, security services, and food services.

Districts provided schools with varying amounts of budget authority. Most often, schools received few discretionary funds. Victoria, for example, allocated three categories of money—curriculum, administration, and facilities—to each site, but schools could not transfer money from one category to another. Furthermore, these allocations together represented only about 10% of the total school budget. Milwaukee gave each school a line-item budget within which money could be transferred, but only if first approved by the district.

Edmonton, Jefferson County, Prince William County, and Rochester gave schools more local discretion. Each granted schools a budget composed of a base allocation for resource needs consistent across all schools. This allocation did not constitute the total school budget, however. In Prince William County, for example, this base allocation consisted of salaries for specific personnel, including the principal, librarian, guidance counselor, secretarial/clerical staff, and custodial staff. In addition, salaries for the director of student activities, in-school suspension staff, and security personnel were included in the baseline allocation for high schools. A per-pupil allocation was then added to this base allocation to provide funding for instructional staff, related support staff, supplies, equipment, and services for students. Several items were excluded from this site allocation, however, including funds for attendance and maintenance personnel, cafeteria staff, student transportation to and from school, utilities, and repair and maintenance of school buildings and grounds. As a result of these exclusions, the districts that provided the most discretion usually allocated between 85% and 95% of the school budget to the site. But even then, many constraints existed.

Across all schools, a major constraint on school control was that very few discretionary dollars remained after salaries were paid and district restrictions, such as class size, were taken into consideration. Perhaps as a consequence, principals in the schools we studied were active in cultivating resources from outside sources. Almost all of the schools had or were in the process of applying for grants and other funding from the government and private sources. In general, these additional funds helped reduce the constraints of the district allocation and had the effect of increasing the schools' discretionary resources.

Budget Power

To assess the amount of power in schools with respect to budgeting, we first identified who was empowered at the site. We found that a redesign process occurred at the school to accommodate new budget responsibilities. Next, we looked at what control schools had over their budgets, particularly in areas that traditionally have been controlled by the central office.

Who Is Empowered at the School Site?

School-based budgeting involves dispersing power that was once centralized in the district office to the school site. Across the sample districts, who was empowered at the school site was often determined by decision-making structures outside of the school. In most sample districts, either central office or state policy formally identified who would be responsible at the school site for the budgeting process. In seven of the nine districts, the task of developing and monitoring the budget was vested with a school-site council. Two districts, Edmonton and Prince William County, identified the principal as the sole person responsible for the planning and expenditure of all funds. At the district level, such policies typically were set through collective bargaining agreements.

Although empowerment was formally defined, the exemplary schools in our sample worked hard to ensure that power was devolved throughout the organization. Thus, in effective schools where the responsibility for the budget was delegated to a school-site council, the process of developing the budget usually entailed soliciting input from various groups of stakeholders, including parents, so that many constituents participated in the budget decision-making process. Further, the council typically set up a budget subcommittee to organize this process. A few councils empowered the principal to oversee budget development.

In the schools studied, the budget process usually began with the principal's and/or a budget subcommittee's soliciting of input on school priorities. These forums used to get input were both formal (i.e., surveys and scheduled meetings) and informal (i.e., conversations and word of mouth). In most schools, the principal and/or budget subcommittee developed a site budget based on input from various school constituents and presented it to the school council. The school council usually reserved the right to adopt the budget or request that changes be made.

In Edmonton and Prince William County, where principals were solely responsible for the budget, a budget committee composed of the principal and staff members drafted the site budget on the basis of school priorities that had been set by the faculty. This budget then was presented to the faculty for recommendations. Although principals in these districts had the ultimate authority to approve the final budget, they relied heavily on faculty input to guide the process and usually did not contradict faculty wishes. Thus, although principals had veto power, we found in the schools we studied that it was rarely used.

In most of the schools we studied, principals were critical players in the budget development process. Frequently they were required to serve on the council, with duties including chairing the budget subcommittee or implementing budget decisions made by the council. Therefore, although the principal and school staff played the predominant role in budget development, parents and students in exemplary schools were also involved in the process. Although they almost never served on the budget subcommittee, parents and students were surveyed for input on school priorities and needs to guide the process. In general, their participation was restricted to approving the final budget through council membership.

What Control Over the Budget Do Schools Have?

As noted earlier, previous research on school-based budgeting identified four areas of control: authority to determine the mix of professionals and paraprofessionals at the school site, authority over substitute teachers and utilities, the ability to choose where to purchase supplies, and authority to carry over unused funds from one year to the next. In traditionally managed districts, these areas are largely under the control of the central office, but earlier studies of school-based managed districts found a shift of control toward the school site (Hentschke, 1988; Wohlstetter & Buffett, 1992). Table 11.1 indicates the extent to which the districts we studied had devolved control in these four areas.

Districts provided schools with varying amounts of authority over the mix of teachers and other staff at the site. Schools usually had the power to reduce class size by adding teachers, but could not increase class size due to collective bargaining agreements, district policy, or state law. There was more flexibility in the mix of classified staffing positions, including maintenance and clerical staff. Both the elementary and high schools we studied in Jefferson County eliminated some custodial and librarian positions so that they could add more staff to

Table 11.1. Power Summary Measures for the School-Site Budgeting Process

| | *Power* | | | | |
School District	*Mix of Teachers & Other Staff*	*Substitute Teachers*	*Utilities*	*Source of Supply*	*Carryover of Unused Funds*
Bellevue, Washington	Yes	Yes	No	Yes	Yes
Chicago, Illinois	Yes	No	No	Yes	No
Denver, Colorado	No	Yes	No	Yes	No
Edmonton, Canada	Yes	Yes	Yes	Yes	Yes
Jefferson County, Kentucky	Yes	Yes	No	Yes	Yes
Milwaukee, Wisconsin	Yes	Yes	No	Yes	Yes
Prince William County, Virginia	Yes	Yes	No	Yes	Yes
Rochester, New York	Yes	Yes	No	No	No
Victoria, Australia	No	Yes	Yes	Yes	Yes

the classrooms, such as teacher aides. A school in Rochester eliminated a custodial position and used the extra money to purchase additional supplies and equipment.

Schools frequently had difficulty increasing the number of teachers at the site because most districts allocated teacher salaries using a district-wide average. According to interviews with district budget specialists, this allocation method was used to prevent schools from trying to save money by hiring more inexpensive, and possibly less qualified, teachers. Although this provided schools with hiring flexibility in terms of experience, it prevented site flexibility in the number of positions. Unlike the private sector, where changes in staffing patterns are a major component of high performance, schools were not able to save money through teacher salaries and therefore could not really change staffing much because money for an additional teacher had to come from another source. Similarly, in districts where teacher salaries were not allocated to the site, schools were unable to make significant changes in their professional staffs.

Almost all of the districts in our sample decentralized money for substitute teachers to individual schools. This enabled schools with low rates of teacher absenteeism to accrue money allocated for substitute teachers and to use it for other purposes. At the same time, schools that went over this allocation usually had to access other funds in order to balance their budgets. There was some form of a "safety net" in all of the districts that served to protect schools from financial hardship. Bellevue and Jefferson County gave schools control over funds for professional leave activities, and the district covered the cost of uncontrollable items such as illnesses and emergencies. In Milwaukee and Rochester, schools were allocated a set number of substitute teacher days per teacher per year, based on the district average. These districts then paid for any days exceeding this amount. Schools in Edmonton and Prince William County were provided with funds to cover the cost of short-term absences, but the district picked up the cost of substitute teachers after the regular teacher had been absent for more than three consecutive days.

In interviews, faculty members stated that substitute teacher funds, if carefully spent, could be used to enhance budget flexibility by empowering schools to trade off substitute teachers for other resources. This was one area in which schools had some real budgetary flexibility, but it represented only a small portion of the budget. We did find evidence suggesting that teachers had begun to feel the collective impact of their individual decisions. As one teacher explained, "If a teacher calls in sick and does not come to work, then that teacher has made the decision to use school money for a substitute teacher."

As shown in Table 11.1, it was more common for districts to decentralize funds for substitute teachers than for utilities. Generally speaking, we found that schools did not want control over utilities. Among school-level participants, there was a preference for controlling funds related directly to managing instructional activities, but not for controlling funds related to the physical plant. This sentiment restricted school-site authority over the budget process, however. Much of the budget was already constrained through restrictions on teacher salaries, and, as a result, schools had relatively small amounts of discretionary funding. Central office jurisdiction over utilities further constrained the dwindling discretionary pot at the school site.

Whether schools could choose where to purchase supplies, staff development, and maintenance services was another element of budgeting power. Most of the districts we studied allowed schools to make purchases from vendors outside the district, but the central offices usually had mechanisms in place to discourage schools from doing so. Only Rochester required schools to use the district warehouse and central office for supplies. Districts frequently monitored the amount of money that was spent on outside vendors to ensure that costly errors were not made. In Bellevue, schools could make purchases only under $100 outside of the district. Similarly, schools in Jefferson County and Prince William County had to use a bidding process designed by the central office for purchases over $5,000 and $2,500, respectively. This bidding process required schools to solicit a minimum number of bids, and the central office usually had final approval. According to interviews with central office administrators, districts put in place these deterrents to prevent schools from spending more than they needed to on a particular good or service. These costs amounted to less than 5% of the whole school budget, however, and appeared to constrain the budget unnecessarily without any clear focus on results.

Some schools bought supplies outside the district even if they were discouraged from doing so. In Milwaukee, for instance, schools were strongly discouraged from purchasing maintenance services outside because the central office felt schools paid a premium for these services. Schools continued to use these outside services, however, because the response was so much quicker, and as a result it was more cost-effective for them to do so. According to an interview with the budget specialist in the central office, this use of power at the school site had forced the district maintenance department to become more competitive. Not only is this what is supposed to happen in the ideal school-based budgeting process, but studies in the public sector suggest that this type of response builds a central office culture focused on providing services instead of on reinforcing rules (Barzelay, 1992).

As shown in Table 11.1, over half of the districts in this study, which had been identified as having exemplary school-based management practices, had unspent funds revert back to the central office at the end of the year. In Rochester, state law prohibited the carryover of unspent funds. Chicago allowed state Chapter 1 funds to be carried over, but general funds reverted back to the board of education. Denver was in the preliminary stages of allowing schools to carry over unused funds and was piloting the program in a couple of schools.

In other districts where schools were able to carry over funds from one year to the next, there were often restrictions. These restrictions included allowing schools to carry over funds only in certain accounts, such as equipment and supplies, or restricting the total amount that could be carried over. In Prince William County, for instance, schools could carry over only a small amount—$1,000 for elementary schools and $3,000 for high schools.

Many schools took advantage of the opportunity to carry over unused funds, regardless of whether restrictions existed. One elementary school in Edmonton accrued a $25,000 surplus over a 5-year period. Similarly, schools in Milwaukee carried over $6 million district-wide in one year. As a result, schools were able to make purchases that otherwise would not have been possible by adding unspent money to their discretionary resources. Furthermore, the evidence suggests that schools were making budget decisions carefully each year to ensure there was money to carry over. Schools that had the power to carry over unused funds also usually had to carry deficits into the next fiscal year as well. A school in Jefferson County, for example, overspent by $2,100 in one year. This deficit subsequently was rolled over into the following year's budget.

In sum, there was a gap in the schools studied between the high-involvement model and the actual amount of power devolved to the site. There continued to be many restrictions on the budget, resulting in a very small discretionary fund for the school. As a result, resource allocations had not changed substantially because schools did not have the required flexibility. Although there was a gap between high-involvement and actual school-based budgeting practices, districts were working to close this gap slowly.

Budget Information

Districts need to give schools with budgetary powers the information they need to create, implement, monitor, and evaluate their own budgets. Access to a computer network on which schools can input their budgets and shift funds from one account to the next provides schools with immediate, current fiscal information (Wohlstetter & Mohrman, 1993). Not only does this save time and paper shuffling, but it can also be used to provide schools with information about other performance measures, such as attendance rates and parent survey results (Odden, 1994).

Most of the exemplary school-based managed districts we studied had already developed a computer network linking schools to the central office or were planning to do so. There was a great deal of variation across districts in how far advanced they were in this process. Victoria's Schools of the Future on-line system included revenues listed by their source, budgets for each program, an automated invoicing and purchase ordering system, a student scheduling system, and a process for recording student information. Denver was still a couple of years away from having schools on-line, but was planning for it.

In most districts where schools were on line, the technology only provided information about the budget allocated to the site and did not allow schools to make budget changes. Thus, although schools could create a budget or view their accounts, they could not make purchases or transfer money from one account to the next. In Chicago, the computer network was used only to input the school site budget. After that, expenditures were processed through a batch system. Although schools were on-line for budget information in Rochester, for example, the district budget specialist did not think that schools were really using this resource.

In addition to information transmitted via computer networks, most districts provided schools with other budget information. This included both planning information, such as a district budget manual that took schools through the steps of developing a site budget, and monitoring information, such as monthly budget updates (if this information was not available on-line). Often the budget manuals emphasized that the budgeting process should be used as a tool for achieving local priorities and goals. Edmonton's manual required schools to list specific school priorities, measurable school results related to each priority, primary indicators used to determine the extent to which the result had been achieved, and descriptions of the activities and strategies used to achieve the results. The school was then supposed to create a budget to accomplish these goals.

Monthly budget updates were provided in some districts to enable schools to assess their own status. Rochester, for example, provided schools with a computer printout each month that listed how much had been spent to date. Every expenditure was provided in detail so that the schools knew how much had been spent on supplies, service contracts, and every other code in the budget. In addition, schools in Rochester had access to data regarding student enrollment and attendance. Several districts, however, did not provide information as frequently or comprehensively. The budget specialist in Milwaukee, for example, felt that the schools needed better information for the current year, and the district was working to improve this service.

Evidence suggested that schools receiving information used it. The elementary school principal in Jefferson County, for example, provided the school-site council with monthly budget updates, including the balance by line-item. However, in Chicago, the teachers were basically unaware of the monthly status of the budget and focused instead on curriculum and instruction issues.

Access to information about innovative budget processes was another form of information that a few districts provided to schools. This information was used to help schools improve their own budgeting processes. A couple of districts promoted and encouraged sharing information by providing informal opportunities for schools to learn from one another. The central office in Bellevue facilitated sharing by serving as a clearinghouse referring schools to each other. As a consequence, many schools in Bellevue used similar budgeting systems despite the wide flexibility given to them by the district office. Similarly, in both Jefferson County and Prince William County, experts from outside the district, including the superintendent from Edmonton, were brought in to provide new perspectives on the budgeting process.

There was, however, evidence that most districts' political cultures made it difficult for schools to share with one another. In Milwaukee, for example, people we interviewed at the elementary school described an extremely competitive system that made sharing across schools unpopular. Rochester schools were forced to share information about how they developed their budgets through a "freedom to access of information" act, but the information had to be formally requested from the district, which was politically difficult for schools. As a result, information sharing was idiosyncratic and dependent upon school initiation and district support.

Another kind of information available to many of the schools we studied was feedback from constituents. Feedback was used in some districts and schools to help set priorities for the upcoming year. Chicago, for example, required school-site councils to convene at least two "well-publicized" meetings every year to gather input from the entire school community on the School Improvement Plan, the school budget, and the annual school report. Edmonton also required public budget meetings; further, the district conducted yearly district-wide surveys of staff, students, parents, and community members.

Exemplary schools used such feedback to develop their guiding framework, or mission statement, and to inform the budget process. A guiding framework provided direction to the budgeting process because it forced the school to determine its priorities and to allocate its budget accordingly. In Edmonton, the school-site budget was viewed as a tool for meeting local needs and priorities. Feedback from constituents in the form of survey information was used within the school to help develop budget priorities.

In sum, information served a twofold purpose for most districts. Though it was recognized that schools needed information to be effective in the budgeting process, concern was also expressed about the importance of the district's oversight role. In Edmonton, problems in misallocations at school sites led to increased central office control. Frequent reporting of information provided the district with an accountability mechanism. Therefore information also had a compliance orientation typical of information sharing in traditionally managed districts, reflecting once again the gap between high-involvement and actual budgeting practices. The computer networks had the potential to meet both the need for central office oversight and the need to provide schools with frequent, comprehensive information. Ideally, they could provide schools with quick access to budget information while still allowing the central office to monitor school-site budget activities easily. This was one way that districts were scaling up to reduce the gap between high-involvement and actual budget information practices.

Budget Skills and Knowledge

In the smoothly functioning site-based managed school, professional development is typically a bottom-up activity in which people at the school site define their own training needs and how services will be delivered (Wohlstetter & Mohrman, 1994). With respect to budgets, we found that the district office continued to provide most of the training and professional development. Thus, although many schools in our sample could go outside the district to purchase services and had at least some discretion over professional development funds, they continued to rely on the district for budget training.

To assess the nature of professional development in relation to budgeting, we determined the types of staff development activities that were needed, whether these activities were being offered in the districts, and, if so, whether they were ongoing, sustained activities. To begin with, participants in the budgeting process need a wide range of knowledge and skills in order to create a budget effectively. Because budgets at the school site are usually developed in committee, this includes both group process skills, such as consensus building and learning how to work in teams, and technical skills specifically related to budgeting.

Almost all the districts provided schools with at least some training to assist participants in the budgeting process, but over half did not provide technical training. In Bellevue, an orientation was held for district schools covering such areas as the contract and policy procedures for site-based management teams; decision-making, consensus-building, and conflict resolution skills; how to process information during council meetings; and leadership training. The district did not provide much technical training for school-based budgeting. Similarly, Rochester had a department in the central office for school-based planning to provide training in process skills to the school-site teams, but very little technical training for budgeting. This lack of technical training frequently led to frustration among school staff about their lack of understanding of the budget process. For example, although central office staff in Rochester felt that school-level participants were very knowledgeable about the budget formula and did not need training, teachers at the elementary school we visited were, in fact, frustrated by their lack of budget skills.

A few of the districts provided schools with both process and technical training. Much of the technical training was designed to teach schools how to create a budget using the district's guidelines for school-based budgeting. This training included seminars on how to use the computer systems and how to develop a budget according to district specifications.

Some of the districts we studied provided schools with some initial in-service training, but it was not sustained. In these districts, very little additional staff development was provided after the initial training sessions, even though participants changed routinely each year. Some respondents cited the lack of support staff in the central office as the primary reason for so little follow-up. Although Lawler's (1992) findings suggest that professional development is needed only until the staff are competent in their new roles and responsibilities, it appeared that some of these districts were terminating these activities too soon.

Several models of staff development emerged in the districts we studied. Sometimes staff development was a central office-initiated activity, but more often schools initiated their own. District-initiated staff development usually dictated which school-level participants should attend, and often only a few were selected to attend training on the budget. In Edmonton and Victoria, primarily principals were given training, whereas Milwaukee and Prince William County provided training to both school principals and business managers. A few Edmonton principals were selected for year-long positions in the central office so that they could be more aware of how the district operated before returning to their school sites.

Other staff development activities were school initiated. Schools requested assistance from the district or other service providers, and the training was developed and tailored to the school. Most school-initiated staff development was in the form of one-on-one assistance. Some districts offered telephone numbers that schools could call to get questions answered, and central office personnel were available to come to the school site. The central office in Prince William County had two people who spent almost all of their time answering budgeting questions on the phone, and Edmonton had one person dedicating 90% of his time traveling to schools to provide training. Some training was tied to demand. For example, in Chicago, the department of purchasing was available to present purchasing seminars, and the budget office in Prince William County could hold additional budget in-services if schools requested them. Similarly, the district's budget personnel in Bellevue were available to make presentations at principal and school council meetings and other similar gatherings upon request.

Although, schools generally relied heavily on the central office to provide training for budget-related skills, much of the training was school initiated, in the form of requests either for one-on-one assistance or for increases in the number of training sessions held. Because of the lack of technical training in most of the districts, staff development was relatively fragmented and largely dependent on the availability of one-on-one assistance. As a result, there was a large gap between high-involvement professional development practices, in which staff development is continuously provided until the school-site staff have achieved the expertise needed, and the actual practice in the districts. There was little evidence that districts were scaling up to close this gap, but central office personnel were beginning to recognize that more assistance was needed.

Rewards

A decentralized reward structure enables schools to reward staff for skills and performance according to local priorities. In general, two characteristics of the formal reward structures were decentralized in the districts we studied. First, districts did not pay teachers or principals for additional skills learned. There was no assessment of budget skills and no bonus tied to mastery of such skills. Second, some districts paid teachers for additional work. Such policies were usually initiated and worked out through collective bargaining agreements. Another characteristic of site-based rewards was that they tended not to be numerous financial in nature. In general, schools provided "pats on the back" to their teachers and other staff. The elementary school in Jefferson County provided teachers with flowers for Mother's Day and an appreciation dinner, and the high school teachers were recognized by the Parent/Teachers' Association during National PTA week. Among our sample schools, there were a few instances of financial rewards. The high school in Milwaukee, for example, chose to use one sixth of its local budget to compensate council members for their time. Similarly, schools in Bellevue issued stipends for leadership roles that were played. Many schools also used staff development opportunities as a reward. Staff, however, did not always perceive these opportunities as part of the reward structure. At the high school in Denver, several teachers did not consider staff development money to be a reward.

Many of the site-based managed schools we studied theoretically had the power to reward faculty but chose not to exercise it. During interviews, several principals mentioned that they avoided such distinctions among faculty because they usually led to feelings of "winners and losers." Furthermore, the organizational culture frowned upon such differentiation.

In order for school-based budgeting sites truly to control the reward/compensation system, the high-involvement framework calls for a shift from district policy and collective bargaining agreements to a school-based policy in which the reward system for faculty is aligned with school goals. Currently, there is some experimentation occurring with decentralized compensation/reward systems. These are usually district-driven reforms, and they are not often present in school-based managed districts. Some districts in Colorado, for example, are experimenting with delegating authority over compensation structures to school sites, but Denver is not. In fact, the schools in Denver wanted to compensate teachers for not using their sick leave or for working overtime and were constrained by district rules and regulations. Thus the evidence suggests that innovative reward structures are being adopted as separate, stand-alone reforms instead of as one component of a more comprehensive approach to systemic school reform.

Conclusion

School-based budgeting, like school-based management, is a tool to help schools achieve high performance—not an end in itself. Although school-based budgeting can be used to help schools accomplish desired goals by enabling them to allocate money according to local priorities, stakeholders at all levels must be willing to engage in the effort. The central office personnel have to be willing to devolve power and provide support in the form of knowledge, information, and rewards to the schools, and similar processes need to occur among constituents within the school.

In this study of exemplary school-based managed schools, we found evidence of a broadened definition of school-based budgeting, but there was still a tremendous gap between school-based budgeting within the high-involvement framework and what was actually occurring in the districts. Districts had decentralized some budget power, but schools had little discretion after district, and sometimes state, constraints were taken into consideration. There was a scaling-up process occurring, however, as districts experimented with devolving authority over various items. Similarly, information sharing was often restricted by the political culture and use of technology within the district, but several districts were working to close the gap between high-involvement and real practices by expanding the use of technology in the budget process.

Although there was not as much evidence to suggest that districts were scaling up to reduce the gap between the need for continuous, ongoing staff development and the current fragmented practice of providing professional development according to availability and demand, there was a growing recognition that more training was needed, and there was potential for growth in this area. Finally, there appeared to be very little experimentation with reward structures in schools, but there was movement toward the high-involvement framework as some schools were beginning to manipulate budgets in ways that allowed participants to be rewarded for skills.

In conclusion, there are several policy implications for local, state, and national actors from this study of school-based budgeting. First, power that is devolved needs to be real power so that schools can allocate money according to site needs and priorities. Second, the flow of information can be improved with the use of computer systems that provide quick, up-to-date information that is needed to make good decisions. A guiding framework—provided by a state or district curriculum guide, for instance—also informs the site-based budgeting process because it helps the school to develop its mission, which in turn helps schools establish priorities and make budget decisions. Third, the money for professional development needs to be set aside to ensure that it is continuously provided so that participants can improve their budget decision-making processes. Finally, more experimentation is needed in terms of rewards. We have experiments with teacher compensation systems going on, but not in districts that have decentralized aggressively. There appears to be a need to marry the two reforms into a comprehensive strategy to create high performance schools.

References

Barzelay, M. (1992). *Breaking through bureaucracy: A new vision for managing in government.* Berkeley: University of California Press.

Bradley, A. (1994, September 14). Equation for equality. *Education Week,* pp. 28-32.

Brown, D. J. (1990). *Decentralization and school-based management.* London: Falmer.

Brown, D. J. (1991). *Decentralization: The administrator's guidebook to school district change.* Newbury Park, CA: Corwin.

Clune, W. H., & White, P. A. (1988). *School-based management: Institutional variation, implementation, and issues for further research* (Rep. No. RR-008). New Brunswick, NJ: Rutgers University, Consortium for Policy Research in Education.

David, J. L. (1990). Restructuring in progress: Lessons from pioneering districts. In R. F. Elmore (Ed.), *Restructuring schools: The next generation of educational reform* (pp. 152-206). San Francisco: Jossey-Bass.

Firestone, W. A. (1994). Redesigning teacher salary systems for educational reform. *American Educational Research Journal, 31,* 549-574.

Hannaway, J. (1993). Decentralization in two school districts: Challenging the standard paradigm. In J. Hannaway & M. Carnoy (Eds.), *Decentralization and school improvement: Can we fulfill the promise?* (pp. 135-162). San Francisco: Jossey-Bass.

Hatry, H. P., Morley, E., Ashford, B., & Wyatt, T. (1993). *Implementing school-based management: Insights into decentralization from science and mathematics departments* (Rep. No. 93-4). Washington, DC: Urban Institute.

Hentschke, G. C. (1988). Budgetary theory and reality: A microview. In D. H. Monk & J. Underwood (Eds.), *Microlevel school finance: Issues and implications for policy* (pp. 311-336). New York: Ballinger.

Knight, B. (1993). Delegated financial management and school effectiveness. In C. Dimmock (Ed.), *School-based management and school effectiveness* (pp. 114-141). London: Routledge.

Lawler, E. E. (1986). *High involvement management*. San Francisco: Jossey-Bass.

Lawler, E. E. (1992). *The ultimate advantage*. San Francisco: Jossey-Bass.

Lawler, E. E., & Mohrman, S. A. (1993). *A new logic of organizing: Implications for higher education.* Los Angeles: University of Southern California, Center for Research in Education Finance, Consortium for Policy Research in Education.

Levin, H. M. (1987, June). *Finance and governance implications of school-based decisions.* Paper presented at the meeting of the National Advisory Committee of the Work in America Institute, New York.

Little, J. W. (1989). District policy choices and teachers' professional development opportunities. *Educational Evaluation and Policy Analysis, 11,* 165-179.

Mohrman, S. A., Lawler, E. E., & Mohrman, A. M. (1992). Applying employee involvement in schools. *Education Evaluation and Policy Analysis, 14,* 347-360.

Murphy, J. (1991). *Restructuring schools: Capturing and assessing the phenomena.* New York: Teachers College Press.

Odden, A. (1994). Decentralized management and school finance. *Theory Into Practice, 33,* 104-111.

Ornstein, A. C. (1974). *Race and politics in school/community organizations.* Pacific Palisades, CA: Goodyear.

Prasch, J. (1990). *How to organize for school-based management.* Alexandria, VA: Association for Supervision and Curriculum Development.

Raywid, M. A. (1990). Rethinking school governance. In R. F. Elmore (Ed.), *Restructuring schools: The next generation of educational reform* (pp. 152-206). San Francisco: Jossey-Bass.

U.S. General Accounting Office. (1994). *Education reform: School-based management results in changes in instruction and budgeting* (GAO/HEHS Publication No. 94-135). Washington, DC: Government Printing Office.

Wohlstetter, P., & Briggs, K. (1994). The principal's role in school-based management. *Principal, 74*(2), 14-17.

Wohlstetter, P., & Buffett, T. (1992). Promoting school-based management: Are dollars decentralized too? In A. Odden (Ed.), *Rethinking school finance: An agenda for the 1990s* (pp. 128-165). San Francisco: Jossey-Bass.

Wohlstetter, P., & Mohrman, S. A. (1993). *Site-based management: Strategies for success* [Finance brief]. New Brunswick, NJ: Rutgers University, Eagleton Institute of Politics, Consortium for Policy Research in Education.

Wohlstetter, P., & Mohrman, S. A. (1994). *School-based management: Promise and process* [Finance brief]. New Brunswick, NJ: Rutgers University, Eagleton Institute of Politics, Consortium for Policy Research in Education.

Wohlstetter, P., & Odden, A. R. (1992). Rethinking school-based management policy and research. *Educational Administration Quarterly, 28,* 529-549.

Wohlstetter, P., Smyer, R., & Mohrman, S. A. (1994). New boundaries for school-based management: The high involvement model. *Educational Evaluation and Policy Analysis, 16,* 268-286.

TWELVE

The Politics of School-Level
Finance Data and State Policy Making

CAROLYN D. HERRINGTON

State policy makers are increasingly interested in better understanding how the dollars they appropriate for public schooling are being expended and what relations exist between the expenditures and improved student learning. Over the past three decades, real per-pupil school expenditures have risen dramatically, yet there is no evidence that the increases have purchased more effective service delivery (Odden, 1992). Although policy makers' frustration has been growing over this entire period, the lack of results from the substantive policy reforms and increased expenditures that went hand in hand with the state reform packages of the early 1980s is the most proximate cause of the frustration. This frustration has been rendered even more acute by international comparisons that suggest that other Western industrialized countries are achieving more impressive academic results with even smaller expenditures. Policy makers' frustration has been further stimulated by media coverage of these issues in national publications such as *Forbes* and *U.S. News and World Report*.

To understand in a meaningful way the relationship between schooling outcomes and expenditures, policy makers have expressed specific interest in having more data on financial expenditures at the school level. They argue that only at the micro or school level can the relationship between the money expended and the learning outcomes that result be understood. Although most states are just beginning to discuss how to collect and use such data, the state of Florida, over 20 years ago, set in place a process to gather and analyze school-level financial data to aid in school-, district-, and state-level decision making.

The purpose of this chapter is to investigate the interests and concerns of state policy makers in utilization of school-level finance data as a tool for educational reform, drawing upon lessons that may be learned from the 20-year history of the state of Florida. The first section reviews why the issue is currently rising on the agenda of state policy makers, places it in the larger context of U.S. educational reform thrusts of the past two decades, and provides an overview of extant research on related issues. The second section describes Florida's 20-year experience in collecting and disseminating school-level finance data. The last section draws lessons learned from Florida about the potential utility of school-level finance data as a policy-making and managerial tool for educational reform.

Why Are State Policy Makers
Interested in School-Level Finance Data?

State policy makers are increasingly determined to understand what happens to educational funds as they cascade from the state capitol to school districts and on into schools. The resistance of the U.S. educational system to significant gains in student learning despite significant increases in funds has given rise to a number of theories as to where the money is going. The most loudly touted theory is that noninstructional activities are absorbing the additional monies, with the most favored culprit being district central administrative activities (Finn, 1991). This theory gives vent to long-standing tensions between an idealized educational system in which classroom teachers and students form the bulk of the system and the larger, more institutionalized and bureaucratic form of public schooling that has emerged since World War II.

Another hypothesis is that special education costs have skyrocketed since the advent of federal mandates in the 1970s requiring states to provide schooling to all children with disabilities (Parrish & Verstegen, 1994). A variant borrowing from both the administrative and special-student theories is that overall increases in students with special educational needs, including not just students with disabilities but also poor students, students with limited English proficiency, students

from troubled families and communities, and students with severe
emotional and disciplinary problems, have forced school systems to
divert resources from core instructional tasks to the provision of
noninstructional services such as guidance, social and health services,
and security.

When offered by state policy makers, this line of argument is often
tinged with anger that funds appropriated for schooling are being
used for other social ends, ends that the same policy makers may have
opposed in the form of a social service program appropriations request. However, there are insufficient empirical data to support any
of these propositions. The inability to fix responsibility has led to
increasing acrimony between lawmakers and educators.

A second question prompting state policy makers' interest in school-
level finance data concerns student equity or the vertical distribution
of dollars across school sites. Again, there is suspicion by state policy
makers that state efforts undertaken to achieve interdistrict equity
may be thwarted by within-district policies that favor some schools
over others. In particular, there is suspicion that schools that serve
middle-class children are favored in district resource utilization over
schools serving children from less advantaged communities. Although
this is a more recent concern, it illustrates standard intergovernmental
dynamics in which governments with larger jurisdictional areas suspect that lower forms are less able to implement or less committed to
issues of equity. State policy makers' concerns have taken on a sharper
edge as the judicial system has shown less and less toleration for
inequities in school inputs and as the issue of adequacy has joined
equity as a basis for state school finance lawsuits (Berne & Picus, 1994;
Clune, 1993). Intraschool equity has also become more critical for state
policy makers with the passage of the Goals 2000: Educate America
Act of 1994, which will require states to develop school-level delivery
standards. These standards, designed to ensure that all schools are
receiving educational resources sufficient for students to attain the
higher-learning standards represented by the goals, will force more
cross-site analyses.

Finally, policy makers' interest is also heightened by a broader
strategy to stimulate parent and community activism as an engine of
reform. It is hoped that pressure at the community level will be more
successful than state mandates in fostering restructuring reforms and
in ensuring school-level equity. Thus public dissemination of these

data is usually seen as part of the overall strategy for utilizing school-level finance data.

The above summary represents issues being raised by senior elected and appointed officials at the state level. But to understand better the increasing saliency of the interest in school-level financial data, we must situate the issue in relationship to broader currents of thought. Several overlapping currents of thought reinforce each other and reinforce policy makers' interest in school-level finance data as a policy tool for improving public schools.

One is the disillusionment with the now decade-long attempt by state policy makers to improve schooling through the application of across-the-board state mandates. The apparent lack of success of this approach has given credence to those who have argued that state-level mandates are inherently unproductive because they exclude the most important actors in the system—school-level personnel—from decision making. Across-the-board prescriptions, goes the argument, ignore the considerable diversity that exists from school to school in student socioeconomic, cultural, and language diversity, teacher expertise and motivation, academic expectations, and institutional norms. A state mandate that might be an effective instrument of state policy objectives in one school may be counterproductive in another school. Following this line of thought, some argue that prescriptions should shift from the state to the school level and that the role of the state should become that of developing policies supportive of site-based decision making.

For policy makers, these considerations are consonant with currents of thought within the larger arenas of public policy and private sector management circles that hold that, in general, the role of central management should be rethought. This line of thinking argues that, in the public sector, state activity should be narrowed and the emphasis should be on vision setting, standard setting, and enabling, with the production of information a key responsibility. Information is to be used for measuring progress, cross-site comparisons, and accountability (Osborne & Gaebler, 1992). In an era of increasing public skepticism concerning public sector effectiveness, this more limited and focused role for government has an inherent appeal for elected officials. In the corporate sector, according to recent organizational analyses, U.S. companies that have successfully survived the intense global competition over the past decade have done so by creating leaner, less hierarchical, and more fluid and flexible organizational structures, and have pushed more responsibility and authority to lower units of the organization (Peters & Waterman, 1982). One of the key roles of central management has been the provision of ample, accurate, and timely information to these units to allow them to respond quickly and in a more targeted fashion to changing external conditions.

At the same time, it is critical not to overstate the level of interest manifested by policy makers. The level of interest should be more accurately described as relatively low though increasingly persistent. Evidence for this caution can be drawn from two different sources. First, public interest polls, to which elected officials are very sensitive, do not suggest that issues of efficiency or even of school-level equity are high on the public's agenda. In comparison to issues regarding discipline, safety, and drugs, efficiency does not even register (Johnson & Immerwahr, 1994). Second, problems that may surface as school-level data become more widely available properly fall under the jurisdiction of district, not state, leaders, and the development and implementation of school-level policies are more immediately the responsibilities of local school boards. States have traditionally ceded to local boards on issues that require school-level differentiation and have proceeded only with great reluctance to infringe on this arena.

The potential gains that might be anticipated also need to be calculated modestly. As Kirst (1988) pointed out, the very nature of the instructional enterprise has proved resistant to input-output analyses; the manner in which fiscal data are maintained is designed to reflect budgeting needs, not resource utilization; and the educational research community has shown surprisingly little interest in providing analytic support for such efforts. One example of the difficulty in applying fiscal data to learning outcomes is that most of a school's resources are expended in teachers' salaries and that the level of funds is dependent, more than anything else, on average tenure of the teachers, which in turn may not be related to instructional gains.

Moreover, whereas school-level finance information is a relatively recent area of interest for educational researchers and policy makers, research into the use of analytical information as a support for the policy-making process and as a political strategy itself has been investigated by social scientists over the years, and the findings from these lines of research suggest that gains to be achieved may be seriously compromised by diverse stakeholders. Previous research indicates the data can be captured by those who must provide it and that the information itself is far from being politically neutral (Weiss, 1989; Weiss & Gruber, 1984; Weiss & Tschirhart, 1994). Information is almost always constructed by those who have control over the process and who thus may exert considerable influence on how the data are collected, displayed, and released. Technical issues such as units of analysis, frequency of reporting, and comparability reflect different value systems, may become politically charged, and may thwart some and advantage others. Decisions on how the data are treated, aggregated, analyzed, and arrayed may be just as critical as the actual availability of the data in determining whether they will answer the policy makers' questions.

Finally, research to date on attempts to make the information itself an agent of reform by using it to stimulate community and parent grassroots activism has not documented strong effects. In the field of health, collection, analysis, and public dissemination of comparative cost data have been tried as a means to spur patient activism to exert pressure on health institutions to contain costs, but this strategy has met with very modest results (Weiss & Tschirhart, 1994).

In summary, state policy makers are frustrated by lack of results from previous infusion of funds, suspicious about where the new dollars have gone, and concerned about intradistrict equity. It is hoped that the availability of school-level finance data will help address the questions of whether the funds going into schooling are being utilized productively or swallowed up by nonproductive administrative activities. It is also hoped that the data will help policy makers address the issue of whether substantial variations exist in per-pupil spending across sites. Furthermore, state policy makers are encouraged by modern management theories to allow more managerial discretion at lower levels; indeed, they are being told that a key role of central management is providing ample, timely, and accurate data to lower units. On the other hand, it is important not to overstate the level of interest among state policy makers or the potential utility of the data. Although constantly present, at no particular time does the issue of school-level finance data rise above more pressing items on state policy makers' agenda. Furthermore, the technical challenges of linking the fiscal data to meaningful resource allocation decision making are formidable. Finally, the effectiveness of comparative numbers-based strategies in other areas suggests limitations of this approach as a policy and political strategy.

The Case of Florida:
20 Years of School-Level Data Collection

Florida, perhaps more than any other state, merits attention in regard to the use of school-level finance data because of its long history of political commitment to school-based management and its sophisticated and sustained technical capacity for the generation of school-level data. This section chronicles the historical development of the state's fiscal management information system, drawing upon a number of historical documents and interviews with the principals involved.[1]

Design

State policy regarding school-level fiscal information systems in Florida was developed in the early 1970s as part of a comprehensive redesign of the relations between the state and its public schools. The goals of this redesign were both political and substantive. Prior to the 1970s, state policy makers had relied almost exclusively upon the educational community for information and analysis for state policy aking. However, following a decade of student unrest, court-ordered desegregation, and the first statewide teachers' strike in the United States, political leaders wanted to replace a now-discredited educational community with an objective and rational system of policy making through data-based planning, implementation, and evaluation. In order to recoup public respect, the state was to establish clear educational goals with corresponding standards to measure their attainment as well as an objective means to assess them. Fiscal equity was seen as a necessary ingredient in a rational system emphasizing efficiency and effectiveness. To ensure that every student and every school would have an equal chance of meeting the higher standards and could not evade responsibility for failure to achieve, the state aid formula was rewritten to ensure that each student received the same amount of fiscal support independent of local economic disparities. The formula provided differential funding dependent on special needs of the individual student or the differing costs of the program in which the student was enrolled. School-level managerial flexibility was to be maximized so that responsibility for outcomes would be clearly fixed at the school level. The state was to review its existing statutes and rules, eliminate unnecessary state mandates, and encourage school-based management throughout the state.

The substantive aims of the redesign followed the political aims. The current system of schooling was believed to be ineffective and inefficient. For example, according to the political leadership of the time, "The basic structure of education involving a teacher, a textbook and a classroom could no longer meet the needs of Florida's fast-moving and affluent society" (White, 1975, p. 83). In keeping with the long-standing ethos of local control in Florida, the state did not look to state-level mandates for a prescription for educational reform. Instead, it devised a policy framework that would stimulate innovation while fixing responsibility at the local level through fiscal and programmatic deregulation. The school, not the district or the state, was to be the locus of improvement and accountability. Innovation and experimentation at the school level would create promising new practices that, if validated by the district or state as contributing to student achievement, could be shared and adopted by other schools. To stimulate experimentation, school districts were to be given incentives from the state to allow individual schools maximum operational and budgetary flexibility and were encouraged to allow schools to engage in comprehensive planning. The state withdrew a number of mandates regarding salary schedules and supervisory responsibilities. To allow local innovations to be evaluated and disseminated, the state department's role was rethought. The state department's administrative functions were to be reduced and a greater emphasis was to be placed on fostering continuous and comprehensive inquiry into efficiency and effectiveness at the school, district, and state levels. Legislative language was enacted requiring the state department personnel to "divest themselves of as much administrative trivia as possible to concentrate on study, research, evaluation, [and] overall coordination to policy decisions" (White, 1975, p. 82).

This emphasis was to be technically supported at the state level by three independent but interrelated functions: student assessment, information management, and research and development. The state was to develop a comprehensive statewide student assessment system. It would administer criterion- and norm-referenced tests to all students on all critical subject matter and in sufficient detail and with sufficient frequency as to serve as a constant monitor of progress in learning, as well as a diagnostic tool for school leaders and a means for accountability for state funds. The assessments would be based on state-level learning goals, educational objectives, and standards. The assessment system would allow for within-school, within-district, within-state, and within-country comparability (Florida Department of Education, n.d.).

The information from the state assessment system would be fed into a large and comprehensive information system. Comprehensive databases would include school characteristics, student demographics, and finance data at the school, district, and state levels. The provision of comprehensive, timely, and accurate data, both fiscal and programmatic, to the school level was deemed essential to the deregulatory thrusts of the state-local redefinition of roles and to the pinpointing of accountability and school improvement at the school level. The information would support a school-based management capacity to analyze and diagnose current processes and procedures to determine their efficiency and effectiveness and to relate dollars to learning outcomes. School-site personnel would have the managerial discretion to make necessary adjustments to improve school operations and increase student learning. In addition, public dissemination of the data through required annual school report cards and school-based advisory councils, whose membership would include parent and community residents, would further ensure local responsiveness and help restore credibility. Parents and other community leaders would become informed advocates for and even participants in the educational planning and improvement process. The state would provide sophisticated technical assistance in collecting and maintaining the data utilizing the newly emerging computer technologies (Governor's Citizens' Committee, 1973).

The final state function was the establishment of a research and development capacity at the state level. The state-level research program would use the assessment data to guide the search for effective practice and the fiscal data to identify schools and school districts whose practices were unusually efficient. If promising practices were empirically validated through research, then the findings would be applied to improve practice throughout the state. The research and development program would also be charged with the piloting of innovative practices and cost-effective alternatives.

Implementation

The state spent most of the next two decades putting into place the system as outlined. However, though the state remained committed in principle to the system, in practice the press of time, the constraints of funding, and changes in leadership resulted in some components' being more actively pursued than others.

The first leg of the tripod, the assessment program, expanded rapidly and became the largest and most thorough state system of student assessment in the United States (Wise, 1979). By the end of the decade, every student was being assessed four times during the 12 years in the three basic subjects of math, reading, and writing. The second leg was equally well established. The state developed a comprehensive management information system, automating the reporting of data among the school, district, and state levels under the direction of a master plan that required adoption of more advanced technologies and aimed at the eventual establishment of a student-based information system. The Florida student-based managed information system today is considered perhaps the most technologically sophisticated and comprehensive system in the United States (W. Fowler, personal communication, 1994). Annual school report cards that included cost data, student demographics, and student achievement were released to parents, community members, and the media annually.

The third leg, the research and development function, never materialized. The legislature established an educational research and development program in 1969 and appropriated the first funds in 1970 to 1971. Two specific charges were assigned to the research and development program: (a) the development of preliminary objectives and test items for assessment and (b) the piloting of alternative educational practices. Assessment data and the research on alternative practices were to be linked to fiscal data. The original concept was that the school-level finance and other data would be analyzed in light of what the assessment data showed. Any findings that could be established would then be fed back into the planning process, achieving what is referred to today in the quality sciences as continuing improvement.

In 1971, the Florida legislature enacted provisions requiring school-level fiscal data reporting and analysis. It specifically required the preparation of an annual public report of the assessment results by grade and subject area for each school, each district, and the state, with an analysis and recommendations concerning the costs and differential effectiveness of instructional programs. However, in 1974, these provisions were amended. The requirement for the analysis of the school's assessment results and the linking of the results with cost and differential effectiveness analysis was dropped. Furthermore, in 1976, in yet additional legislation, concern with cost-effectiveness was re-placed with cost accounting.

Interviews with senior policy makers in the state substantiate the fact that the analytic function was never properly funded or sustained. The research and development office, though established in law, was funded at a very low level and then disbanded within a few years. Its functions were reduced, and the responsibility for them was sub-sumed under the office of student assessment. The research and development function thus lost its identity as a distinct entity.

Lessons Learned About the Utilization of School-Level Finance Data

1. *State political interests do not necessarily support the development of a capacity for systematic inquiry that is necessary to convert school-level fiscal data into knowledge useful for policy.* Though for over 20 years Florida has had a relatively comprehensive system in place providing data on school expenditures and student performance, there is no evidence that it has stimulated any systematic analysis at either the state or the local level of the relationships between student achievement and resource allocation patterns. As first envisioned by the state planners, assessment data were to be rich enough so that if they were combined with school- and student-level data, researchers could identify prac-tices that were both effective and efficient. However, analytical and feedback usage of fiscal data was never exploited. The commitment to use the data systematically for exploring the relations between the dollars and the learning outcomes was not sustained.

Even though the state now had data by which to press for greater accountability for results from the school system, it continued to behave in the traditional manner of responding to identified needs by providing more funds. For example, in 1976, the state used the per-formance data from the assessment system as a basis for creating a state compensatory education program that provided additional funds to schools whose students achieved below the standards. In other words, in lieu of using its information system to search for system problems that might explain variation among institutions in student perform-ance, the state chose to compensate districts with low-performing students with additional funds. Likewise, the data on performance were used to hold students, not systems, accountable. The primary stimulus for the creation of the school-based information system had been political: It was an attempt to restore public trust and credibility in the public school system. This was more easily achieved by holding students accountable than by holding the system accountable. Decreeing that only students who had mastered certain content would be promoted did restore credibility to the grading and promoting practices, but it did little to improve the educational system.

More perniciously, the negative consequences of low performance fell not on the school system but on individual students. By the end of the 1970s, laws were passed denying high school graduation to students who could not pass the high school state assessment, and promotion in grade was denied students who could not meet minimal grade-level standards. By the middle of the 1980s, over one quarter of the students had been held back at least 1 year between kindergarten and third grade. Yet the state did not try to investigate what was happening within the schools that could result in so many students not achieving at acceptable rates.

Though the rhetoric of state policy makers stressed the need for efficiency and accountability for performance, there is scant evidence to suggest that the state had the structure by which to pursue these goals. As pointed out by a former Florida state superintendent, the electoral cycle of most elected officials does not lend itself to the investment of substantial amounts of money in a research and development process that may not bear fruits for many years. It is clear that in the case of Florida, the press for greater accountability took the form of measures leading to greater procedural accountability in lieu of greater program improvement. The political pressures for accountability led to a focus on the assessment of individual student achievement, not to a focus on improved delivery of instruction.

2. *Educator professional norms do not support the development of a capacity for the systematic inquiry that is necessary to convert school-based fiscal data into knowledge useful for management.* After the state had abandoned the intention of maintaining a research unit itself, it tried to enhance local capacity for critical reflection and decision making based on the school-level data. First, it attempted to improve the quality of school principals by requiring advanced education and experience through a state-mandated certification program. Fiscal knowledge was an integral part of the preparation. The building principal was to understand school finances and be able to make reasoned fiscal decisions. However, in interviews with school administrators,

it became clear that the emphasis was on accounting and budgeting, not on probing the relationships between the inputs and the outcomes. Second, the state in the late 1970s offered at no charge to the school districts an experimental computer software program designed to help building principals better understand the resource utilization patterns in their individual schools. According to state officials, district personnel showed only limited interest in availing themselves of the software, and this program withered due to lack of interest.

Other studies of administrator professional norms substantiate a relative lack of interest in these issues by school administrators. Boyd and Hartman (1988), in their article on the politics of educational productivity, found little evidence to suggest that school administrators spend time or effort on issues relating to productivity and stated that the political, sociological, and budgetary contexts within which administrators operate provide them with little or no incentives to do so. Further, at the district level, superintendents may have even less incentive to focus the spotlight on cross-school discrepancies. This would only stimulate greater scrutiny by the school board, the media, and parents. It might well be in the best interests of organizational stability and staff harmony to shift attention away from across-school comparisons.

3. *The publication and dissemination of data on school-level finance do not necessarily stimulate public interest in or public pressure for school improvement.* According to district finance officers interviewed, the release of school-level fiscal data, including average per-pupil expenditure at the school level, did not mobilize community-based groups. Though the data were widely disseminated, through both school report cards brought home by students and the media, the data did not stimulate greater interest in fiscal issues or discussion of school improvement. This corroborates other research in Dade County (Miami) that in general failed to find evidence that the public dissemination of school-level data stimulated public interest or pressure for reform (Herrington, 1993). The faith placed in public dissemination of data as a means of stimulating pressure for improvement may have been unwarranted.

One can conclude that substantial barriers exist to useful application of available data and that the barriers are as much social and political as technical. At the local level, there is neither lay interest in nor professional competence to attack the methodologically thorny issues of relating inputs to outputs, and if there were, the press of more immediate concerns would not allow the time to undertake the analyses. Likewise, at the state level, the tenure of elected officials or the press of other more demanding issues militates against the development of a long-term, large-scale research and development program.

Where Now?

It is clear that over the next decade a number of states will be attempting to establish school-level fiscal information systems. The increasing interest among policy makers in issues of cost-efficiency makes such systems increasingly desirable, and the remarkable advancements in information technology make them feasible. However, will such systems provide substantive support to policy makers to aid them in their deliberations or to educators to aid them in making resource allocation decisions? The above analyses suggest a guarded response to that question. Although the state of Florida has had a management information system that has collected, stored, and reported school-, district-, and state-level fiscal data for almost two decades, it has not deployed the capacity in a manner that has provided meaningful policy or managerial support. The previous section documents a lack of will and a lack of sustained commitment to the ongoing research and development process necessary to produce useful information out of the fiscal data.

To be useful in answering questions of policy makers and school administrators, raw fiscal data such as Florida's system is capable of producing must be embedded in an ongoing, dedicated program of research and development. For example, one of the most politically charged issues to which state policy makers are being asked to respond is the question of how large a percentage of funds should be spent in administrative or overhead costs. However, having the data to say that 5%, 10%, or 50% is expended in nondirect classroom instructional activities is meaningless in the absence of research that can show the degree to which such nondirect instructional activities are contributing to increased student learning. In the absence of the research necessary to make the data meaningful, the newly available data will no doubt fuel even more heated debate about administrative "blobs" or bureaucratic ineptitude, but little light will be shed on the central question of how schools can best be organized to sustain optimal student learning. Likewise, simply having data available will no doubt lead to more cross-site comparisons, but the knowledge that one school is spending more (or less) on a particular function is not meaningful unless one can establish the relationship between the expenditures and the desired outcomes.

Given the need for a research and development program, the next question is, Who should conduct this research? The federal and state governments and local school districts are the obvious candidates. The federal government has traditionally identified educational research as an appropriate responsibility but in practice has failed to meet that responsibility. According to the recent study of educational research conducted by the National Academy of Education (1991), the federal government's investment in disciplined inquiry and research-driven experimentation is small, particularly as compared with its research investments in other public sector areas such as defense, health care, energy, and agriculture. Furthermore, no other group at the national level is picking up the responsibility. Foundations tend to fund demonstration projects, with limited research on comparative effectiveness and affordability. State governments have no tradition of funding basic research and little tradition of funding applied research. State efforts have generally been limited to data collection, replication and dissemination, and evaluations of existing programs or monitoring of small-scale pilot projects. School districts remain the third possibility. School districts, on the whole, however, lack the capacity. Central staff is often small and overwhelmed with operational responsibilities. The larger districts, which presumably have greater capacity by dint of scale, are often highly troubled due to the host of problems besetting urban America.

It is my contention that the greatest combination of incentive and capacity exists at the state level. Unlike the federal government, which has a limited investment in the public schools and limited leverage over the system, and unlike the school districts, which have limited capacity for undertaking research or funds to support it, the state has a considerable degree of both. States are heavily invested in the system and exercise virtually unlimited control over it. Funding the public school systems in the state is usually the single largest activity of the state. State governments such as Florida dedicate over 50% of their general revenues to schools. States would be direct beneficiaries of the new knowledge gained from research; funds used to conduct the research would be presumably recaptured by increases in efficiency and effectiveness.

Though states lack a tradition of funding basic or applied research,[2] they may be more ready to take on such a responsibility. Politically, the pressures to restrain expenditures and avoid tax increases are intense, and the notion that the public sector must be able to demonstrate the effectiveness of its programs is in ascendancy. However, of perhaps more import is that state governments are reaching a level of maturation at which they may better appreciate the benefits of research. The modern edifice of state government that exists today is basically a creation of the 1960s. Its creation was stimulated by the federal government's war-on-poverty program requirements for state-level oversight and monitoring and the one-man, one-vote ruling of the Supreme Court that weakened the small-government, agrarian influences in state legislatures.

States now have a cadre of senior, appointed professionals who have a 20-year tenure in state government and who realize that much of state expenditure goes into programs for which the state has little evidence of effectiveness. Furthermore, many senior appointed officials have some university graduate school training and more fully appreciate the value of basic and applied research. This cadre of senior professionals, spurred by the elected officials eager to restrain public sector growth and to demonstrate public sector effectiveness, can better appreciate the return on investment of a long-term, large-scale, sustained program of research and development.

If policy makers are to use school-level data to answer the questions posed at the beginning of this chapter, such as whether schools have unnecessarily large bureaucracies or whether variations across sites in resource allocations correspond to greater productivity, simply having access to the data will not be sufficient. States must commit to a substantial research and development process that allows the fiscal data to be analyzed within the larger context of student demographics, school organization, and the technology of teaching and learning.

Notes

1. This section draws upon material in Florida Department of Education, n.d.; W. Fowler, personal communication, 1994; Governor's Citizens' Committee, 1973; White, 1975; and Wise, 1979; and interviews with senior state fiscal policy analysts in the offices of the state department and the governor's office and with the fiscal administrators in Florida. The interviews were conducted in spring and summer of 1994.

2. States do fund basic research through their support of public university faculty time for research. However, the prevailing norms of faculty roles and academic freedom militate against any programmatic application of this resource.

References

Berne, R., & Picus, L. O. (1994). *Outcome equity in education*. Thousand Oaks, CA: Corwin.

Boyd, W. L., & Hartman, W. T. (1988). The politics of educational productivity. In D. H. Monk & J. Underwood (Eds.), *Microlevel school finance: Issues and implications for policy* (pp. 271-308). Cambridge, MA: Ballinger.

Clune, W. H. (1993). The shift from equity to adequacy in school finance. *The World and I, 8*(9), 389-405.

Finn, C. E. (1991). *We must take charge: Our schools and our future*. New York: Free Press.

Florida Department of Education. (n.d.). *Development of the Florida statewide assessment program: A chronology from 1971*. Tallahassee: Author.

Goals 2000: Educate America Act of 1994 (Pub. L. No. 103-227).

Governor's Citizens' Committee on Education. (1973). *Improving education in Florida*. Tallahassee, FL: Author.

Herrington, C. D. (1993). Accountability, invisibility, and the politics of numbers: School report cards and race. In C. Marshall (Ed.), *The new politics of race and gender*. Washington, DC: Falmer.

Johnson, J., & Immerwahr, J. (1994). *First things first: What Americans expect from the public schools*. New York: Public Agenda.

Kirst, M. W. (1988). The internal allocation of resources within U.S. school districts: Implications for policymakers and practitioners. In D. H. Monk & J. Underwood (Eds.), *Microlevel school finance: Issues and implications for policy* (pp. 365-389). Cambridge, MA: Ballinger.

National Academy of Education. (1991). Research and the renewal of education: Executive summary and recommendations. *Educational Researcher, 20*(6), 19-22.

Odden, A. (1992). *Rethinking school finance*. San Francisco: Jossey-Bass.

Osborne, D., & Gaebler, T. (1992). *Reinventing government*. Reading, MA: Addison-Wesley.

Parrish, T. B., & Verstegen, D. A. (1994). *Fiscal provisions of the Individuals With Disabilities Education Act: Policy issues and alternatives*. Palo Alto, CA: Center for Special Education Finance.

Peters, T. J., & Waterman, R. H. (1982). *In search of excellence: Lessons from America's best-run companies*. New York: Warner.

Weiss, C. H. (1989). Congressional committees as users of analysis. *Journal of Policy Analysis and Management, 8*, 411-431.

Weiss, J. A., & Gruber, J. E. (1984). Using knowledge for control in fragmented policy arenas. *Journal of Policy Analysis and Management, 3*, 225-247.

Weiss, J. A., & Tschirhart, M. (1994). Public information campaigns as policy instruments. *Journal of Policy Analysis and Management, 13*, 82-119.

White, A. O. (1975). *Florida's crisis in public education: Changing patterns of leadership*. Gainesville: University Presses of Florida.

Wise, A. E. (1979). *Legislated learning: The bureaucratization of the American classroom*. Berkeley: University of California Press.

THIRTEEN

Implications for Policy
WHAT MIGHT HAPPEN IN AMERICAN
EDUCATION IF IT WERE KNOWN
HOW MONEY ACTUALLY IS SPENT?

JAMES W. GUTHRIE

Possible Pictures of the Future

Imagine the year 2010, when the following three scenarios occur in the United States.

State senator James LaMorte is sitting at an Apple computer in his Atlanta legislative office. He chairs the Senate Appropriations Committee, and the markup session for the fiscal 2011 budget begins the next morning. He is working on a spreadsheet that displays a 10-year pattern of public school spending by subject matter and grade level. His network link to the state education database enables him to access categories of spending data and an assortment of school process and outcome data such as student performance on state subject matter achievement tests. These data are stored in a manner that permits disaggregation to the school site of origin.

The Georgia Association for Guidance (GAG), an intensely focused interest group representing guidance counselors, contends that added spending for counselors would enhance the proportion of female students majoring in math and science. They are lobbying for a categorical spending feature in the upcoming appropriations bill.

Generally, Senator LaMorte detests earmarked spending limitations on school-site personnel. Nevertheless, he decides to explore the matter. Both his sisters were themselves quite gifted mathematically, and he has always been interested in expanding the career opportunities of women. Consequently, he is quite open to any reasonable means that would enhance gender equity on this dimension.

Senator LaMorte asks himself the question: "Will added spending on counselors be likely to enhance female science and math enrollments and achievement levels?" If the answer is "yes," he is quite willing to increase state appropriations for these purposes. To answer this question, he has accessed 10 years of school spending data and an assortment of other input and output information from the state education department data file. He makes the key strokes necessary to array these data on a school-by-school basis, scrolls to the new S4P (Super Social Science Statistical Program) under TOOLS, and applies the programmed weighting controls for student social background characteristics. He then begins to search for Georgia high schools with the highest and lowest proportions of female science and mathematics majors.

Once he has identified the top and bottom 10 secondary schools on this dimension, he quickly computes the mean per-pupil guidance expenditure in each set of schools. He uses his statistical package again in order to control for student achievement levels and concludes, alas, that level of guidance spending bears no relationship to either gender decisions or achievement levels.

Ten years of precise accounting for functional subject matter spending, school by school, simply do not reveal any systematic relationship between added levels of spending on guidance counselors and student decisions about academic major, numbers of courses taken, or subject matter achievement. All of these results hold even after the most stringent statistical controls for student characteristics are applied.

Senator LaMorte searches further through his database, looking for possible relationships with high levels of student math and science achievement, and finds that the most likely spending-linked variable is teacher training in advanced science and mathematics courses and in-service education in these areas.

Senator LaMorte firmly believes in permitting school-site professional educators to make resource allocative decisions. Furthermore, he has little doubt that literally dozens of Georgian principals have already done the kinds of analyses that he has just conducted in the past 15 minutes. However, he had now verified for himself that added resources, if allocated in a categorical aid bill directed specifically at guidance spending, would be unlikely to lead to favorable outcomes. He now has an answer for when he meets the next morning with GAG advocates. They will not be happy with his response and his refusal to include them in an earmarked section of the appropriations bill. Still, he thinks, the data he has just analyzed are every bit as available to them as to him. Why have they not done the analyses themselves? Then they might have had a better idea.

Twenty-five hundred miles to the west, in his office in the Los Angeles Municipal Court building, Anthony Serrano is sitting at his networked computer. Almost two decades have passed since the Los Angeles Unified School District consented, in *Rodriguez v. Los Angeles Unified School District*, to allocate financial resources on an equal per-pupil basis. Serrano, the grandson of a leading plaintiff in a famous interdistrict equal-protection school finance suit, is a court-appointed master charged with ensuring that the school district is complying with the intradistrict equal-protection agreement.

The school district has been fumbling for years in achieving per-pupil spending parity. To do so has been an intense challenge because senior teachers filed their own suits claiming a violation of union contractual agreements regarding seniority transfer privileges. The school-by-school budgeting that resulted from the original *Rodriguez* consent decree left many schools in the San Fernando Valley in the upper income reaches of the city short of the resources to employ senior teachers with their higher salaries. In effect, parents on school-site councils generally opted for smaller class sizes as opposed to higher-paid, more senior teachers and the inevitable concomitant of large classes. Many of the district's more senior teachers found that they were having to accept the forced-choice positions available to them in central city schools, and they were not pleased with the prospect of having either to move their residence or to undertake a long daily commute. Of course, a number resigned, but a significant percent filed suit and delayed the consent decree implementation as a result.

Now, in 2010, most of these problems have been resolved by the court, and Serrano is using the LAUSD data bank to test for anomalies in school-site budgets. The consent decree still permits a degree of disparity. Judge Ito, formerly of the criminal justice division but now hearing civil cases, has decided that the same decision rule that applies to school spending for the state of California—95% of all pupils in the state have to fall within a prescribed per-pupil spending band—will also hold inside a school district. It is Serrano's task to monitor this band and report to the court if resource allocation disparities exceed the limit. He is now preparing his quarterly report for the court.

In midcontinent, in a Chicago suburb, Emma Coons sits at her computer. The screen is filled with school-by-school budget and program comparisons. As she scrolls through available data regarding spending and program profiles of Chicago area secondary schools, she reflects fondly upon the distinguished career of her grandfather, John E. Coons, a forceful and thoughtful advocate for school choice plans. Here she is, as a school choice adviser, living out the hopes of her famous relative by advising families regarding the fit between their social preferences and the offerings and results of area public and private schools.

If we overlook the author's effort at humor, these three scenarios illustrate the policy and practical prospects of accurate school-by-school financial and program data. Such information could substantially transform the American education policy landscape. It could empower advocates for greater equality of educational opportunity. It could unleash a tide of far more sophisticated analyses regarding efficiency and "production" of schooling. It could empower clients and facilitate choice. Moreover, while unleashing these forces, it could promote both sophisticated and informed public discussion regarding the purposes and desired outcomes of schooling and perhaps trigger-added politicization of and conflict in American education.

The purpose of this chapter is to summarize the current state of school budget information and the limitations imposed upon policy makers as a consequence, to speculate regarding the low demand for more sophisticated information, and to extrapolate regarding the policy consequences of an advanced system of school-by-school financial and program accounting.

How It Is Today

Financial administration of a school district, as with almost any formal organization, consists of two conceptually distinct activities: (a) budget planning and (b) budget administration. In a district such as New York City, each of these activities may be performed by separate specialized teams involving hundreds of officials. In a small school district, the superintendent and secretary may perform all functions. Regardless of how many or how well trained and specialized the actors or participants, neither budget planning nor administration typically involves schools as a unit of accounting control or analysis.

Planning and accounting are far more likely to be undertaken district-wide. It is unusual to be able to read a school district budget and determine the amount of money spent in a school. When a superintendent is asked, "What do you spend at X school?" the likely answer is to name a figure that specifies the amount of discretionary funding for instructional supplies and expenses. This typically is only 1% to 2% of the total spending at a school. The overwhelming proportion of resources allocated for operating the conventional school is linked to professional and classified salaries and fringe benefits. It is unusual for these personnel-related spending amounts to be specified on a school-by-school basis. A few districts do specify them, but they are unusually avant garde.

Budget Planning

Budget planning is the forward-looking component of the budget cycle. Here an organization determines what it intends to spend in the forthcoming fiscal year.

School districts with a thousand or more enrolled students frequently resort to a mechanical or formulaic budget format. They rely on uniform allocation rules that give the appearance of treating each school, and by deduction each student, equally. A district will formulate allocation rules: for example, that each 25 enrolled students will generate a teaching position at a school site; that every 400 students entitles a school to a librarian, a counselor, or an assistant administrator; that every 15 students will generate a teacher aide; that so many square feet of building will generate a custodial position; and that so many acres will generate a groundskeeper or gardener.

In addition to these full-time-equivalent (FTE) personnel allocations, the formulas distribute a specified amount of revenue per pupil for discretionary items such as textbooks, instructional supplies, and perhaps field trips and consultant days. A school's "budget" is the aggregate of the personnel positions and discretionary funding it is due by virtue of such informal decision rules.

The allocation of revenues to cover activities such as employing substitute teachers, paying utilities, and engaging consultants is likely to remain centrally budgeted. It is an unusual principal who has knowledge of how much is annually being spent on these items for his or her school.

These uniform distribution decision rules are often reinforced by state statutory components (e.g., maximum class sizes specified by the legislature), collective bargaining contracts, and historic precedent in either the district or its surrounding region. However rational these decision rules appear, and even if they square with best practice and the experience of thoughtful educators, they are not scientifically validated. They have little or no basis in research.

These uniform allocation rules have two principal advantages. They give the appearance of uniformity. Everyone is treated the same way. A principal, parent, or teacher is provided with little apparent reason to complain. Any question regarding equity of treatment can be answered with, "Well, we have an allocation rule. Your school was treated like every other school. If you do not like the result, then you can ask the school board, legislature, or congress for an exception." Such an admonition generally serves to discourage debate.

The other advantage to formulaic allocation is that it centralizes authority. In U.S. public schools, the mechanical allocation norms are, in fact, followed for allocating personnel. Consequently, for every 25 (or whatever number) of students generating a teaching position, the school is in fact likely to be allocated a teacher.

Of course, the alternative is to utilize uniform decision rules to determine the resources for which a school is eligible, convert this result to actual dollar resource levels, and then permit the unit to determine how, in fact, it chooses to allocate the resources. An individual school under such a plan might choose to trade people for things, things for people, or people for different kinds of people. However, such school-site decision making is quite unusual in the United States.

Budgeting Administration

The purpose of budget administration is to ensure that an organization adheres to whatever budget plan it develops. Budget administration calls for a series of "control" points. These are the domains of accountants, auditors, payroll specialists, and purchase agents. Spending decisions are controlled by such agents, who use the budget, and by reference all appropriate law, to ensure that a proposed expenditure is in fact both approved by the budget and legal. The overwhelming result is to keep "control" central.

Public school accounting practices in the United States are principally a product of advisory publications of the U.S. Office (now Department) of Education. These advisories regarding accounting procedures have been adopted and, in many instances, adapted by state agencies. The consequence is an almost uniform school accounting system across the United States.[1]

This relatively uniform code of accounts serves at least two purposes admirably. First, it accurately tracks revenue sources, ensuring that categorical funds are separated from general discretionary revenues. This enables governmental agencies to ensure that revenues are deployed in the manner and for the purposes that governments decree. Second, it ensures that school revenues are expended in a legal manner. Current functional and object codes permit careful tracking of expenditures, should such detailed auditing be necessary.

What Is Wrong With This (Financial) Picture?

The inability to obtain spending data school by school is a major impediment to efficient planning, equitable distribution, and client choice. In effect, the inability to determine precisely what is spent at a school prevents American education from being efficient, fair, or just. Few seemingly simple matters have such far-reaching consequences. More accurate spending information is an unusually small reform step possessing the potential for huge policy and practical rewards. Of course, such a small step might also trigger substantial added conflict. However, we will say more about that later.

The Impediment to Efficiency

The absence of school-by-school spending and accompanying program information imposes so many barriers to rational operation and determination of efficiencies that it is difficult to catalogue them all here. Suffice it to say that research, effective practice, and realistic accountability are all handicapped by the absence of sensible and accurate disaggregated data.

An Illustration About
Production Function Research

In 1966, the so-called Coleman Report (Coleman et al., 1966) was released by what was then known as the U.S. Office of Education. This endeavor, authorized by Congress as a part of the 1964 Civil Rights Act, was then the largest social science undertaking in history. The analytic team was led by the world-famous sociologist James S. Coleman. The congressional charge was to map the extent of educational inequality in the United States.

Among its activities, the Coleman team attempted to understand the relationship between financial resources and student achievement. Even though Coleman and his colleagues attempted to control for student background characteristics, their research effort proved badly flawed. For financial data, they used what was available to them—district-wide, highly aggregated expenditures per pupil. These proved to be quite inaccurate portrayals of the levels of resources actually spent on particular pupils. Consequently, without any malice whatsoever, the Coleman Report finding that financial resources had little relationship to level of pupil performance, separate from the social background of the student, was simply unsupportable. Inaccurate data eroded the nature of the finding. This did not impede the acceptance of the finding itself. The prestige of Coleman, the massive data sets involved, the sophistication of the analytic techniques utilized, and possibly, a predisposition by policy makers to believe that schools waste money all combined to create a receptive audience, even if the message had not properly been proved.

Despite the inaccurate information, the Coleman finding was widely trumpeted by the policy community. For literally decades following issuance of the report, it has been cited as evidence that added financial resources make no difference in pupil performance. Other researchers have attempted valiantly to employ more sophisticated models with more accurate data. Nevertheless, it is still difficult to conduct the research in the manner needed because of the widespread absence of school-by-school financial data.

Professional Ineffectiveness Through Uniformity

The absence of school-by-school data and of spending discretion on the part of school principals renders American education unnecessarily ineffective. In effect, currently employed, aggregated, budgeting accounting procedures reinforce a virtual uniform blanket model of schooling. Levels of experimentation are unusually limited by the dictates of uniform allocation rules. Principals and staffs are stifled in whatever creative efforts they might desire to make to rearrange resources.

Ill-Conceived Process Accountability

The absence of school-by-school data and school-site budgeting eviscerates useful accountability. By budgeting and accounting for resources centrally, school districts provide administrators with a built-in excuse for lack of pupil performance. Under current arrangements, school decisions are effectively central office decisions, perhaps even school board and state legislative decisions. It is thus easy for a principal to hide behind such centrally promulgated rules and explain that the lack of student achievement is not his or her fault. Rather, the absence of results is a consequence of the district's decision rules. The principal is acting only as a conduit, overseeing educational and operational decisions made elsewhere.

School-based management exposes dramatically the decisions of those at schools. Principals, teachers, and parent councils are all subject to careful scrutiny in a system that simultaneously measures student performance and permits school-based decisions. The threat of such true accountability may well explain the absence of enthusiasm on the part of professional educators for school-by-school data and school-based management.

The Impediment to Equality

Present-day budgeting procedures disguise dramatic spending disparities. Certainly, aggregating spending to district-level means disguises the high spending on legally protected categories such as the handicapped. However, less well understood are the dynamics of intradistrict spending disparities that penalize low-income students.

The principal "culprit" in intradistrict unequal spending, or at least the silent accomplice, is the aggregated spending means kept by districts and the use of previously described uniform allocative criteria. By relying upon uniform personnel allocation rules and then driving the decision rule through to practice by allocating actual positions rather than revenues, school districts disguise spending inequities accompanying teacher salaries.

In most school districts, particularly large districts where disproportionate percentages of low-income youth reside, teachers' pay is a function of number of years of service and numbers of college credits beyond a bachelor's degree. These two factors have little bearing upon instructional proficiency. However, they possess the advantage of being measurable. Thus they are widely used, regardless of their validity in measuring competency or productivity.

Teachers, also as a frequent product of collective bargaining, have often gained the right to transfer to open teaching positions on the basis of their seniority of service. This condition frequently permits teachers with the greatest number of years of service to transfer to school within a district with students or working conditions that they find agreeable. Aside from whatever just deserts are involved for individual teachers, the system constitutes a conspiracy to defraud inner-city students of a just share of revenues. In those unusual instances in which actual accounting has taken place school by school, low-income students often find themselves in schools with lower-paid teachers. This is true simply because their teachers are the least senior, and thus the least paid.

A few court cases have questioned the equity of such arrangements. The earliest was *Hobson v. Hansen* (1966), a Washington, D.C., intradistrict equity case. The court decided in favor of plaintiffs and required that the Washington, DC school district reallocate teachers so that their salary distributions were more equitably aligned with the socioeconomic status and race of schoolchildren. The court was insufficiently imaginative to mandate a useful reform such as school-site budgeting, which offered the prospect of achieving both greater equality and greater efficiency.

A more recent West Coast consent decree in *Rodriguez v. Los Angeles Unified School District* (1992) holds brighter promise of a productive remedy. Here, the school district has agreed to make a transition to school-based budgeting and accounting.

The regular practice of school-by-school accounting and school-based decision making, coupled with other reforms, might actually rectify these types of intradistrict injustices and simultaneously render schooling more effective.

The Impediment to Liberty

Private schooling has a long history in the United States. Nevertheless, almost 90% of America's students attend public schools. Many individuals cannot afford otherwise. Many of those who can afford a choice of schools have exercised their option by purchasing a home in a desirable school district. They exercise choice through their pocketbook. Thus there remains a substantial residue of less-than-wealthy households who use assigned public schools but who might prefer a choice if they could afford it.

Increasingly, public school districts attempt to accommodate this desire for greater choice by using magnet schools or some other optional assignment mechanism. This may prove more satisfying than simply assigning schools to households. However, a school choice plan would be measurably enhanced by school-by-school financial and program information. Such an arrangement would enable households to make more informed choices. They could choose the school with a resource allocation pattern most to their liking. Parents and students preferring more senior teachers might be willing to trade larger classes for their preference. Conversely, households favoring small class size might trade teacher experience. Yet other sets of parents might choose a school heavily invested in technology. Whatever customer preference, all would be better served with better information.

Why No Serious Demand for Change

Given the substantial and sustained disadvantages accompanying aggregated, school district-wide data, why has there not been a sustained outcry for change? Why have public officials not demanded more precise and disaggregated information? Why has school-by-school accounting not been higher on the reform agenda? More definitive answers to these related questions will no doubt have to be provided by historians writing in some future time. Meanwhile, it is possible to pose several hypotheses to explain the absence of more policy-relevant financial data. Before we offer these tentative explanations, we should note that these hypotheses are tightly tied to political conditions. Technically, it has been practical to account for school spending more precisely for literally decades. Little technical planning or accounting complexity is involved in providing decision makers with school-by-school financial information. The problem is one of will, not way.

Possible Explanations for the Financial Accounting Status Quo

Progressive Era Residue

"Scientific management" and depoliticization discouragement were the watchwords of a sweeping set of turn-of-the-century reforms that dramatically altered the governance and management of American public education. The full range of changes is chronicled by historians such as David Tyack in *The One Best System* (1974) and Raymond Callahan in *Education and the Cult of Efficiency* (1962). Suffice it to summarize here that a coincidence of events combined Progressive Era political reforms, industrial engineer Frederick Taylor's "scientific management," school district consolidation, and the advent of urban school district professional administration in a forceful reform package. One component of this package was to redefine and restrict decision-making legitimacy for school board members. They were intensely socialized to avoid the prerogatives of management and repeatedly admonished only to make "policy." Detailed decisions regarding what should be allocated or how it might be allocated to a school were regarded as intrusions on management prerogatives. Hence, asking that a new accounting system concentrate on school-by-school measures would probably have been used as a threat to mount a recall election.

Present-Day Political Homeostasis

School-by-school financial information holds the prospect of upsetting the political status quo. System ignorance of detailed distributional consequences enables teachers and their unions to adhere to the above-described transfer privileges. Principals make few requests for more complete disaggregated financial data because such information flow might expose them to greater accountability expectations.

Superintendents and central office staff may believe that their currently held decision-making prerogative would be threatened by greater school-site autonomy. Similarly, parents of upper socioeconomic status students may not be eager to have the existing balance changed out of a belief that they are currently advantaged. In short, the political system has accommodated to ignorance. Added information threatens this balance. Hence, there is not great clamor for change.

Sheer Ignorance and Naiveté

Few school board members have had experience with the financial side of organizations before assuming their positions. Their training and expertise reside in other areas. Hence, they seldom know to ask for disaggregated data. For their part, business experts may often assume that school data are arrayed in a disaggregated manner. They are used to cost centers and decentralized management. Many of them may simply assume that such procedures are commonplace. In schools, of course, they are not. However, only those individuals close to school decision making know of the absence of disaggregated data. The president of a large local business is seldom sufficiently engaged with schools to learn the difference.

So What If Things Were Different?

More and more accurate knowledge of how education resources were allocated could be a mixed blessing. The prospect is favorable if the policy system links disaggregated budget information with disaggregated decision making, and school-site budgeting with school-site decision making. However, if the policy community uses school-site financial data simply to make more prescriptive decisions from the center and to invent even more narrow programs of categorical aid, then more accurate information may serve only to rigidify American education even further.

Positive Policy Possibilities

The favorable consequences are in the realms of efficiency, equity, and, possibly, liberty. Accurate school-by-school, or even classroom-by-classroom or student-by-student, data would permit far more research about education "production." This would be particularly true if schools were sufficiently unfettered, even encouraged by incentive systems, to experiment with far more models of instruction than now generally exist. Researchers would have more settings, more accurate information, and, possibly, a wider range of instructional models to assess.

More accurate, and more appropriate, information would also create an opportunity for greater professional leadership on the part of educators, teachers, and administrators. Knowledge of, and greater control over, resource decisions would empower educators and enable them more productively to match resources to the needs of the students.

More accurate information would also create the possibility of an effective accountability system that placed responsibility for results on schools. Similarly, as illustrated in the opening fictional Serrano scenario, more accurate and disaggregated data would permit far greater monitoring of equality of opportunity.

Finally, more accurate information, particularly regarding school-level spending, would permit more accurately matching the preference of clients with the offerings of schools. This could serve as a productive platform for enhancing the choices of households.

Possible Dysfunctional Policy Outcomes

More accurate data might well provoke more sophisticated debates among the public and its representatives regarding the purposes of schooling. If the hypothetical Senator LaMorte wanted to know how much money was being spent on science instruction in Georgia, in contrast with home economics or social studies, he might have stirred a controversy regarding the question, "What knowledge is of most worth?"

Under current arrangements, we can claim to include virtually every subject in the public school curriculum. All we have to do is mention or mandate that subject X should be taught. With a disaggregated, accurate, school-by-school accounting system, we could proceed further to explore how much money was actually being allocated for and spent on the instruction of subject X. Under such circumstances, spending on subject X might conflict with the spending priorities of others who would like more spent on subject Y. Proponents of subject Y, once understanding that their interests were being slighted in terms of resource flows, might well complain and undertake some form of political protest in behalf of their interest. None of this currently occurs because there is seldom any accurate information regarding spending level on particular subjects or activities.

Such political controversy need not be negative. Indeed, one can argue that it is good. An appropriate role of the political system is to resolve conflicts regarding the allocation of values. Hence, if more accurate information provokes conflict regarding values, the political system can accommodate the interests involved, and the polity can enjoy the added commitment of participants.

Nice talk, but tell it to the residents of Bosnia or Rwanda, nations torn by conflict because the political system could not resolve questions of values and allocation of scarce resources. The question is the level of conflict provoked. If it becomes too intense, it could prove dysfunctional. Public schooling would become even more politicized, losers would be less willing to allocate resources to its support, and social cohesion might be jeopardized as a result.

Accurate information, if mishandled, also could lead to greater levels of rigidity in schools. If policy makers took the opportunity resulting from accurate resource flow information to proscribe even more tightly the uses of resources and to require not only equal spending per pupil in each school but also equal spending for science, math, social studies, home economics, foreign language, and so on, the system would lose what little flexibility now remains. The opportunity to tailor resource flows to the needs and preferences of individual students could be reduced even further. Incentives for educators to exercise professional discretion would be further diminished, and the productivity of the system could be decreased.

Summary

More accurate financial information, disaggregated to operational levels, is a management and policy tool with enormous potential for both good and evil. Mishandled, it could stultify American education yet further. Appropriately used, it could be a remarkably liberating component contributing to a golden era of productivity, justice, and client satisfaction. Of course, like many policy innovations, it is more likely to be something in between.

However, regardless of its potential benefits or disadvantages, unless a larger group of advocates emerges than now is immediately evident, policy system and education professionals will not ever have to face the issue. Homeostatic forces are not now encouraging that such information will ever be provided. Some kind of champion must emerge before the shaping of consequences will be a challenge to the school finance community.

Notes

1. But even though all school accounting systems are fundamentally part of the same genus, for those who attempt to interpolate finance data across state boundaries, accounting system idiosyncrasies and definitional differences can be maddening.

References

Callahan, R. E. (1962). *Education and the cult of efficiency.* Chicago: University of Chicago Press.

Coleman, J. S., Campbell, E. Q., Hobson, C. J., McPartland, J., Mood, A. M., Weinfeld, F. D., & York, R. L. (1966). *Equality of educational opportunity.* Washington, DC: Government Printing Office.

Hobson v. Hansen, 252 F. Supp. 4 (1966).

Rodriguez v. Los Angeles Unified School District, No. C611358 (Los Angeles County Sup. Ct. May 5, 1992).

Tyack, D. B. (1974). *The one best system: A history of American urban education.* Cambridge, MA: Harvard University Press.

American Education Finance Association Board of Directors, 1995-1996

OFFICERS

Mary P. McKeown, *President*
Lawrence O. Picus, *President-Elect*
George R. Babigian, *Executive Director*
David S. Honeyman, *Immediate Past President*

DIRECTORS

1996 Term
Catherine P. Clark
Faith E. Crampton
Mary F. Fulton
Stephen L. Jacobson
Neil Theobald

1997 Term
Chris Malkiewich
Michael O'Loughlin
Kathleen C. Westbrook
Terry Whitney
R. Craig Wood

1998 Term
Patrick Galvin
Carolyn Herrington
Maureen McClure
John Schneider
Stephanie Stullich

Sustaining Members
Jewell C. Gould
Paul Houston
Edward Hurley
Will S. Myers
Thomas A. Shannon
Don I. Tharpe

Patricia Anthony, AEFA Journal Executive Editor
Koy M. Floyd, *AEFA Newsletter Editor*

Index

CORWIN
PRESS

The Corwin Press logo—a raven striding across an open book—represents the happy union of courage and learning. We are a professional-level publisher of books and journals for K-12 educators, and we are committed to creating and providing resources that embody these qualities. Corwin's motto is "Success for All Learners."

This book may be kept